ADR IN EMPLOYMENT LAW

Cavendish
Publishing
Limited

London • Sydney • Portland, Oregon

ADR IN EMPLOYMENT LAW

Chris Chapman
LLB, FCIArb, Solicitor

Jerry Gibson
MA, FCIPD, MCMI, FRSA
Acas Director for London

Stephen Hardy
JP, LLB, PhD, FRSA, ILTM, MCIArb
Senior Lecturer in Law
University of Manchester

Cavendish
Publishing
Limited

London • Sydney • Portland, Oregon

First published in Great Britain 2003 by
Cavendish Publishing Limited, The Glass House,
Wharton Street, London WC1X 9PX, United Kingdom
Telephone: + 44 (0)20 7278 8000   Facsimile: + 44 (0)20 7278 8080
Email: info@cavendishpublishing.com
Website: www.cavendishpublishing.com

Published in the United States by Cavendish Publishing
c/o International Specialized Book Services,
5824 NE Hassalo Street, Portland,
Oregon 97213-3644, USA

Published in Australia by Cavendish Publishing (Australia) Pty Ltd
3/303 Barrenjoey Road, Newport, NSW 2106, Australia

British Library Cataloguing in Publication Data
Hardy, Stephen T
ADR in employment law
1 Labour laws and legislations – Great Britain
2 Dispute resolution (law) – Great Britain
3 Mediation and conciliation, industrial – Great Britain
I Title II Gibson, Jerry III Chapman, Chris

344.4'1'018914

Library of Congress Cataloguing in Publication Data
Data available

ISBN 1-85941-778-7

1 3 5 7 9 10 8 6 4 2

Printed and bound in Great Britain

FOREWORD

The use of alternative dispute resolution (ADR) methods to resolve issues between parties without recourse to complex and often costly court procedures is becoming ever more widespread in Britain today. Disputes between family members, neighbours, consumers and providers, estate agents and homeowners/buyers can all now be resolved through techniques such as mediation, arbitration, complaints procedures and the involvement of an Ombudsperson.

In the field of employment relations, Acas and its predecessor bodies have been providing such a service since 1896, and for disputes around individual employment rights since 1972. This new book is aimed at those wishing to learn more about the latest extension of ADR in the individual employment rights field – the Acas arbitration scheme for the resolution of unfair dismissal disputes. It provides a step by step guide to the new scheme, which was launched in 2001, as well as outlining the skills and techniques used in the arbitration process.

With good employment relations back in the spotlight following the enactment of the new Employment Act in July 2002, the challenge will be to help employers, unions and lawyers become more familiar with ADR methods. This book does this. Its authors, from multi-disciplinary backgrounds and experiences, bring reality to employment law and provide useful guidance on how ADR can best be applied in employment matters. Overall, this book marks a new opportunity to re-assess where litigation fits in and what can be done before reaching that last resort.

I strongly recommend this book.

Rita Donaghy, OBE
Chair of the Advisory, Conciliation and Arbitration Service

PREFACE

Both the Employment Act 2002 and the Employment Rights (Dispute Resolution) Act 1998 introduce amendments to 'the existing legal framework relating to dismissal procedures, agreements and other alternative methods of resolving disputes about employment rights'. Behind these initiatives lies a modernisation of the current tribunal framework to individual employment dispute resolution, a potential new role for Acas in terms of internal disciplinary and grievance procedures and the introduction of an Acas scheme providing for arbitration in the case of 'disputes involving proceedings or claims which could be the subject of proceedings before an employment tribunal'. The initiatives also encourage dispute resolution as an alternative to litigation before employment tribunals. Notwithstanding the provisions of the 1996 Arbitration Act, the Acas scheme is conducted alongside this framework and its provisions are guided by the ethos and principles established under current alternative dispute resolution (ADR) and practice.

Given this Woolf legal era of ADR, lawyers have some idea about what arbitration involves. Employment law practitioners will have to grapple with new methods of working, including answering some salient procedural and legal questions such as: who decides on arbitration as an option? What powers does an arbitrator have? What process/model(s) exists? What procedures underlie the arbitration scheme? What remedies are available? What costs exist? Is there an appeal route?

This new practice text will not only address these central questions and describe and explain ADR within the context of employment law, but also guide employment law practitioners through the new arbitral scheme governed by Acas and the new dispute resolution envisaged under the Employment Act 2002. Whilst this text covers neither the well-established collective conciliation and arbitration arrangements, nor the legal framework governing employment disputes involving trade unions, it breaks new ground by evaluating the emerging ADR schemes concerned with individual employment relations.

Our thanks go to Rita Donaghy for her Foreword and generous support, as well as to Myf(anwy) Milton for her encouragement with the initial proposal. Phil Bull's technical computer expertise saved the day and our publishers, particularly Jeremy Stein and Jon Lloyd, were patient and courageous enough to publish in this developing area.

Appreciation, as ever, goes to our families for their patience and support throughout.

The material in the Appendices is reproduced with kind permission of Acas and The Stationery Office.

The law is stated as at 1 January 2003.

Chris Chapman, Jerry Gibson and Stephen Hardy
Manchester
February 2003

CONTENTS

TABLE OF CASES

TABLE OF LEGISLATION

TABLE OF ABBREVIATIONS

Acas	Advisory, Conciliation and Arbitration Service
ADR	Alternative dispute resolution
CA	Court of Appeal
CAC	Central Arbitration Committee
CLS	Community Legal Service
DAC	Departmental Advisory Committee
DE	Department of Employment
DTI	Department of Trade and Industry
EA	Employment Act 2002
EAT	Employment Appeal Tribunal
EDR	Employment dispute resolution
ERA	Employment Rights Act 1996
ER(DR)A	Employment Rights (Dispute Resolution) Act 1998
ETA	Employment Tribunals Act 1996
ETS	Employment Tribunals Service
EU	European Union
HL	House of Lords
HMSO	Her Majesty's Stationery Office (now The Stationery Office)
HRA	Human Rights Act 1998
IDH	Internal disciplinary hearing
IT	Industrial Tribunal
LCD	Lord Chancellor's Department
NAAFI	Navy, Army and Air Force Institutes
TEU	Treaty on European Union 1992
TUC	Trades Union Congress
TULR(C)A	Trade Union and Labour Relations (Consolidation) Act 1992
TUPE	Transfer of Undertakings (Protection of Employment) Regulations 1981

CHAPTER 1

RESOLVING EMPLOYMENT DISPUTES AND ADR

Considering the 1889 Arbitration Act, Scrutton LJ commented that: 'The courts do not allow the agreement of parties to oust the jurisdiction of the courts. Arbitrators, unless expressly authorised, have to apply the laws of England.'[1] In 2001, the Advisory, Conciliation and Arbitration Service (Acas) scheme for unfair dismissal came into force across England and Wales,[2] despite delay caused by the need to consider the implications of the Human Rights Act 1998. Such an advent marks the arrival of alternative dispute resolution (ADR) in employment law. In attempting to explain the impact of ADR on employment law, and in order to identify some of the potential problems which arise when new policy conflicts with well-established practice and procedure, this text discusses the following points:

- the underlying policy aims of the government's new laws on dispute resolution;
- the Acas scheme for unfair dismissal;
- the employment tribunal reforms; and
- the impact of the Woolf civil justice rules in the movement towards encouraging ADR methods of working.[3]

This examination concentrates particularly on the impact of ADR upon current employment law practice, raising questions on human rights, the notion of 'fairness', the available remedies and the future of employment relations. With a review of this new 'third way' in employment dispute resolution, this text will draw some interim conclusions on the future of ADR in modern employment law.

1.1 THE BACKGROUND – THE CURRENT LEGAL FRAMEWORK

Both the Industrial Tribunals Act 1996 and the later Employment Rights (Dispute Resolution) Act (ER(DR)A) 1998 made several changes to employment tribunal procedure but, more significantly, the 1998 Act proposed a scheme for Acas arbitration of unfair dismissal claims. The origins of the legislation date back to the growing concern in the mid-1990s, on the part of the then Conservative government, that the delays caused by the dramatic increase in the caseload of industrial (now 'employment') tribunals and the growing complexity of the law meant that the original objectives of the tribunal system

---

1   *Czarnikow v Roth, Schmidt & Co* [1922] 2 KB 478, CA.
2   The Acas scheme for Scotland is currently being drafted, since Scotland has its own arbitration law.
3   From 1996 to 2000, there have been some 233 ADR orders in the Commercial Court (see Genn, 2002).

were no longer being met. Consequently, a Department of Employment (DE) Green Paper[4] reviewed its operation and considered various options which would relieve pressure on the system, reduce the delays in cases being heard and contain demands on public expenditure.[5] Some proposals, such as the introduction of a statutory requirement for employees to pursue grievances with their employer before a tribunal complaint could be made, were subsequently dropped. However, the suggested voluntary arbitration scheme as an alternative to a tribunal hearing has finally become a reality.

The need for an alternative to employment tribunals was, in fact, first considered by labour lawyers in the early 1980s.[6] Since then, and due in part to the 1990s Woolf reforms, its impetus has gathered pace. For instance, Doyle attributes recent ADR developments, including the unfair dismissal arbitral route, to Lord Woolf's Civil Justice Review of 1996: 'Lord Woolf envisaged a new landscape in civil justice, in which people will be encouraged to start court proceedings to resolve disputes only as a last resort, and after using more appropriate means when these are available.'[7]

With the Civil Justice Council devoting much of its discussion to ADR, such a view is reinforced by the Civil Procedure Rules 1998, which empower judges to order the parties to attempt mediation or another form of ADR, as well as by the Access to Justice Act 1999, which has placed a greater emphasis on ADR. The Labour government, having inherited a Conservative policy initiative, has given the green light for the new arbitration scheme to go ahead. Such a movement towards ADR was furthered by the provisions contained in the Employment Act (EA) 2002.

In 1999, the Lord Chancellor's Department (LCD) Discussion Paper on ADR[8] set out 76 questions about ADR and inquired about what role the government should play in its development. A disappointing total of 133 responses was received, the majority being from lawyers and ADR practitioners. According to its post-consultation report (2000), the LCD remarked that '[the] proponents of ADR far outnumbered detractors'. However, most respondents commented that they did not class arbitration as a form of ADR, although 51% of the respondents had found benefits from using ADR, particularly in terms of time, cost, confidentiality/privacy and convenience. Nevertheless, some lawyer scepticism was noted, suggesting that ADR was amateurish and could be used as a 'delaying tactic'. Above all, the report acknowledged that:

- *arbitration* was suitable in cases involving complex or technical issues;
- *expert determination* was deemed to be the most suitable ADR process to be applied in purely technical or complex disputes or, alternatively, where a speedy award is important;

---

4   *Resolving Employment Rights Disputes: Options for Reform*, Cm 2709, December 1994, London: HMSO.

5   The results of the review were published in the DTI's proposal: *Resolving Employment Rights Disputes: Draft Legislation for Consultation*, DTI, July 1996.

6   For examples, see Rideout, 1986; Hepple, 1987; Lewis and Clark, 1993.

7   Doyle, 2000.

8   See www.open.gov.uk, November 1999.

- *mediation* suited cases where a significant element is the claimant's sense of grievance and the feeling that the other side has not acknowledged their distress, as well as multi-party disputes;
- *Med-Arb* (mediation-arbitration) was suitable for cases where the parties are likely to agree on some but not all of the issues involved.

As for the role of government, it was noted that it should be limited to the provision of information, education and quality control. Following this ADR consultation, the number of cases before tribunals continued to spiral and, consequently, the government announced the Leggatt Review of Tribunals in 2001.[9] The Leggatt Inquiry's remit was 'to review the delivery of justice through tribunals other than ordinary law' and to 'seek to lay down recommendations to ensure there are fair, timely, proportionate and effective arrangements for handling disputes'. Leggatt concluded that employment tribunals operated effectively, but that their increasing workload was a matter of concern. As a result, a further review was commissioned to focus solely upon the operation of employment tribunals. This Employment Tribunal Task Force was headed by leading employment lawyer Janet Gaymer. The Task Force investigated potential reforms to resolve the government's concerns about the rising caseload and the 'need for reform and modernisation'[10] in the employment tribunal system.

As the Lord Chancellor put it: 'The work of the Task Force is consistent with the modernising agenda of the Leggatt Report.' The Task Force was to make recommendations to the Secretary of State for Trade and Industry and the Lord Chancellor on how services could be made more efficient and cost-effective for users. The Task Force's overall objective, according to its remit, was 'to ensure that the employment tribunal system reflects the needs of its users and the changing environment in which it operates'. The Task Force's Report was published on 30 July 2002. In Chapter 7, discussion of this report's recommendations will be considered.

Despite all of these reviews, task forces and consultations, Genn reports that 'The legal profession is still very cautious about using ADR outside commercial practice'.[11] In this latest LCD report, Genn evaluated the Commercial Court's practice of issuing ADR orders and reviewed the 38 cases to date under the Court of Appeal's mediation scheme, which has been in operation since 1996. On a more optimistic note was the fact that since 1996, there have been over 233 ADR orders made by the Commercial Court, of which 52% were settled and only 5% went on to trial, having failed at ADR. Consequently, Genn commented that 'a modest level of voluntary take-up of the ADR scheme continued ... and ... positive experience of ADR does not appear to be producing armies of converts'.

---

9 Leggatt Review, 2001 (see www.tribunals-review.org.uk).
10 Secretary of State, Mrs P Hewitt, MP, www.employmenttribunalsystemtask force.gov.uk/news.htm.
11 Genn, 2002.

1.2   ADR – ITS MEANING

ADR collectively refers to mediation, conciliation and arbitration, as well as a combination such as Med-Arb. ADR describes the situation where a third party is involved to assist the parties in a settlement of their dispute. Arbitration provides for the provision of the final determination of a dispute by a private tribunal. According to the Community Legal Service's *Guide to Alternatives to Court*,[12] 'There are many different types of alternative dispute resolution scheme. The one (or ones) you choose to use will depend on: how you want your problem dealt with; and what sort of problem you have'.[13]

The evidence presented so far suggests that the application of ADR to employment law is questionable. An ADR scheme operated by Acas for alternative resolution of unfair dismissal claims exists. However, such a scheme was born out of a concern about the substantial rise in the caseload of tribunals although, ironically, unfair dismissal claims themselves had increased only marginally over the previous decade. For instance, in the 1980s, the maximum volume of cases in any year was 35,000, as opposed to the maximum volume of 71,000 cases in the 1990s.[14] In 2001, 98,000 IT1 applications were recorded.[15] Shortly after the new scheme was suggested, the number of claims reaching tribunals rose (temporarily) to the point where, in some regions, there was anecdotal evidence of representatives seeking adjournments because there was insufficient time for the preparation of cases.

The view that somehow ADR, namely arbitration, will restore the Donovan ideals 'lost' by employment tribunals also appears to be open to question, either because there is insufficient evidence to show that, for example, tribunals are no longer speedy, cheap or accessible, or because it is not clear to many at present how arbitration will have any greater success in achieving those ideals. Paradoxically, it is often unfair dismissal cases which are less complex, less time-consuming and more easily brought by unrepresented applicants than, for example, claims of discrimination, especially disability discrimination. In Chapter 2, the 1998 enabling Act and its policy aims will be considered, as well as the new emerging force of change being brought in under the EA 2002.

One aim of this book is to help advisers to examine more closely the components of the Acas scheme and to identify those unfair dismissal situations and cases where its very differences from the employment tribunal process make it a preferred route for advisers and their clients.

---

12   CLS Information Leaflet No 23 (English version).
13   *Ibid*, p 5.
14   See *Labour Market Trends*, 1989 and 1999.
15   Acas, *Annual Report*, 2002.

1.3   ARBITRATION ACTS FROM 1697 TO 1996

According to Marshall, 'An arbitration is the reference of a dispute or difference between not less than two persons for determination after hearing both sides in a judicial manner by another person or persons, other than a court of competent jurisdiction'.[16] The first Arbitration Act was enacted in 1697 and was first consolidated in 1889 following the initial codification under the Common Law Procedure Act 1854. The later 1950 consolidation became more famous. The 1950 Arbitration Act established international arbitrations under the Geneva Convention. This latter initiative was furthered to include the New York Convention in 1975.

However, the watershed for arbitration came in 1996, following the recommendation of the Mustill Committee, with the enactment of an extensive, newly reformed Arbitration Act. Introducing the 1996 Act, Lord Fraser of Carmyllie observed that: 'The Act follows a logical sequence. The language is clear and simple. Above all it is based on the proposition that arbitration is a valid alternative to litigation as a means of resolving those disputes which inevitably arise in business ... The principle of party autonomy is central to the [Act]. The parties who are in dispute are able to decide how the arbitration should be conducted ... What potential users want is a system which is speedy and cost-effective, is final and fair.'[17] As Marshall puts it, '[the Act is] a refreshing new start for law and practice of arbitration in England, Wales and Northern Ireland'.[18] The Act was passed on 17 June 1996 and came into force on 31 January 1997,[19] applying only to arbitrations after this commencement date. The Act applies to both domestic and international arbitrations.[20]

Overall, the 1996 Act represents a comprehensive and coherent legal statement of the principles of arbitration to be adopted in England, Wales and Northern Ireland. Its clarity and simplicity were praised, as was its central judicial non-intervention principle. The advantages of arbitrations under this important Act are that they provide the following:

- a non-legal process;
- speedy dispute resolution;
- cost-saving; and
- a private hearing.

In repealing Pt I of the 1950 Act, the 1996 Act divides its 110 sections into four parts, consisting of general provisions, arbitration agreements, recognition of awards and enforcements of awards. Its adjoining four schedules clarify its

---

16 Marshall, 2001, p 1.

17 *Hansard* (HL), 1996, vol 568, col 761.

18 Marshall, 2001, p 2. Note the deliberate omission of Scotland, since the Scottish legal system has its own pre-existing equivalent primary legislation in its Arbitration (Scotland) Act 1894 and its Scottish Arbitration Code 1999. In any event, since 1998, under the Scotland Act, arbitration has become a devolved matter.

19 By the Arbitration Act 1996 (Commencement No 1) Order 1996.

20 Hence, ss 85–87 of the Act, referring solely to domestic arbitrations, were not brought into effect, so as to avoid the exclusion of international arbitrations under the 1950 and 1975 pre-existing Acts.

general principles of fair resolution, consent of the parties and non-judicial intervention. Section 4 of the Act provides for 'mandatory provisions', which are listed in Sched 1 to the Act.[21]

These include:

- the staying of legal proceedings;
- the power to extend time limits;
- the application of the Limitation Acts;
- the power to remove an arbitrator (before a court);
- the parties' liability to fees and expenses of an arbitrator;
- arbitrator immunity;
- the objection to jurisdiction of an arbitration tribunal;
- the determination of preliminary points;
- the general duty of tribunals;
- the attendance of witnesses;
- withholding and enforcing the award; and
- challenging the award.

Section 3 defines the 'seat of arbitration'. This is the all-important geographical location, or jurisdiction, to which the arbitration is tied. It is the seat which prescribes the procedural law applicable to the arbitration. Such a 'seat' (juridical seat) is often determined by the parties, the arbitrator or the arbitral tribunal, or agreed contractually in a relevant clause prior to the dispute.

1.4   ADR AND EMPLOYMENT LAW – THE 1998 ACT AND THE ACAS SCHEME

Since the inception of the 1996 Act, much interest has grown in both commercial and employment legal sectors in relation to the applicability of ADR, namely arbitration. Consequently, the main focus of interest in the ER(DR)A 1998 was the proposal that in certain cases where the parties so agree, Acas rather than the employment tribunals should have a role in adjudicating on unfair dismissal claims. Thus, s 7 of that Act enabled Acas to prepare a scheme for arbitration of unfair dismissal claims that could otherwise be brought before a tribunal. The Act also provided that the Secretary of State may, by Order, allow for other types of claim to be the subject of such arbitration. It is important to note that this new role for Acas is quite separate from its long-standing role in seeking to settle and conciliate unfair dismissal claims prior to a tribunal hearing, and that Acas will continue to perform this function, which in itself is a form of ADR. The main thrust of the scheme is that where the parties to an unfair dismissal (or other designated) claim agree in writing to submit the dispute to arbitration,

---

21 See ss 9–13, 24, 28–29, 31–33, 37(2), 40, 43, 56, 60, 66–68 and 72–75.

Acas will refer the claim to an arbitrator. The primary legislation remained silent on how such an arbitration scheme might work. However, in order to submit a dispute to the Acas arbitration scheme, the parties must do so through a legally binding procedure, which must be in the form of either a compromise agreement (as defined by statute and referred to further below), or else after the intervention of an Acas conciliation officer.[22] In this way, submitting a dispute to the Acas scheme requires exactly the same formalities to be followed as would be required for an actual settlement of a claim, the thinking behind such a requirement clearly being to protect claimants from being pressured to agree to Acas arbitration of their dispute. The operation of the scheme is to be triggered only when Acas receives a copy of the conciliated settlement or compromise agreement. The 1998 Act and the EA 2002 are fully discussed in Chapter 2. The Acas arbitral scheme launched in May 2001[23] established clear terms of reference for the arbitrator, under which they will be able to decide whether the dismissal is fair or unfair, and where it is found to be unfair, they will be able to award reinstatement, re-engagement or compensation. However, if there is any dispute as to jurisdiction, such as whether or not the applicant was an 'employee', then the parties would consider whether the matter should be referred to an employment tribunal. The parties will be expected to participate fully in the arbitration process by, for example, exchanging documents and details of the witnesses who will be called.

Acas has already responded to the need to staff the new scheme by appointing 60–70 additional arbitrators,[24] who are not necessarily lawyers but who have experience in employment relations. The arbitrator is to be responsible for the conduct of hearings, and parties will be allowed to be represented and to call witnesses. The approach will be inquisitorial and there will be no direct cross-examination, although questions may be put through the arbitrator. The decision will be issued to the parties only, hence a measure of privacy is achieved. So far as awards of compensation are concerned, these will be determined in accordance with the traditional tribunal principles and subject to the same financial limits. Similarly, where reinstatement or re-engagement is ordered but not complied with, the order will not be capable of being enforced directly but, as with tribunal orders, will give rise to the possibility of enhanced compensation. The scheme contemplates that there would be no appeal either on a point of law or fact, although if a party considers that there has been a 'serious irregularity' in the conduct of the arbitrator or substantive jurisdictional issues, an appeal to the High Court under ss 67–68 of the Arbitration Act 1996 is possible. Appeals and remedies will be discussed in Chapter 6.

The benefits of using this new scheme are laid out more fully in Chapter 3, but the main benefits, like those under the 1996 Arbitration Act, are thought to be speed, cost, privacy and greater informality. To date, there have been 20 cases

---

22 See ER(DR)A 1998, s 8.
23 See Earnshaw and Hardy, 2001, pp 289–304, for further details, including an initial review of the scheme. Further, see Baker, 2002, pp 113–34.
24 That is, in addition to around 30 members of its existing Arbitration Panel who deal with 'trade dispute' arbitrations.

under the Acas scheme. Consequently, Acas intends to relaunch its scheme sometime in the future,[25] since it believes that the General Election in 2001, which coincided with the original launch, distracted attention, which thus probably accounts for the initial low uptake to date.

1.5   THE EMPLOYMENT ACT (EA) 2002 AND ADR

The government's Employment Bill (now the EA 2002) was introduced to the House of Commons in November 2001,[26] marking 'the most radical change to unfair dismissal law in 25 years'.[27] Part II of the Bill set out long-awaited, controversial rules relating to tribunal reform in the shape of costs and expenses before employment tribunals and the Employment Appeal Tribunal (EAT).[28]

In particular, ss 24–28 introduce strengthening measures on conciliation as a pre-tribunal stage. For instance, s 24 encourages the postponement of hearings before employment tribunals pending conciliation. Consequently, this acts as a preface for 'dispute resolution' in Pt III of the 2002 Act. Part III of the Act, in particular s 29, provides for a statutory dispute resolution procedure. Schedule 2 sets out the detailed procedure, including a 'standardised procedure' for disciplinary meetings and appeals, dismissals and grievance handling. Section 30 ensures that 'every contract of employment shall require the employer and employee to comply, in relation to any matter to which a statutory procedure applies', a significant incentive towards compliance being that in cases of non-compliance, the tribunal will reduce or increase the award by 10% of any unfair dismissal compensation awarded to the non-complying party.29 Furthermore, the Act amends s 98 of the Employment Rights Act (ERA) 1996 in order to accommodate failure under the statutory scheme and enables such procedural non-compliance to give rise to an automatic unfair dismissal. The exemption of the smaller employers, that is, those with fewer than 20 employees, for written statements of employment is revoked. During the parliamentary passage of the EA 2002, the Joint Committee on Human Rights,30 following concerns being raised by the President of Employment Tribunals for England and Wales,31 considered whether the Bill potentially limited applicants' rights of access before employment tribunals. For example, Prophet J suggested that cl 33 of the Bill might violate Art 6(1) of the European Convention on Human Rights 1950 (ratified by the UK in 1951), given the proposal to deprive employees of their right to litigate before a tribunal where they have not complied with an employer's statutory internal procedure. The Committee found that such concerns were not supported.

---

25 *Personnel Today*, 12 March 2002, p 2.

26 HC Bill 44, 2001.

27 See Hepple and Morris, 2002, pp 245–69.

28 Sections 22–23.

29 Section 31(2), (3) and (4).

30 Twelfth Report (see www.publications.parliament.uk/pa/jt200102/jtselect/jtrights/85/8502.htm).

31 His Honour Judge John Prophet.

1.6 ADR AGREEMENTS?

It is anticipated that an increase of compromise agreements will accompany the latest reforms towards ADR in employment law. For this reason, the ER(DR)A 1998 made some changes to the requirements surrounding their validity. The compromise agreement procedure was introduced into employment law by the Trade Union Reform and Employment Rights Act 1993, which provided a mechanism for the settlement of claims in respect of certain statutory employment rights, including unfair dismissal, discrimination, equal pay and unauthorised deductions from pay. The settlement would be binding on the parties only if certain conditions were met; however, the agreement had to be in writing and the complainant was required to have received independent legal advice from a qualified solicitor or barrister as to the terms and effect of the agreement, in particular, its ability to bar an employment tribunal claim. The procedure became popular and was widely used, although the legislation as initially enacted left a number of ambiguities. These were addressed by the 1998 Act and several other important changes were introduced.

First, the Act widens the range of persons who can validly give advice to a complainant. It is no longer necessary to receive 'independent legal advice from a qualified lawyer'; rather, the requirement is to receive 'advice from a relevant independent adviser'.[32] A 'relevant independent adviser' is defined as one of the following:

- a qualified lawyer (that is, a solicitor or barrister);
- a trade union officer;
- an employee or member who has been certified by the union as competent to give such advice and is authorised to do so on behalf of the union;
- a worker at an advice centre who has been certified by the centre as competent to give such advice, and is authorised to do so on behalf of the centre; or
- a person of a description specified in an Order made by the Secretary of State.

However, an adviser is *not* independent:

- if he is employed by or acting in the matter for the employer; or
- in the case of a union or advice centre, if the union or the advice centre is the employer; or
- in respect of advice from a worker at an advice centre, if the employee makes a payment for the advice received from that worker.

The practical effect of these changes is, in essence, to allow for trade unions and advice centres to give advice to employees on compromise agreements. The monopoly enjoyed by lawyers on the giving of such advice is thereby lost. Further, the requirement that the adviser be covered by a 'policy of insurance' is replaced by a requirement that the adviser be covered by a 'contract of insurance, or an indemnity provided for members of a professional body'. The

---

32   See ER(DR)A 1998, s 9.

main purpose of this change is to make it clear that the protection afforded to solicitors by the Solicitors' Indemnity Scheme is indeed valid for the purpose of signing off compromise agreements. There had been some concern as to whether the scheme complied with the technical definition of a 'policy of insurance'.

1.7   PRELIMINARY HUMAN RIGHTS ISSUES

Whilst the current hope is that the Human Rights Act (HRA) 1998, which came into operation on 2 October 2000, will not become a breeding ground for the raising of minor technicalities without substantive merit, it is already clear that the effects of the Act will be far-reaching. For example, in *Smith v Secretary of State for Trade and Industry*,[33] the question was raised as to whether employment tribunals met the 'requirement of independence' under Art 6 of the European Convention on Human Rights,[34] since the lay members of the tribunal are appointed and paid by the Secretary of State, who may, in certain cases, also be a party. In addition, the Court of Appeal in *Lawal v Northern Spirit*[35] concluded that it was incompatible with Art 6 of the Convention for an employment tribunal to hear a case where the advocate representing one of the parties also sat as a part-time chairman and had previously sat with one of the wing members hearing the case (now overruled by the Court of Appeal, although one judge did dissent). Such cases reiterate the need for impartiality and independence.

Concerns about the extent to which the ADR scheme will comply with Art 6 appear to focus on the need to ensure its 'voluntariness'[36] and the decision to go for an inquisitorial approach in which the parties will not be permitted direct cross-examination of witnesses. Lewis and Clark, whilst accepting that adversarialism, backed up by cross-examination, is the traditional model of the common law trial, draw on case law from the European Court of Human Rights to argue that, at its most fundamental level, adversarialism simply implies that 'one party should be allowed to comment upon the evidence and arguments of the other party with a view to influencing the eventual decisions'. Since the Acas scheme envisages that parties will be permitted to comment on each other's evidence, and to put questions through the arbitrator at the hearing as well as being invited to comment prior to the hearing on matters raised in the written statements of case, Lewis and Clark[37] submit that the requirements surrounding the right to a fair hearing will be met. One of the central questions about the arbitration of unfair dismissal claims is 'how will decisions be made?'. The standard terms of reference (which cannot be varied) are:

---

33 [2000] ICR 69.
34 That is, the right to a 'fair hearing'.
35 [2002] IRLR 714.
36 In this respect, Acas believes that a 'waiver' of the right to have the claim adjudicated by an employment tribunal should be signed by applicants and respondents.
37 Lewis and Clark, 2000.

The arbitrator shall decide whether the dismissal was fair or unfair, and in doing so shall have regard to the general principles of fairness and good conduct in employment relations, including, for example, the Acas Code of Practice, *Disciplinary and Grievance Procedures*, and the Acas Handbook, *Discipline at Work*, instead of applying legal tests or rules. Apply EC law. The arbitrator shall not decide the case by substituting what he would have done for the actions taken by the employer. Where the dismissal is found to have been unfair, the arbitrator may award reinstatement, re-engagement or compensation. Nothing in these Terms of Reference affects the operation of the Human Rights Act 1998.[38]

These questions will be addressed in detail in Chapters 2–5.

Even though there is no mention made of the ERA 1996 or the Trade Union and Labour Relations (Consolidation) Act 1992, it would appear that arbitrators must, however, pay heed to EC and human rights law where they are relevant, although they should not otherwise apply a legal standard. What seems to be envisaged is that the decision to dismiss will be judged in accordance with an employment relations standard which may also take account of the good practice of the industry.

Two possible scenarios appear to arise in consequence. The first is that the application of an employment relations standard will, or may, produce a different result in a given case from the application of the existing legal standard. Currently, an employer knows, or should know, the basis upon which a dismissal is to be judged fair or unfair and can act accordingly. On the other hand, it could be argued that in reality, there will be little difference between the two standards. After all, in considering 'the circumstances of the case', when deciding whether an employer acted 'reasonably', accepted practice within the industry is frequently a relevant factor. Moreover, although it is certainly true that the Acas Code of Practice does not figure specifically in the legal standard for determining the fairness of a dismissal, the EAT has specifically ruled[39] that an employment tribunal misdirected itself in law by failing to have regard for the Acas Code of Practice in reaching its decision. In the view of the EAT, the Code formed the basis on which the employer's conduct should be judged and should be taken into account, even if not referred to by the parties. In Chapter 5, these practical issues will be considered and some guidance will be given.

1.8   ADR AND THE FUTURE OF EMPLOYMENT LAW

ADR is surely increasing in its significance and impact in employment law. The EA 2002 supports the government's commitment to 'create highly productive, modern and successful workplaces through fairness and partnership at work'. In terms of dispute resolution, the government seeks to 'make it easier to settle disputes in the workplace',[40] the emphasis being placed on 'in' the workplace.

Such government commitment heralds a new era for the application of ADR in employment disputes. The Act itself, according to the government, 'aims to

---

38   Acas, 2001(b), para 26.
39   In the case of *Lock v Cardiff Railway Co Ltd* [1998] IRLR 358 (see s 207 of the TULR(C)A 1992).
40   See www.dti.gov.uk/er/employ.

help to build constructive employment relations and avoid the need for litigation through better communication in the workplace and improved conciliation'. This will be achieved under the 2002 Act by encouraging internal resolution of workplace disputes, by facilitating a better understanding of the employment relationship and, above all, by 'providing for timely and amicable settlement'. The detail of the Act will be evaluated in Chapter 2 and some conclusions in terms of its furtherance of ADR in employment law will be drawn in Chapter 7.

CHAPTER 2

UNDERSTANDING THE EMPLOYMENT RIGHTS (DISPUTE RESOLUTION) ACT 1998 AND THE EMPLOYMENT ACT 2002

The thought of going to a tribunal to resolve a dispute is most employers' and employees' worst nightmare. Yet, on average, over 100,000 applicants/ respondents undertake such a journey every year. As long ago as 1968, the then government's White Paper, *In Place of Strife* (very appropriately termed), recommended a free, informal and speedy forum for dealing with unfair dismissal claims. Industrial tribunals (now employment tribunals) emerged out of the former National Industrial Relations Court as that forum. That was the era when lawyers rarely practised employment law. Since then, with a growth in legislation, exhaustive legal intervention generally, high levels of employment litigation and an emerging number of employment law specialists, over 100,000 cases have arisen annually and this once virtuous system has become overloaded. Consequently, alongside these changes, an exhaustive body of case law has developed. The end result is that whilst some individuals relish their day in tribunal, others find the experience altogether too daunting and frustrating. This contributes to Acas resolving some 75% of cases before they get to tribunal. Against this background, the Employment Rights (Dispute Resolution) Act (ER(DR)A) 1998 was born.

2.1 THE EMPLOYMENT RIGHTS (DISPUTE RESOLUTION) ACT 1998

The ER(DR)A, enacted on 8 April 1998, sought to make significant changes to the procedures relating to employment tribunals. In particular, it proposed a scheme for Acas arbitration of unfair dismissal claims which has now come into effect. The Act sought to make employment tribunals work more efficiently and speedily, and to reduce the level of tribunal litigation by introducing an arbitral scheme for unfair dismissal, given that unfair dismissal cases account for most of the caseload each year.

2.1.1 Peer's Bill

The ER(DR)A 1998 made several changes to employment tribunal procedure but, more significantly, it proposed a scheme for Acas arbitration of unfair dismissal claims. It was introduced by Lord Archer of Sandwell to the House of Lords as a Private Peer's Bill, with government support, in July 1997, and came into force on 1 August 1998. The origins of the legislation date back to the growing concern in the mid-1990s, on the part of the Conservative government, that the delays caused by the dramatic increase in the caseload of industrial tribunals, and the growing complexity of the law, meant that the original objectives of the tribunal system were no longer being met. The main focus of interest in the ER(DR)A 1998 was the proposal that in certain cases, where the parties so agree, Acas rather than the employment tribunals should have a role in adjudicating on unfair dismissal claims. It is important to note that this new role for Acas is quite separate from its long-standing role in seeking to settle and conciliate unfair dismissal claims prior to a tribunal hearing, and that Acas will continue to perform this function even when the new scheme is in operation.

The decision to introduce a new arbitral option, and the upholding of its virtues,[1] has not put an end to controversial debate about the effectiveness of the employment tribunal system. In its defence, MacMillan contends that the Donovan ideals of accessibility and cheapness have remained intact, and that outside London the so called 'problem' of a backlog of cases simply does not exist.[2] Tackling accusations of lack of informality, he argues that if formality means making decisions in accordance with the law, then the alternative is for disputes to be resolved 'on the basis of apparently unfettered pragmatism or, if you are a cynic, the unchallengeable whim of an arbitrator'. If there is indeed a problem, then, in MacMillan's view, this lies not in how tribunals operate but in the continual extension of the tribunals' jurisdiction to areas of law which Donovan could never have envisaged.

2.1.2 Agreement

This new arbitral route relies on voluntariness and an agreement amongst the parties to proceed down an arbitral route. This formal agreement marks the start of a tight set of deadlines in order to allow the dispute to be resolved in theory in as little as eight weeks. The detailed guidance on such an agreement and the ensuing arbitral procedures are considered, explained and evaluated in the following chapters.

2.1.3 Compromise?

Any ADR scheme promotes conciliation and settlement. Some critics consider this to be compromise. Compromise in such circumstances should be viewed in a positive rather than a negative manner. For instance, in an employment dispute, surely it is logical that the parties – the employer and the employee – meet and exchange their views (or convey them through a third party) and then attempt, even if unsuccessfully, to resolve the matter without initiating formal litigation. Furthermore, this act promotes such intervention between the normal internal hearings and the progression towards claiming unfair dismissal before an employment tribunal. As Lewis and Clark[3] ask, 'why seek an alternative?', simply because the parties want a quick, cheap and less legal forum for dispute resolution, or at the very least desire to attempt it prior to litigation, if all else fails.

---

1   See Lewis and Clark, 2000.
2   MacMillan, 1999, pp 33–56.
3   Lewis and Clark, 2000, p 2.

The ER(DR)A 1998 also sought to amend and promote the law relating to compromise agreements, insofar as they should be more regulated but more widely accepted and applied to confirm arbitral and/or settlement arrangements. This will be discussed in Chapter 3.

2.1.4   The Acas scheme

The ER(DR)A 1998 makes Acas responsible for establishing a statutory arbitral route for unfair dismissal, for managing it and for recruiting the relevant arbitrators. Subsequently, an Order was put to and approved by the Secretary of State and Parliament, and the scheme became operative on 21 May 2001. The scheme marked a watershed, given that it formally introduced arbitration as the 'third way', promoting dispute resolution instead of litigation in employment dispute resolution. The Acas scheme, as it is now widely referred to, is examined in Chapter 3.

2.2   THE EMPLOYMENT ACT (EA) 2002

The Employment Bill[4] was introduced into the House of Commons on 8 November 2001 and completed its Commons Third Reading by early February 2002.[5] The Bill was then introduced to the House of Lords on 13 February 2002 and completed its Lords stage in July,[6] with the Bill receiving Royal Assent on 8 July 2002. The Act will come into force fully during April 2003. As the government proclaims: 'The Employment [Act] is a wide ranging package. It covers work and parents, dispute resolution in the workplace, improvements to employment tribunal procedures, including the introduction of an equal pay questionnaire, provisions to implement the Fixed Term Work Directive, a new right to time off for union learning representatives, work focussed interviews for partners of people receiving working-age benefits and some data sharing provisions.'[7] Overall, the Act supports the government's commitment to 'create a highly productive, modern and successful workplace through fairness and partnership at work ... and make it easier to settle disputes in the workplace'.[8] Such a varied cocktail makes for interesting times ahead, if only in terms of dispute resolution.

2.2.1   Dispute resolution

Since this book is concerned with ADR in employment law, the significance of the EA 2002 with reference to its dispute resolution proposals will now be addressed. The Act seeks to 'amend the Employment Tribunals Act 1996 and to make provision for the use of statutory procedures in relation to employment

---

4   Bills 44 and 86.

5   Commons Committee, 24 January 2002 and Report, 3rd Reading, 12 February 2002.

6   Second Reading, 22 February 2002; Grand Committee, 22 April, including nine sessions (13, 14, 18, 20, 21, 25 and 26 March and 11 and 22 April 2002); and Report Stage, 30 May and 11 June 2002.

7   See www.dti.gov.uk/er/employ.

8   *Ibid.*

disputes'.[9] Sections 29–41 cover dispute resolution.[10] These are supplemented by four Schedules.[11]

2.2.2 Hansard

As with all parliamentary business, *Hansard*'s coverage has been extensive, yet the debates have been relatively short. It is under the Committee's scrutiny, mainly in the Lords, where the salient issues have been debated and amended. When a Lords Grand Committee sits for 10 sessions, producing over 50 amendments and four revised versions of the same Bill,[12] then the controversy/interest rating is very high.

2.2.3 Committee

The House of Commons Standing Committee F carefully scrutinised the Employment Bill. At its meeting of 13 December 2001, during its consideration of cl 29,[13] reference to the existing Acas Code on disciplinary procedures – *Disciplinary and Grievance Procedures* – was discussed. It emerged that both the Law Society and the TUC shared some concerns about whether such a proposal would undermine the existing Acas Code. The Minister[14] responded that '48% of employers who go to an employment tribunal do not have internal procedures ... There is no evidence that setting a minimum wage or any other minimum standard drags everything down to the minimum'. Given the Minister's observations, it is quite clear that such a statutory minimum procedure is championed and that ADR in employment disputes should become common practice prior to litigation, since in 48% of cases, according to government data, tribunal time was concerned with the absence of procedures which might well have resolved the situation. The Acas Code will need to acknowledge the existence of such procedures in any future revised draft.

Meanwhile, the House of Lords Grand Committee was similarly active in its deliberation on the Employment Bill. In fact, at its meetings of 15 and 20 May 2002, their Lordships raised some 38 amendments on cll 34–39. Of significance were the amendments by Lords McCarthy and Wedderburn and Baroness Turner, relating to the statutory disciplinary procedure limiting the Secretary of State's powers of intervention and ensuring clarity of the standards by which a tribunal will consider breach of the new statutory minimum requirement. Evidently, the concerns that such a new dispute resolution mechanism should be unambiguous and allow for improved dialogue between the aggrieved parties in order to settle the matter emerged quite strongly during the Parliamentary Committee scrutiny process.

---

9   HL Bill (53/1) Preamble.
10 Part 3 of the Bill.
11 Schedules 2–5.
12 See www.parliament.the-stationery-office.co.uk/pa/cm200102/cmstand/f/ cmemp.htm and www.publications.parliament.uk/pa/ld200102/ldbills/077/ amend/am077-c.htm.
13 Statutory dispute resolution procedures.
14 Alan Johnson, MP, Minister for Employment Relations.

2.2.4 Provisions

The Act aims to 'build constructive employment relations and avoid the need for litigation through better communication in the workplace and improved conciliation'.[15] In ensuring that a 'modern user-focused' employment tribunal will emerge, all of these aims will be achieved by:

- encouraging internal resolution in the workplace;
- facilitating a better understanding of the employment relationship;
- altering the way in which unfair dismissals are determined;
- providing for timely and amicable settlements; and
- providing a speedier, more efficient delivery of service.

These policy goals are therefore to be attained by introducing a minimum standard for internal disciplinary and grievance procedures in each workplace, and by encouraging employees to raise issues with their employer before applying to litigate against them before an employment tribunal. Moreover, the Act seeks to ensure that employers follow basic procedures prior to dismissals and to any form of disciplinary action, hence promoting ADR in employment disputes. Thus, the Act clearly heralds a policy shift in favour of ADR in employment law and moves away from total reliance on litigation-focused dispute resolution.

2.2.5 Processes

The Act, in aiming to provide better workplace dispute resolution mechanisms, sets out statutory minimum standards to be met, thereby establishing new processes for dispute resolution. Consequently, employers will have to provide clear disciplinary and grievance procedures. Furthermore, they will have to manage them with 'fairness' and procedural accuracy. Given such renewed legalities being formalised in statute, whilst current best practice mirrors such requirements, it is clear that the government desires to ensure that the employer and employee exchange dialogue rather than litigate in the first instance. To that end, employers will have to exchange views with the aggrieved employee and thus will be drawn towards resolution and settlement rather than litigation.

More significantly, the 2002 Act presents a new logistical process for dispute resolution at work. For instance, since this new law will demand improved internal decision-making, then such dialogue at the earliest opportunity encourages conciliation/ADR in the later stages and thus acts as a filter for those more acrimonious cases to prevail in the closing stages in tribunal in due course. Clearly, such a strategy sits squarely with the 1998 Act and the Acas arbitral scheme for unfair dismissal claims. Such a new era of internal employment dispute resolution requires the parties to put their respective cases succinctly and less legalistically. Chapters 4 and 5 will cover these new skills and processes.

---

15 See www.dti.gov.uk/er/employ.

2.3   EMPLOYMENT DISPUTE RESOLUTION (EDR)

As this chapter has demonstrated in its examination of the existing and forthcoming statutory provisions, a revitalised emphasis, dating back to the Donovan ideals of the 1960s, is re-emerging in the form of so called EDR. Internal disciplinary hearings will have to meet renewed minimum standards in future, in order to ensure that they exist and are practised, as well as the focus being on internal conciliation prior to litigation. Alternatively, the application of ADR principles and schemes as methods of dispute resolution rather than litigation before tribunals is being encouraged and promoted by government. In Chapter 3, it is pointed out that this thinking is not new and consideration is given to Acas's alternative scheme for ADR in unfair dismissal cases. In Chapters 4 and 5, the new EDR skills and legal processes required are presented.

2.3.1   The changing litigation landscape

In summary, we are now entering a new phase of legislation-supported ADR for workplace disputes on individual employment issues. Employers and employees are encouraged to make far greater efforts to resolve disputes within their own place of work. Where this proves to be impossible, and the employee feels the necessity to resort to the law, conciliation will be promoted within a fixed period to concentrate the minds of all the parties concerned on a speedy resolution of the problem. Should this further ADR approach not succeed, a formal hearing will follow within a prescribed time limit, and for unfair dismissal cases, there is now a choice of type of formal hearing. All of this new architecture is designed to promote ADR, so that fewer employers and employees will in future face the 'nightmare' of a full legal hearing before a tribunal.

2.3.2   New skills

As is explained more fully in Chapters 4 and 5, parties participating in employment arbitration will have to learn new skills. The absence of cross-examination will mean more emphasis on the respective arguments of the parties, as presented in the statement of case, to facilitate definition of the issues in such a way that the arbitrator will ask the relevant questions of witnesses.

2.3.3   Impact on employment law and practice

Clearly, a changing landscape in terms of EDR and the new skills required will impact upon existing and entrenched employment law and practice. Lawyers, human resources practitioners and trade union officials alike will have to re-adjust, re-educate and re-deploy their learning, practice and experiences to an ADR method of employment dispute resolution. Whilst this will be no easy task, as many commentators have suggested,[16] it is, as Chapter 4 demonstrates,

---

16 See Earnshaw and Hardy, 2001; Baker, 2002.

achievable. Yet, more significantly, it can only be achieved where open-mindedness is first accepted as a pre-condition to change. The merits and demerits of the new scheme of dispute resolution are assessed in both Chapters 3 and 4.

CHAPTER 3

BACKGROUND TO THE ACAS SCHEME

In this chapter, the Acas scheme for unfair dismissal, providing an alternative to tribunal determination for unfair dismissal claims, is presented and examined.

3.1   FIRST STEPS TO A SCHEME

The concept of using arbitration as a means of resolving disputes relating to the disciplining and dismissal of individual employees is by no means new. In 1993, Lewis and Clark[1] outlined the use of the voluntary Acas arbitration arrangements in such cases, at that time around 60–70 per year, mainly arising from provisions contained in national, industry-wide collective agreements. The experience of these authors and of their fellow arbitrators hearing such cases led them to propose voluntary arbitration as an alternative which parties could jointly opt for as opposed to the statutory route of the industrial tribunals for resolving individual employment rights disputes. Key differences between the two processes include the following:

- the use of an employment relations standard as opposed to a legal one in deciding a dismissal;
- speedier, less adversarial and more inquisitorial arbitration hearings;
- the savings that such hearings can provide in terms of both time and money; and
- the scope that they can provide for a wider range of remedies than are available under the statutory route.

As noted in Chapter 1, the concept of an alternative arbitration route was found attractive by the then Conservative government, which included it first in a Green Paper, *Resolving Employment Rights Disputes: Options for Reform*, Cm 2707. Later, following favourable comment from a wide spectrum of employment relations practitioners, it was included in the DTI Consultative Document, *Resolving Employment Rights Disputes* (July 1996). In the event, the concept of an alternative arbitral scheme, to be prepared by Acas, was finally given effect in a Private Peer's Bill – supported by the new Labour government – which became the Employment Rights (Dispute Resolution) Act (ER(DR)A) 1998. In drafting such a scheme, which the Act restricted initially to cases of unfair dismissal, Acas 'tried to adhere to the central features of trade dispute arbitration which are that it is voluntary, speedy, informal, confidential and free from legal argument'.[2] It was always recognised that some safeguards would have to be built into the scheme and its operation in recognition of the fact that employees who wished to opt for arbitration under the scheme had to give up their right to pursue an alternative unfair dismissal claim in the employment tribunal. It was

---

1   Lewis and Clark, 1993.
2   Acas, 1998.

initially envisaged that such safeguards could, in part, be provided by incorporating into the scheme, or into the Secretary of State's Order giving it effect, appropriate provisions of the Arbitration Act 1996, including a right of challenge to the arbitrator's decision on the grounds of serious irregularity. Responses to the Acas Consultation Document, which contained an outline of the proposed scheme, covered many aspects. There were, however, two major aspects on which many respondents sought clarification. The first concerned the 'test' which the arbitrator would use to decide whether a dismissal was fair or unfair and how it would differ from that applied by employment tribunals, especially in relation to the 'range of reasonable responses' guidelines from the EAT in *Iceland Frozen Foods v Jones*.[3] The second major area of concern related to the way in which arbitrators who found dismissals to be unfair, and who decided not to award reinstatement or re-engagement, would calculate compensation. The outline scheme merely stated that 'the amount of any award of compensation will be reasonable in all the circumstances, taking into account the established practice of, and any statutory limits imposed on, employment tribunals'. In both instances, respondents to the consultation argued that unless there was more clarity about these and other issues, it would be difficult to fairly advise parties of the strengths and weaknesses of the alternative routes, either in general terms or in the particular circumstances of their case. In addition, it was argued, the consistency of decision-making on such issues in the employment tribunals, which is assisted by a legal framework of precedent, would be lacking in arbitration cases where decisions relied on the arbitrator 'having regard to the Acas Code of Practice, *Disciplinary and Grievance Procedures* and the Acas Handbook, *Discipline at Work*'.

3.2   DETAILED DRAFTING OF THE SCHEME

In drafting the final scheme for the Secretary of State to approve and then lay before Parliament in the form of an Order, the need for greater clarity in how arbitrators would make salient decisions which would inform their awards was only one of a number of considerations. Two key issues related to the impact on the scheme of both the Human Rights Act (HRA) 1998 and of EC law where the right not to be unfairly dismissed emanated from an EC right, such as dismissal on the grounds of sex discrimination, dismissal related to the transfer of an undertaking or for exercising a right under the 1998 Working Time Regulations. In the former instance, Acas had initially received advice that the voluntary nature of the scheme and the presence of an alternative statutory route of redress meant that the scheme was unlikely to contravene the European Convention on Human Rights, and in particular Art 6 (the right to a fair trial). Subsequent advice, following the passing of the HRA 1998, indicated that a more formal waiver of such rights by the parties to an arbitration under the scheme would be required, in order to formally indicate their understanding of the differences in principle and practice between the employment tribunal and

---

3   [1982] IRLR 439.

arbitration routes. These would be set out in detail in guidance material which would be issued to parties contemplating using the scheme, and a standard form of waiver would be provided. With regard to issues of EC law, Acas was advised that the parties could not 'contract out' or otherwise ask the arbitrator to ignore its provisions in the same way that they had agreed in the waiver to the arbitrator using non-legal industrial relations principles, as opposed to reliance upon legal precedents, to decide the case. Whilst parties would be strongly advised that such EC law issues should be taken through the employment tribunal route, where they did arise before or during an arbitration hearing, provision would be made for a legal adviser to be appointed to advise the arbitrator on matters of EC law. A similar arrangement would apply for issues relating to the circumstances of the case, as opposed to the conduct of the arbitration, where there were issues appertaining to the HRA 1998.

The need to make provision for issues arising under EC law and the HRA 1998, and the related need for the provision of legal advisers, introduced the requirement for a route of appeal in respect of the arbitrator's consideration of points on these issues raised in the context of their award. However, it was important for the principle of finality in arbitration to be preserved in all other circumstances whilst at the same time protecting the interests of parties who had waived their rights as a condition of entry to the scheme. This was achieved by incorporating sufficient provisions of the Arbitration Act 1996 to make the scheme effective, and by training arbitrators under the scheme in standard arbitration practice. Appeals against the arbitrator's award would consequently not be possible, but challenges on the specific grounds of substantive jurisdiction or serious irregularity could be made. To meet the needs of respondents to the Acas consultation exercise, standard terms of reference for the arbitrator to use in every case were introduced. In addition, the guidance material issued to those people contemplating using the scheme was expanded to indicate the types of documentation and areas of witness expertise which the parties might wish to have at their disposal during the hearings. Guidance was also given on the way in which arbitrators would use their own experience of accepted standards in the workplace when reaching a decision. Detailed guidance, which mirrored the practice in employment tribunals, on the remedies available to arbitrators where an award of unfair dismissal was made was also included.

Given all of the above considerations, the final scheme and the guidance material which supported it emerged as a far more complex set of documentation than many who had followed its progress from Lewis and Clark's original proposals, and through both government and Acas consultation papers, might have envisaged. Whilst its final form may be off-putting to some, much of the detail is geared for the exception rather than the rule. At the heart of the scheme remains a genuinely alternative process to an employment tribunal hearing. Feedback suggests that many commentators can see the value, in a variety of unfair dismissal cases and for a variety of reasons, often related to the particular circumstances of a particular case, of what remains an essentially non-legalistic, non-adversarial, confidential and potentially relatively inexpensive alternative to the employment tribunal route.

3.3   THE RECRUITMENT AND TRAINING OF ARBITRATORS

Acas arbitrators are not employed by Acas but are appointed by them on a case by case basis from a standing panel. Initial estimates of likely caseloads indicated the need for a panel of around 100 to hear cases under the scheme. With some 30 of those on the existing trade dispute arbitration panels, traditionally drawn mainly from the industrial relations/human resources disciplines of academia, indicating a desire to be included on the scheme panel, there was a need to recruit the remainder. The appointments were subject to the recently introduced guidelines from the Commissioner for Public Appointments which required the process to be transparent, accountable and non-discriminatory. From an Acas perspective, it was vital to the success of the scheme that the parties should have complete confidence in the arbitrator appointed to hear their case. It was recognised that this would depend not only on the arbitrator's knowledge and experience of employment relations and the practical application of the Acas Code of Practice and Handbook to everyday situations at work, but also on their handling of the arbitration process itself. In respect of the latter, this was as much a function of their professional conduct in managing the process as of their interpersonal skills when relating to the wide social and economic spread of the parties in unfair dismissal cases. Whilst these attributes, together with an understanding of the law, are also required of employment tribunal chairmen and members, the burden placed on an individual sitting alone with no professional or administrative support on the day is arguably greater. For the purposes of recruitment and selection, and given this wide variety of requirements, a framework of competences for the role was drawn up by an occupational psychologist. In doing so, a programme of interviews with existing arbitrators and Acas administration staff was conducted, together with observations of arbitration hearings. The framework produced a set of three competence families: intellectual (judgment and analytical thinking); interpersonal (relationship management, credibility, oral and written communication); and personal (self-reliance, adaptability, planning and organising and specialist knowledge).

Advertisements in the national press, professional journals and selected local and minority publications produced over 3,500 requests for recruitment packs, from which around 1,500 competence-based application forms were returned. Using the competence framework, these were reduced to a shortlist of some 180 candidates, who attended a one-day assessment centre in groups of six. The centre employed a range of individual and group exercises to further test the candidates against the competence framework, resulting in a final shortlist of between 60 and 70 people to join the panel for the scheme. The successful candidates came from a variety of backgrounds, including human resources and line management, trade union officers, independent consultants, academics, lawyers and a few former employees of Acas. A number of them belonged to more than one of these categories, and there were representatives from the private, public and not-for-profit sectors of the economy. Many also, in one way or another, had experience of unfair dismissal cases under the employment tribunal route. This proved very useful when comparing and contrasting both processes and potential outcomes under the alternative routes during the training programme. After appointment, initial training and guidance material in all aspects of the scheme, and in good arbitration practice, was provided by experienced trade dispute arbitrators, together with legal and policy advisers and Acas staff responsible for the drafting and implementation of the scheme. A programme was then put in place to allow those new to the panel to shadow experienced arbitrators when they were hearing cases, and to prepare draft awards for discussion with experienced colleagues and Acas staff. As the scheme gathers momentum, regular conferences will be held to allow arbitrators to exchange knowledge and good practice with their peers.

3.4   AN OUTLINE OF THE ACAS SCHEME

A detailed description of the scheme and guidance for those who have opted to use it are contained in the Acas publication, *The Acas Arbitration Scheme for the Resolution of Unfair Dismissal Disputes: A Guide to the Scheme*. For ease of reference, the key features of the scheme are outlined below:

- The scheme provides an alternative to an employment tribunal hearing in cases of unfair dismissal.
- The arbitration process is confidential, relatively fast, cost-efficient, non-legalistic and informal.
- Entry to the scheme is entirely voluntary and there must be agreement by both parties to the dispute to go to binding arbitration.
- The employee/s must either have an existing application to the employment tribunal pending or must claim that they have grounds to potentially lodge such an application.
- Entry to the scheme is via an arbitration agreement reached with the assistance of an Acas conciliator or in the format of a compromise agreement drawn up by appropriate representatives.
- Both parties must sign a waiver form which confirms their agreement to go to arbitration and their understanding of the process.
- The arbitration agreement must be received by the Acas Arbitration Section within six weeks of it being concluded by the parties.
- On receipt of a valid arbitration agreement, Acas will appoint an arbitrator from its Arbitration Panel. Parties will not have a choice of arbitrator.
- Where an employee has a claim or claims in addition to unfair dismissal, any other claim(s) must be settled, withdrawn or heard by an employment tribunal.
- The scheme is not designed to deal with complex legal issues.
- In agreeing to go to arbitration, the parties waive any jurisdictional issues: for example, whether the employee had qualifying service, whether any application to the employment tribunal was submitted within time limits, etc.
- The scheme is not designed to deal with issues of EC law. If such issues arise, the arbitrator may appoint a legal adviser to provide guidance.

- Where issues arise under the HRA 1998 (apart from procedural matters set out in the scheme), the arbitrator may appoint a legal adviser to provide guidance.
- In addition to the information on the employee's application to the employment tribunal (IT1) and the employer's response (IT3) (where an application to the employment tribunal has been made), the parties will be invited to submit a written statement of their case in advance of the hearing.
- Parties to the dispute must comply with any instruction given by the arbitrator and will be expected to co-operate in the production of relevant documents and the attendance of appropriate witnesses.
- Hearings will be held at a location convenient and accessible to the parties and will not normally last for more than half a day.
- Each party meets their own costs in attending the hearing; however, if a dismissal is found to be unfair, the arbitrator can include in the calculation of any compensation a sum to cover the costs incurred by the employee personally in attending the hearing.
- The arbitrator has the power to set dates and locations of hearings if the parties do not co-operate in these arrangements.
- If parties do not attend a hearing without good cause, the arbitrator has the power to continue the hearing and decide whether a dismissal was fair or unfair, or where an employee fails to attend without good cause, the case can be treated as dismissed.
- The arbitrator will use an inquisitorial rather than adversarial approach – there will be no cross-examination of witnesses by a party or representative, or swearing of oaths; rather, the arbitrator will question the witnesses.
- Instead of applying strict law or legal precedent, the arbitrator will take account of general principles of fairness and good practice in the workplace, including the principles set out in any relevant Acas Code of Practice and the Acas Handbook (relevant here means those in existence at the time of the dismissal).
- Exceptions to the non-application of strict law concern EC law or the HRA 1998 where these are relevant.
- Following the hearing, the arbitrator will issue a binding 'Award' summarising each party's case, the arbitrator's main considerations, the decision and, if unfair, the remedy. The award will be confidential to Acas and the parties.
- If a dismissal is found to be unfair, an arbitrator can order the same remedies as an employment tribunal. These are reinstatement, re-engagement or compensation.
- There are very limited grounds for challenging an arbitrator's award and parties cannot appeal against an arbitrator's binding award on points of law except in cases where EC law or the HRA 1998 is relevant.

3.5   USAGE OF THE SCHEME TO DATE

Despite some expressions of disappointment that the scheme has, at least on paper, turned out to be more complex than might have been anticipated from both the original proposals of Lewis and Clark and some of the draft outlines included in subsequent consultation exercises, many commentators from across the employment relations spectrum have welcomed its introduction. A common reaction has been one of 'horses for courses', with one or more of the scheme's features being cited as making it preferable to an employment tribunal hearing in the particular set of circumstances of a specific case. In one instance, this might be the more informal nature of the proceedings, in another, the confidential nature of the hearing and the award and, in a third, the convenience to the parties of a speedy local hearing. Thus, many experienced representatives have intimated that whilst they would not – at least in the early stages, before some detailed research on the scheme's usage has been published – consider recommending it to their clients as a matter of course, they would do so where the circumstances of a specific case made the arbitration route an attractive one.

Notwithstanding the conditional support described above, take-up of the scheme to date has been slow. By August 2002, only 16 cases had been received by Acas for hearing. Whilst some of this reluctance to use the arbitration route may well be accounted for by representatives being cautious until they have learnt of the experiences of others, the fact that the public launch of the scheme coincided with the end of the 2001 General Election campaign may have served to reduce widespread awareness of its introduction. Now that some cases have been heard, it may well be time to combine the publication of a digest of first impressions with a relaunch of the scheme.

CHAPTER 4

RIGHTS AND WRONGS IN
EMPLOYMENT ARBITRATION

This chapter examines further the main features of the Acas arbitration scheme. It deals with the essential features, highlighting in particular how the scheme differs from the conventional forum for resolving employment-related dismissal disputes: the employment tribunals. Drawing on the documentation published by Acas and conventional arbitration practice, suggestions are made as to what may constitute best practice for dealing with the various stages of unfair dismissal arbitration. Essentially, most of the material can be derived from the scheme itself, assisted by the material in *The Acas Arbitration Scheme for the Resolution of Unfair Dismissal Disputes: A Guide to the Scheme* (the Guide). As we will see in Chapters 5 and 6, however, there are some areas – in particular when dealing with remedy – where the scheme is silent and where the decision may depend on the discretion of the individual arbitrator.

4.1   THE CONTENT OF THE ARBITRATION AGREEMENT

4.1.1   A valid agreement

(1) Whereas in employment tribunal proceedings the applicant determines whether to secure resolution of the dispute by an external procedure, irrespective of the wishes of the employer, arbitration is an entirely voluntary process which requires the agreement of both parties.

(2) Acas will only accept an agreement to refer the dispute to arbitration if it satisfies the requirements contained in paras 20 and 21 of the scheme and amplified in paras 19–36 of the Guide. A checklist is set out in a box in para 29 of the Guide.

(3) A suggested wording for the arbitration agreement is included in Appendix 2 to the Guide:

The parties hereby agree to submit the dispute concerning the alleged unfair dismissal of [name of employee] to arbitration in accordance with the Acas Arbitration Scheme having effect by virtue of the Acas Arbitration Scheme (England and Wales) Order 2001 (SI 2001/1185).

(4) By virtue of para 21 of the scheme, the arbitration agreement must satisfy these requirements:

(a) it must be in writing;

(b) it must relate to an existing dispute;

(c) the agreement must not seek to alter or vary any provision of the scheme;

(d) it must have been reached either:

(i) through a conciliated agreement following action by Acas; or

(ii) through a valid compromise agreement (see below);

(e) it must be accompanied by waiver forms completed by *both* parties in the form of Appendix A to the scheme (a standard removable pink tear-off form is included in the Guide).[1]

An invalid agreement

(1) If the agreement fails to comply with any of these provisions, it does not constitute a valid reference to arbitration under the scheme; the parties will either have to settle the matter by other means, or take or continue tribunal proceedings.

(2) The wording of the scheme appears to envisage that the parties can still pursue the dispute in the tribunal if Acas rejects the arbitration agreement on the basis that it does not satisfy the requirements set out above, assuming that the proceedings in the tribunal have been stayed rather than withdrawn. If proceedings have not been commenced, which is unlikely to be the case in most instances, the only practical obstacle is likely to be the three-month time limit for commencing proceedings.[2]

The effect on tribunal proceedings

(1) The practice in the employment tribunals since January 2002, where an unfair dismissal dispute has been referred to arbitration, is to make a standard order in terms that stay the proceedings on the basis that the parties have referred the dispute to arbitration.

(2) What the parties cannot do once the agreement has been accepted by Acas is withdraw from the arbitration and return to the tribunal to resolve the unfair dismissal claim, any more than they can ask the tribunal to resolve any jurisdictional issues that arise during the arbitration, or any other issue not covered by the scheme.

(3) If, however, there has been a preliminary hearing before the tribunal, for example, on the issue of jurisdiction – is the application in time, or is the applicant an employee? – then the parties can still, either through Acas or through a compromise agreement, refer the main dispute as to whether the dismissal was fair to arbitration.

(4) However, a reference to arbitration assumes that the parties have agreed to waive any issue relating to, for example, whether the claimant was an employee or had sufficient service to claim unfair dismissal (para 14 of the Guide).[3]

All of these requirements are highlighted and amplified in the Guide.

---

1   Acas, 2001(b), Appendix 2.
2   ERA 1996, s 111.
3   Acas, 2001(b), Appendix 2.

4.1.1 Conciliated agreement

Under s 18(2) of the Employment Tribunals Act (ETA) 1996, an Acas conciliation officer is under a duty to endeavour to promote a settlement in respect of a number of categories of tribunal applications; a claim for unfair dismissal is covered by s 18(1)(d). Under s 18(6) the conciliation officer shall, where appropriate, have regard to 'the desirability of encouraging the use of other procedures available for the settlement of grievances'. If the conciliation officer facilitates the referral to the Acas scheme by the parties, it will be usual to incorporate that agreement in the standard documentation, similar to that already familiar to parties and tribunals, which will record the agreement to submit to arbitration.

4.1.2 Compromise agreement

A compromise agreement which complies with the statutory requirements will also constitute a valid reference to arbitration. To comply with s 203 of the Employment Rights Act (ERA) 1996, a compromise agreement must:

- be in writing;
- relate to the particular proceedings;
- recite that the employee or worker has received independent legal advice from a qualified lawyer or a relevant independent adviser as to the terms and effect of the proposed agreement, and in particular its effect on the employee's ability to pursue his rights before an employment tribunal;
- be covered by a policy of insurance or indemnity provided for members of a profession or professional body in force when the adviser gives the advice, covering the risk of a claim by the employee or worker in respect of loss arising in consequence of the advice;
- name the qualified lawyer or relevant independent adviser; and
- state that the conditions regulating compromise agreements under the ERA 1996 are satisfied.

'Independent' means:

- in the case of a qualified lawyer, not also acting for the employer or an associated employer in relation to the particular matter; or
- in the case of a trade union adviser, not being the other party or connected with the other party; or
- in the case of an advice centre worker, not being the other party or connected with the other party, and not receiving payment.

'Qualified lawyer' means:

- a barrister or solicitor (England and Wales); or
- an advocate or solicitor (Scotland).

Barristers or advocates may be either in practice or employed to give legal advice. Solicitors must hold a practising certificate.

'Relevant independent adviser' means:

- a qualified lawyer as defined;
- an officer, official, employee or member of an independent trade union; or
- an advice centre worker, whether employee or volunteer, or such other description of person as the Secretary of State may specify.

The trade union or advice centre must have certified in writing that the person is competent to give advice and is authorised to do so on behalf of the trade union or centre.

4.2 WAIVER OF RIGHTS AND NOTIFICATION OF THE ARBITRATION AGREEMENT

4.2.1 Waiver

(1) Paragraph 21(v), which sets out the requirements for entry to the scheme, specifies that both parties must submit completed waiver forms in the form of Appendix A to the scheme. The Guide helpfully reproduces the appendix as a pink detachable form at the back of the publication.[4] Both parties receive a copy from Acas.

(2) Whether or not the parties have submitted waivers is a matter for Acas, not the arbitrator.

(3) Appointment of an arbitrator is conclusive of the issue of whether there has been an effective referral to arbitration, subject to the power of an arbitrator to rule on the issue of whether the agreement has been submitted in time (see below at 4.2.2). The waiver expressly provides that both parties agree to the following:

(a) That the proceedings are both private and final.

(b) That the parties have no say in the choice of arbitrator from the Acas panel (unlike in private commercial arbitration).[5]

(c) That the proceedings will be conducted differently from tribunal proceedings, in particular in the following respects:

(i) the proceedings will be informal;

(ii) attendance of witnesses and production of documents is not compulsory, subject to the power of the arbitrator to take account of a party's failure to co-operate;

(iii) evidence is not given on oath and, in particular, there is no cross-examination;

(iv) the arbitrator will take the initiative in finding the facts and asking questions;

---

4   Acas, 2001(b), Appendix 2.
5   See Chapter 3.

(v) decisions will only contain the main considerations that led to the decision; there will not be detailed reasons;

(vi) the arbitrator will have no power to order interim relief.

(d) Once the parties have agreed to go to arbitration, they cannot return to the tribunal.

(e) In deciding the issue of fairness, the arbitrator will be applying the employment relations standard of fairness, as evidenced in the Acas Code of Practice, *Disciplinary and Grievance Procedures*, and the Acas Handbook, *Discipline at Work*, and not strict legal tests (the 'range of reasonable responses'[6] test or the decision in *Polkey*,[7] for example).

(f) There is no right of appeal, beyond the limited ambit provided for in the scheme.

(g) In submitting to arbitration, the parties agree that there are no jurisdictional issues and, in particular, the fact of dismissal is agreed.

4.2.2 Notification to Acas (under paras 24–28 of the scheme)

The scheme places primary responsibility on the parties to ensure that an arbitration agreement is brought to the attention of the Acas arbitration section (para 24), although it also envisages that others may do so:

(1) The agreement can be referred to Acas by either of the parties, their representatives, or an Acas conciliator.

(2) In any event, the agreement, with the requisite waivers and any IT1 or IT3, must be notified to Acas within six weeks of its conclusion.

(3) An agreement is concluded on the date of signature; where there is more than one date because different people have signed it at different times, then the last date is the relevant date.

(4) If the time limit is not complied with, the parties must give an explanation to Acas. Acas cannot waive the time limit; it must refer the papers to an arbitrator appointed to determine whether the agreement should be accepted out of time.

(5) That arbitrator can either decide the issue on the papers or arrange a hearing. If the arbitrator decides that it was not reasonably practicable to notify Acas within the time limit, then the agreement can be accepted under the scheme.

There are a number of points to stress about this complicated procedure:

(1) First, it is the arbitrator, not Acas, who has the sole power to waive the time limit, as it is a quasi-judicial and not an administrative decision.

---

6   *Iceland Frozen Foods Ltd v Jones* [1982] IRLR 439, EAT; *Post Office v Foley; HSBC Bank v Madden* [2000] IRLR 827, CA.

7   *Polkey v Dayton Services Ltd* [1988] ICR 142.

(2) Secondly, the arbitrator will be required to resolve the issue in an award. This has two consequences: first, the arbitrator is exercising a quasi-judicial role, so is obliged to comply with para 48 of the scheme (see 4.3 below); and secondly, that award will be subject to the limited rights of challenge and appeal provided for in the scheme.[8]

(3) Thirdly, the formulation of a 'test of reasonable practicability' has its echoes in the sections on time limits in the statutory scheme for unfair dismissal and claims for unlawful deductions from earnings.[9] The Guide avoids suggesting how this clause might be interpreted in the arbitration context, no doubt because it will be a matter for arbitrators to determine using their independent judicial discretion. In particular, it is silent on the question of whether to invest the phrase with the same interpretation it has received in the legislative context where, of course, the time limit (three months) is longer.

(4) In the *Guide for Arbitrators*, issued to individual arbitrators in May 2001, it is suggested that the arbitrator is able to take into account all the circumstances of the case. This indicates a wider discretion than is the practice in tribunal proceedings, as one might expect from a procedure that does not attempt to replicate tribunal practice and procedure or rely on legal precedent.

Factors that the arbitrator might consider are suggested in the notes and include:

• the reason for the delay;

• the respective prejudice to the parties; and

• the availability of an alternative remedy if the agreement is rejected.

In the latter situation, the problem facing the applicant is either the three-month time limit if there is no existing tribunal application, or the fact that there is a stay of proceedings in the tribunal. Presumably, the tribunal will accede to an application to remove the stay, but it cannot be predicted that that will happen until the problem is confronted in an individual case.

4.3   THE ARBITRATOR'S DUTY

This is spelled out in the scheme at paras 48 and 49, which are virtually identical to the provisions of s 33 of the Arbitration Act 1996.

The arbitrator shall:

(1) act fairly and impartially as between the parties, giving each party a reasonable opportunity of putting his case and dealing with that of his opponent; and

---

8   See Chapter 6 for a detailed review of the law relating to challenges to arbitration awards.

9   ERA 1996, ss 23, 48, 57 and 111.

(2) adopt procedures suitable to the circumstances of the case, avoiding unnecessary delay or expense, so as to provide a fair means for the resolution of the matters falling to be determined:

(a) The arbitrator is expected to comply with that duty at all times and is assisted in this by the general duty placed on the parties by para 50 (see 4.6 below):

- The first part of para 48 invokes and states simply the first of the rules of natural justice, which must be read with paras 38 and 39 of the scheme. These provisions oblige the arbitrator before appointment to notify Acas (which will notify the parties) of any matter which might cast justifiable doubts as to impartiality.

- As Acas has sole responsibility for appointment of the arbitrator and the parties have no input in relation to that choice, unlike in conventional arbitration, the onus is on the arbitrator when selected from the panel by Acas to disclose any material connection which might cast doubt on his impartiality.

- The duty of disclosure is a continuing one and failure to observe the duty, at the outset or subsequently, would support an application to the court for removal of the arbitrator under s 24(1)(a) of the Arbitration Act 1996.[10]

- If the arbitrator has made an award and the parties then wish to challenge the award itself, then arguably they could utilise the procedure in para 163 (challenges for 'serious irregularity').[11]

- As is explained more fully in Chapter 6, before a party can apply to the court for removal of the arbitrator, it must first apply to Acas, then to the court if Acas refuses (paras 40–43 of the scheme).

(b) The second part of the first limb restates the second aspect of the rules of natural justice – the obligation on the arbitrator to allow both parties to put their case and deal with that of their opponent. It is a qualified duty: the duty is to give the parties a reasonable opportunity to put their case, not a 'full opportunity' or 'every opportunity' as the Guide suggests. This distinction is not just semantics. Essentially, the arbitrator with conduct of the hearing will have to use his discretion, ensuring that each party has an opportunity to put their case, but also that the hearing does not lose its essential informality or run the risk of taking longer than the time allocated.

---

10 Arbitration Act 1996, s 24(1): 'A party to arbitral proceedings may (upon notice to the other parties, to the arbitrator concerned and to any other arbitrator) apply to the court to remove an arbitrator on any of the following grounds: (a) that circumstances exist that give rise to justifiable doubts as to his impartiality; (b) that he does not possess the qualifications required by the arbitration agreement; (c) that he is physically or mentally incapable of conducting the proceedings or there are justifiable doubts as to his capacity to do so; (d) that he has refused or failed – (i) properly to conduct the proceedings, or (ii) to use all reasonable despatch in conducting the proceedings or making an award, and that substantial injustice has been or will be caused to the applicant.'

11 Governed by the Arbitration Act 1996, s 68; see Chapter 6 and Appendix 3.

4.3.1 How the parties are expected to assist the arbitrator

The literature produced by Acas envisages that hearings will be concluded in less than a day. To ensure that this objective is met, the following points require emphasis:

- most importantly, the parties are expected to comply with the general obligations under paras 50 and 66;
- specifically, they are required under paras 68–72 to take a number of steps to ensure that the other side and the arbitrator are aware of the nature of that party's case and the witnesses and documents that will be relied on to substantiate it;
- materials and documents not disclosed to Acas prior to the hearing can only be relied on with the permission of the arbitrator.[12]

The second limb of the arbitrator's duty draws on the practice in the courts and employment tribunals of requiring the parties and the adjudicating body to adopt procedures which are cost-efficient and proportionate to the complexity and value of the dispute.[13] The phrase used in both jurisdictions, and derived from the Civil Procedure Rules 1998, is 'overriding objective'; arbitrators will be expected to follow suit not only at the hearing, but also in pre-hearing determinations. The new tribunal rules, which incorporated the overriding objective in tribunal procedures for the first time in July 2001, have only been in existence for one year (although they were applied in spirit long before then).

4.3.2 The overriding objective

The formula has generated a great deal of litigation in the courts in the context of personal injury litigation in particular. The position is different in the employment context, possibly because the formula does no more than echo employment tribunal practice in any event. Arbitrators will develop their own approaches to the overriding objective on a case by case basis, with the obvious caveat that neither arbitrators nor parties will be able to determine how the objective is being met, as awards are not published. Presumably, Acas will be able to detect trends and patterns and may be able to circulate, if not best practice, at least indications of relevant criteria being adopted by arbitrators. It is envisaged by Acas that as the scheme gains acceptance, conferences will be held where arbitrators will be able to exchange information (see Chapter 3). What the formula should do is impress on parties the need to avoid lengthy statements of case and excessive preparation of documents.

---

12 Acas Arbitration Scheme (England and Wales) Order 2001 (SI 2001/1185), para 74.
13 Civil Procedure Rules 1998, r 1.1 (SI 1998/3132); Employment Tribunals (Constitution etc) Regulations 2001 (SI 2001/1171).

4.4   PRIVACY AND CONFIDENTIALITY

Whereas all tribunal proceedings are heard in public and failure to do so will render the proceedings a nullity, all arbitrations and related procedures under the scheme are 'strictly private and confidential'.[14]

In practice, this will mean that the following will happen:

- Only the parties, their representatives, any interpreters, witnesses and legal advisers may attend arbitration hearings. By way of contrast, as long as the tribunal has not made an order to sit in private, anybody can attend to listen to tribunal proceedings. The press can attend and report proceedings, subject to any restrictions imposed while the proceedings are in progress under tribunal reporting restrictions.[15]

- With the agreement of the parties, an Acas official or arbitrator in training may attend the arbitration hearing.[16] It is not envisaged that this facility would extend to the individual Acas conciliator with the conduct of the application. This agreement will have to be forthcoming to enable the ranks of appointed arbitrators to have some practical experience of conducting arbitration before themselves undertaking arbitration under the scheme.

- Arbitrators' awards will be in writing and sent to the parties, but the effect of paras 51–52 and 149 of the scheme is to preserve the confidentiality of that award and obliges the arbitrator also to respect that confidentiality. In contrast, the decision of an employment tribunal, which must be in writing, is not only sent to the parties, but is entered in the register of decisions held in Bury St Edmunds, where it is open to inspection by any member of the public; in very rare circumstances, the decision may raise such an important issue that it may be annotated or even reported in full in one of the specialist legal journals.[17]

- The award is not sent to the employment tribunal where the original proceedings that were stayed pending the arbitration referral are lodged. However, in para 116 of the Guide, Acas makes it clear that it will from time to time publish general summary information about awards, but will not send the award to the employment tribunal where the original proceedings that were stayed pending the arbitration referral are lodged.

- Under para 32 of the Guide, the parties will receive from Acas notification by Acas to the employment tribunal that the dispute has been resolved and, in any event, if the arbitrator awards a remedy of re-employment, the party seeking to enforce that order will have to refer it to the employment tribunal.

- Arbitration awards themselves are only enforceable in the courts, so at that stage the court will expect to see the original signed award from the arbitrator.

---

14 Employment Tribunals (Constitution etc) Regulations 2001, Sched 1, r 10(2); *Storer v British Gas* [2000] IRLR 495; Acas Arbitration Scheme (England and Wales) Order 2001 (SI 2001/1185), paras 51–52.

15 Employment Tribunals (Constitution etc) Regulations, 2001, Sched 1, r 16.

16 Acas Arbitration Scheme (England and Wales) Order 2001 (SI 2001/1185), para 52.

17 *Coker v Lord Chancellor* [1999] IRLR 396; *Nash v Mash/Roe Group* [1998] IRLR 168.

- As the scheme envisages an oral hearing (it is made obligatory by para 53 of the scheme), there is potential for conflict with Art 6 of the European Convention on Human Rights (the right to a fair and public hearing). Fears about this apparent conflict delayed introduction of the scheme for almost a year, and the potential problems have been addressed by the obligation of both parties when submitting a dispute to arbitration to sign the waiver agreement annexed to the scheme, which must be sent to Acas together with the agreement to submit to arbitration. The content of the waiver agreement is addressed at 4.2 above; the confidential nature of the arbitration process is highlighted at the outset of that document.

4.5   FINALITY AND CERTAINTY

(1) Advocates of arbitration, and in particular the Acas scheme, argue that the procedure is intended to be final. The award will not be subject to legal challenge, and once the award has been given, the parties will accept the decision and that will be the end of the matter.

(2) As no proceedings which determine rights can be immune from legal challenge, there are limited rights of challenge to an arbitrator's award in the courts, as we will see in Chapter 6.

(3) Furthermore, para 97 of the scheme emphasises the arbitrator's obligation to ensure that the award gives not only the decision as to whether the dismissal was fair or unfair, but also deals with remedy if the finding is the latter. There should be no loose ends and no subsequent hearings to deal with undecided issues.

(4) This has to be seen in the context of the power given to the arbitrator in theory to issue awards on separate issues, for example, remedy, if the parties are not fully prepared to deal with that at the hearing. To an extent, finality is something that the tribunal system is striving to achieve. The parties to tribunal proceedings are told when an application is listed for hearing that the tribunal will deal with remedy as well as liability if time permits. The hearing is also meant to be final in the sense that it should not be appealed from. There ought to be few appeals from tribunal decisions as the EAT will only hear appeals on a point of law; the ingenuity of advocates as well as judges to identify points of law is, however, legendary.

4.5.1   Will arbitration be more final?

The claim that arbitration is a more final procedure has to be seen in this context:

- In the last year for which figures are available for unfair dismissal applications, there were 11,565 completed tribunal hearings.[18] In 5,294 of those cases, the applicant was successful. Of the balance, 1,040 were

---

18 Employment Tribunals Service, *Annual Report 2000–01*, 2001.

unsuccessful for various jurisdictional reasons. In the remainder (5,231), the applicant was unsuccessful. The total number of completed tribunal hearings in the same year was 35,288. Broadly, although unfair dismissal applications amount to just under 50% of all applications to tribunals, they only account for 30% of cases proceeding to a hearing.

- In the same year, 886 appeals to the EAT were disposed of at the preliminary hearing stage and 1,176 were disposed of at the full hearing. The figures do not give an indication of the spread of the issues in those appeals, but it is safe to assume, as the law is fairly established in relation to unfair dismissal in comparison with other jurisdictions, that unfair dismissal is unlikely to have featured in more than 10% of those cases (approximately 200 overall).

- In the main, appeals are the exception rather than the norm, but it has to be accepted that there will be no appeals from the awards of arbitrators relieved of any obligation to give detailed reasons for their decisions.

- However, both jurisdictions suffer from the same basic deficiency – the absence of any power to enforce decisions. Financial awards by both arbitrators and tribunals must be enforced in the court system; not only that, an arbitrator's award of either reinstatement or re-engagement, if not complied with, has to be enforced by the employment tribunal.[19]

In conclusion, it can be argued that the claim that arbitration will provide a more final and certain outcome than tribunal proceedings is valid because the scope for challenge is so limited, although in practice few tribunal decisions are appealed. It must be accepted, however, that whereas with tribunal proceedings there could be three stages of appeal – to the EAT, to the Court of Appeal and then to the House of Lords – with the possibility of a referral to the European Court of Justice at any stage, including from the tribunal, any appeal to the court against an arbitration award is likely to fall at the first hurdle.

4.6   DUTIES OF THE PARTIES

The essence of arbitration is that the parties attempt to bring the dispute to a resolution with the minimum of delay and intervention by the arbitrator, unlike the courts, which have a number of case management remedies to ensure that litigation does not grind to a halt. The scheme sets out an obligation on the parties in para 50 of the scheme (which draws heavily for its terminology on s 40 of the Arbitration Act 1996):

50   The parties shall do all things necessary for the proper and expeditious conduct of the arbitral proceedings. This includes (without limitation) complying without delay with any determination of the arbitrator as to procedural or evidential matters, or with any order or directions of the arbitrator, and co-operating in the arrangement of any hearing.

---

19   Acas Arbitration Scheme (England and Wales) Order 2001 (SI 2001/1185), para 160; ERA 1996, s 117.

4.6.1 The consequences of failure to co-operate

Arbitration assumes the willingness of both parties to facilitate smooth operation of the procedure, but there are remedies in the scheme to enforce this:

- Any party who fails to comply with the general duty above, with any aspect of the procedure set out in the scheme, or with any order or direction of the arbitrator, risks either the arbitrator drawing such adverse inferences as are appropriate from non-compliance, or the possibility of an adjournment (with no costs sanctions, however).[20]
- Nevertheless, as arbitration anticipates the speedy determination of issues, it is expected that the option of adjournment will be one of last resort, particularly bearing in mind that it may be difficult to re-arrange a hearing date that is convenient.
- In the scheme, it is envisaged that an adjournment would only be resorted to where it would be unfair on either party to proceed (para 66).
- Alternatively, the arbitrator is permitted to 'draw such adverse inferences from the act of non-compliance as the circumstances justify' (para 66).

4.6.2 What form could non-compliance take?

- Failure of either party to co-operate with the arbitrator in fixing the date for a hearing is dealt with in the scheme in para 55 – the arbitrator fixes the date and the venue.
- A party who fails to prepare and submit the necessary statement of case may be prevented from relying on late submission of documents under para 74.
- A party wishing to call a witness at the hearing who was not included on the list submitted to Acas in accordance with para 68 of the scheme may only do so if the arbitrator agrees.

4.6.3 Failure to attend the hearing

- Are the parties obliged to turn up at all for the hearing, and what should the arbitrator do if either or both fail to do so? In practice, the situation is unlikely to occur as the parties have submitted voluntarily to a form of alternative dispute resolution, but the possibility is not inconceivable. The scheme is not entirely clear on what can be done, although there is a provision in the scheme dealing with non-attendance.
- Under para 87, the arbitrator can choose either to continue the hearing in the absence of that party or to adjourn, but the party must have an opportunity to explain and justify non-attendance. It is necessary to look at each of the three possible scenarios in more detail.

---

20 *Ibid*, para 66.

4.7   FAILURE OF THE APPLICANT TO ATTEND

(1) In this situation, para 88 requires the arbitrator, if deciding to adjourn the hearing, to write to the employee seeking an explanation. If not satisfied with the explanation, the arbitrator is permitted to make an award dismissing the claim.

(2) In the alternative, the arbitrator can continue the hearing in the absence of that party but is obliged to take into account any written submissions and documents already submitted by that party.

(3) However, as the scheme requires the party to be given the opportunity to show 'sufficient cause', it must be inevitable that the arbitrator can only proceed under this provision after first adjourning the hearing to require an explanation from the missing employee for non-attendance.

(4) The only challenge we can envisage under the scheme would be that a decision taken in the absence of a party might constitute a material irregularity. In employment tribunal proceedings, a party who does not attend the hearing may be able to seek a review under the limited power in the Rules.[21] As the scheme expressly prescribes the options open to the arbitrator where a party fails to attend, the only obvious ground for challenge would be a failure on the part of the arbitrator to seek an explanation from the party who failed to appear.

4.8   FAILURE OF THE RESPONDENT TO ATTEND

(1) An employer who fails to attend a tribunal hearing risks an adverse finding of unfair dismissal because of the inability to prove the reason for dismissal. In arbitration, there is no power to make such an award by default.

(2) It seems from the drafting of the scheme that the arbitrator will be compelled to proceed in the same way as in the case of failure by the employee to turn up. The hearing will have to be adjourned, an explanation will be sought and the hearing can then continue – with or without the employer – on the basis of whatever information the employer has submitted.

4.9   FAILURE OF BOTH PARTIES TO ATTEND

(1) On the face of it, assuming the parties have delivered statements of case and the supporting documentation, the arbitrator could determine the issue and make an award. The obstacle to that approach is para 53 of the scheme, which provides that a hearing must be held in every case, and expressly prevents the parties agreeing to a purely written procedure. However, although this prevents the parties agreeing to circumvent the procedure, there is no express prohibition on the arbitrator deciding to proceed in that way.

21 Employment Tribunals (Constitution etc) Regulations 2001 (SI 2001/1171), Sched 1, r 13.

(2) The parties might therefore be able to challenge the award on the basis of serious irregularity, which is covered in Chapter 6. The difficulty is that although there is no provision prohibiting the arbitrator from proceeding in this way, there is no power expressly permitting it either. The rules governing employment tribunals do deal expressly with the situation of the non-attendance of parties.[22]

4.10 INAPPROPRIATE CASES FOR ARBITRATION

The arbitration scheme was obviously devised for conventional cases of unfair dismissal, such as conduct, redundancy and capability, whether on the basis of competence or sickness. These are the categories described by Acas in the Guide as 'straightforward cases'. In theory, all unfair dismissal cases can go to arbitration, but there are some cases which are inappropriate for the informal procedure envisaged by the scheme:

(1) Paragraph 19 states that: 'The scheme is not intended for disputes involving complex legal issues.' Acas devotes eight paragraphs of its Guide to the subject of inappropriate cases, and in particular, at para 11, singles out cases that raise questions of EC law.

(2) In the Guide, Acas specifically recommends that the scheme is not intended for cases which raise questions of EC law, and it identifies three examples in particular: dismissal for a pregnancy-related reason; dismissals related to the transfer of an undertaking; and dismissal in connection with the Working Time Regulations.

(3) Nevertheless, the terms of reference of the arbitrator in para 12 require the arbitrator to apply EC law, which is defined in para 10.

(4) In addition, under paras 90 and 94, the arbitrator can either appoint a legal adviser to assist on any issue of EC law or the Human Rights Act (HRA) 1998, or seek a preliminary ruling from the court on any issue of EC law. The arbitrator is unlikely to encounter any topic more complicated than EC law. The issue of EC law and the HRA 1998 is dealt with more fully in 4.16, but it is worth observing that Professor Rees identified 15 dismissal situations which potentially raise issues of EC law.[23]

(5) In the Guide, Acas also advises that the scheme is not suitable for cases where other issues are raised, such as allegations of sex, race or disability discrimination, or claims for unpaid wages.

(6) In summary, parties should not contemplate referring the claim to arbitration unless the following apply:

- there are no jurisdictional issues;
- the dismissal is admitted;
- the dismissal is admittedly for a reason related to the five statutory reasons for dismissal; and
- the only unresolved issue is whether it was fair.

---

22 *Ibid*, Sched 1, r 11(3).
23 Rees, 2000–02.

(7) Acas does, however, deal with the tricky question of constructive dismissal at para 15 of the Guide. Though the Guide has no legal force, the advice is compelling. Acas will accept cases of constructive dismissal under the scheme, provided that the parties, in effect, the employer, agree that there was a dismissal; in other words, the employer accepts that he acted in breach of contract and that the employee was entitled to resign. This is implicit in para 12 of the scheme, which pre-supposes as a requirement of entry to the scheme that there is a dismissal.

4.11   RULES OF EVIDENCE

Paragraph 85 of the scheme is quite succinct and explicit on whether the arbitrator must observe any aspect of the rules of evidence:

(1) The arbitrator is not required to apply any of the rules of evidence, whether in relation to admissibility, relevance or weight. This applies to all material, whether relating to issues of fact or opinion.

(2) In the Guide, Acas sees no need to go beyond the simple statement that the rules of evidence which apply in the courts will not apply in the arbitration hearing.

(3) The Employment Tribunals Regulations[24] and, in particular, regs 11 and 15 provide that the tribunal may regulate its own procedure, seek to avoid formality and, in particular, 'shall not be bound by any enactment or rule of law relating to the admissibility of evidence in proceedings before the courts of law'. Parties and chairmen tend to forget this wide power and there is a tendency in tribunal proceedings, at least where both parties are legally represented, to insist on adherence to the rules of evidence.

(4) In respect of arbitrations conducted under the Arbitration Act 1996, s 34 applies. This section enables the parties to agree to follow the strict rules of evidence, but in default of agreement, the arbitrator (called 'the tribunal' in the Act) has a complete discretion in relation to procedure and evidence.[25]

---

24 Employment Tribunals (Constitution etc) Regulations 2001 (SI 2001/1171), Sched 1.
25 Arbitration Act 1996, s 34: '(1) It shall be for the tribunal to decide all procedural and evidential matters, subject to the right of the parties to agree any matter. (2) Procedural and evidential matters include – (a) when and where any part of the proceedings is to be held; (b) the language or languages to be used in the proceedings and whether translations of any relevant documents are to be supplied; (c) whether any and if so what form of written statements of claim and defence are to be used, when these should be supplied and the extent to which such statements can be later amended; (d) whether any and if so which documents or classes of documents should be disclosed between and produced by the parties and at what stage; (e) whether any and if so what questions should be put to and answered by the respective parties and when and in what form this should be done; (f) whether to apply strict rules of evidence (or any other rules) as to the admissibility, relevance or weight of any material (oral, written or other) sought to be tendered on any matters of fact or opinion, and the time, manner and form in which such material should be exchanged and presented; (g) whether and to what extent the tribunal should itself take the initiative in ascertaining the facts and the law; (h) whether and to what extent there should be oral or written evidence or submissions.'

(5) The fundamental feature of employment arbitration is that the parties are expressly prohibited from cross-examining any of the witnesses.[26] Any questions have to be put through the arbitrator, who will be encouraged, in any event, to adopt an inquisitorial role when defining the issues and asking questions of the parties. If the parties have defined the issues clearly in their respective statements of case, then it ought to be rare for the parties to have many questions to be addressed other than those identified by the arbitrator and put to the respective parties.

4.12   NON-COMPLIANCE AND NON-CO-OPERATION

As we will see more fully in Chapter 5, the scheme imposes on the parties a duty of co-operation. Specifically, the parties are expected to co-operate in arranging the hearing, to comply without delay with any determination of the arbitrator on procedural or evidential matters, and to comply with any other order or directions. One commentator has suggested that the scheme rests on 'trust and co-operation'.[27] As the scheme is a voluntary process, it lacks the sanctions open to the courts or tribunals; however, the arbitrator does have the following options:

(1) if the parties do not co-operate in fixing the hearing date, the arbitrator can go ahead and arrange the date (para 55);

(2) the arbitrator can adjourn the hearing if it would be unfair on any party to proceed (para 66);

(3) the arbitrator can draw such adverse inferences from the act of non-compliance as the circumstances justify (para 66);

(4) if any party fails to supply Acas with the necessary paperwork envisaged by paras 68–71 of the scheme, those materials can only be relied on at the hearing with the permission of the arbitrator (para 74);

(5) if an employer fails to permit the attendance of witnesses at the hearing who can give relevant evidence, the arbitrator can draw an adverse inference, even though the arbitrator has no power to compel the attendance of witnesses (para 77).

The arbitrator is not entitled to find that the case succeeds or fails merely because a party has failed to comply with the general duty or a specific direction or order; the inference must be relevant, appropriate and proportionate. It also would follow that the party in default should be warned of the consequences of non-compliance and the likely inferences that may be drawn for the arbitrator to be able to comply with his general duty under paras 48 and 49 (see Chapter 5).

---

26   Acas Arbitration Scheme (England and Wales) Order 2001 (SI 2001/1185), para 82.
27   McGrath, P, 'Acas: the arbitration scheme' (1999) 7 ELA Briefing 298, quoted in Rees, 2000–02.

4.13   THE ARBITRATION STANDARD OF FAIRNESS

(1) The arbitrator's terms of reference require the issue of fairness to be determined by 'general principles of fairness and good conduct in employment relations'. It is unlikely that this will differ from the general principles in the Acas Handbook, *Discipline at Work*.

(2) This is not the same as the 'range of reasonable responses' test.[28] The arbitrator is no more allowed to substitute his view of what he would have done than is the employment tribunal.[29] It is not, however, 'unfettered pragmatism' or the 'unchallengeable whim'[30] of one individual, as the terms of reference do direct the arbitrator to the Acas Handbook, which the employment tribunal is also required to take into account.[31]

(3) It is important neither to read too much into the debate nor to anticipate major distinctions between the arbitration approach and the tribunal approach, nor inconsistencies in the approach of individual arbitrators. Essentially, arbitrators will expect to see employers follow fair procedures and to take a decision which is proportionate.

(4) It must also be remembered that once the Employment Act becomes law in April 2003, at one level, employers must follow minimum procedural standards, but at the other, extreme tribunals will be able to ignore minor procedural lapses if the decision to dismiss is itself appropriate despite those lapses.[32]

(5) The exception to this general principle is contained in para 95 of the scheme, which comes under the general heading of 'Automatic Unfairness'. It requires the arbitrator to have regard to those provisions of the ERA 1996 and any other legislation which obliges the tribunal to determine that a dismissal is unfair if it is for one of the prescribed reasons, such as pregnancy. It seems that this would require the arbitrator, who is obliged to state the reason for dismissal in the award (para 97), to conclude as a matter of course that the dismissal is unfair if it is for one of the reasons conventionally described as an automatically unfair reason for dismissal.

---

28 *Iceland Frozen Foods Ltd v Jones* [1982] IRLR 439, EAT; *Post Office v Foley; HSBC Bank v Madden* [2000] IRLR 827, CA.

29 Acas Arbitration Scheme (England and Wales) Order 2001 (SI 2001/1185), para 12; *Boys and Girls Welfare Society v McDonald* [1996] IRLR 129.

30 See MacMillan, 1999; for a detailed critique of MacMillan's arguments and the debate on the industrial relations standard of fairness, see Rees, 2000–02.

31 *Lock v Cardiff Railway Co Ltd* [1998] IRLR 358.

32 Employment Act 2002, ss 29–34 and Sched 2.

4.14 THE AWARD

(1) Whether the arbitrator finds in favour of the employee or the employer, the decision must be confirmed in a document termed 'the award', which must be in writing and signed by the arbitrator.

(2) It must:

(a) identify the reason for the dismissal or, if more than one, the principal reason;

(b) in the case of a redundancy dismissal, identify the reason the employee was selected for dismissal;

(c) contain the main considerations which were taken into account in reaching the decision that the dismissal was fair or unfair;

(d) state the arbitrator's decision(s);

(e) state the remedy awarded, together with an explanation;

(f) state the date on which it was made.

(3) A number of points arise from these elements. First, in identifying the reason for dismissal, the arbitrator is conducting a task different from that performed by the employment tribunal, which is required by statute to be satisfied both that the employer has established as a matter of fact the reason for dismissal, but also that it is one of the five potentially fair reasons for dismissal.[33] The arbitrator will merely be recording the factual basis constituting the reason for dismissal: for example, the employee assaulted a manager, or had been absent from work due to illness for a certain period.

(4) The concept of considerations is wider than tribunal summary reasons, but narrower than extended reasons. The award records in a matter of a few paragraphs what factors led the arbitrator to conclude that the dismissal was fair or unfair. It must contain sufficient material to enable the parties to know why the case was decided as it was, or to enable the court to determine whether there is a point of law or a serious irregularity, but arbitrators are not expected to draw up awards in the manner of extended reasons.

(5) The scheme unusually contains powers for the arbitrator to make more than one award, at different times, on different aspects of the dispute, and to make an award on only part of the claim. This is unusual because the philosophy of the scheme is to give the parties a swift, once and for all decision. These provisions draw on arbitration law and practice,[34] where the power is usually limited to interim awards, which are not a feature of employment arbitration. The only time the provisions should be utilised is in the example given in the Guide: where the arbitrator is unable to deal with remedy because of insufficient information. This is one of many instances in the scheme where the language of the Arbitration Act has been incorporated, with only a limited explanation of why it appears.

---

33 ERA 1996, s 98(2).
34 Acas Arbitration Scheme (England and Wales) Order 2001 (SI 2001/1185), paras 98–100; Arbitration Act 1996, s 47.

4.15 DEALING WITH REMEDY

If the arbitrator determines that the employee was unfairly dismissed, the scheme envisages that the award will deal with remedy. As we shall see in Chapter 6, the arbitrator is expected to follow tribunal procedures in a number of respects:

- First, the arbitrator is required by para 101 of the scheme, in language that mirrors the ERA 1996, to explain to the applicant the remedies available and elicit from the applicant the preferred remedy.[35]
- He must then go on to award either the alternative awards of re-employment or reinstatement, or award compensation.
- The arbitrator is required to take into account the same factors as the employment tribunal when deciding which remedy to award, such as the wishes of the employee, the practicability of an award of re-employment and the extent of any contribution of the employee to the dismissal.[36]

Comparing remedies in arbitration with remedies in the tribunal

There are two important distinctions between the approach of the arbitrator and the approach of the employment tribunal:

(1) Although the arbitrator, when awarding compensation, makes an award consisting of a basic amount and a compensatory award, these aspects differ in two respects from their tribunal counterparts. First, under paras 120 and 122 of the scheme, the arbitrator is only required to 'have regard to', not to 'apply' the statutory rules in relation to calculating continuity of employment and the limit on a week's pay.

(2) Secondly, there may be different principles in relation to the treatment of social security benefits received by an employee. One view is that as the scheme does not expressly require the arbitrator to deduct social security benefits, they are not deductible. The alternative view, which we believe will be adopted, is that they are deductible in full for a number of reasons:

    (a) The arbitrator is required to award such a sum as is just and equitable, having regard to the loss sustained (under para 135 of the scheme). It cannot be just and equitable to receive compensation and benefits for the same period of loss.

    (b) It is envisaged by the scheme that social security benefits are to be taken into account. The parties have already been reminded by para 70 of the scheme of the importance of financial information, and examples are given both in the scheme and in the Guide.

    (c) Under para 70(ix)(d), welfare benefits are identified as relevant information. The most obvious example is Job Seekers Allowance. The recoupment provisions cover the position of social security benefits in

---

35 ERA 1996, s 112(2).
36 Acas Arbitration Scheme (England and Wales) Order 2001 (SI 2001/1185), paras 101–15.

the employment tribunal.[37] The employer is notified of the benefits paid, deducts the appropriate amount as directed by the tribunal and reimburses the Benefits Agency. No parallel scheme exists for the arbitration scheme.

(d) Acas believes that the provisions of para 135 require the arbitrator to take benefits into account, presumably by deducting them in full from any claimed loss of earnings in the same way as wages from another employer, notwithstanding that the social security fund is financed by contributions from employees and employers. The problem will be that only the employee will know what benefits have been received, but the scheme documentation does not highlight the requirement for the employee to retain and provide the information, and the arbitrator is not empowered to obtain it from the Benefits Agency (Department of Work and Pensions).

Arbitrators will, therefore, first have to address the issue of principle: should social security benefits be deducted from the compensatory amount and, if so, on what basis? Secondly, if the relevant benefit or benefits are to be deducted, how are the practicalities of obtaining the information to be addressed? This issue is discussed more fully in Chapter 6.

4.16   THE RELEVANCE OF EC LAW AND THE HRA 1998

(1) Paragraph 11 of the Guide stresses that the scheme is not intended for cases which raise questions of EC law, such as unfair dismissal claims based on an EC right.

(2) A number of examples are given in the Guide, such as a dismissal based on sex discrimination; a dismissal in connection with the transfer of an undertaking; and claims that the dismissal was for asserting a right under the Working Time Regulations. As we saw earlier, Rees listed a potential 15 dismissal categories which might raise an issue of EC law.[38]

(3) Acas, in its guidance to arbitrators, contemplates a potential 11 categories. This is one of the intrinsic contradictions in the scheme, as para 12 of the scheme expressly obliges the arbitrator to apply EC law as a specific requirement of the terms of reference, and enables legal advice to be obtained in any case where it becomes relevant.

(4) EC law, for these purposes, is defined in para 10 (the definitions paragraph) as:

- any enactment in the domestic legislation of England and Wales giving effect to rights, powers, liabilities, obligations and restrictions from time to time created or arising by or under the Community Treaties; and

- any such rights, powers, obligations and restrictions which are not given effect by any such enactment.

---

37 Employment Protection (Recoupment etc) Regulations 1996 (SI 1996/2349).
38 Rees, 2000–02.

The second part of this definition is Delphic, but presumably requires the arbitrator to be aware of the Treaty[39] if relevant, of all Directives, of decisions of the ECJ, and of Directives not as yet transposed into UK law if the employer is an emanation of the State.

(5) Fortunately, help is at hand for the non-legally trained arbitrator confronted by an issue of EC law or an issue arising under the HRA 1998. Under paras 90–93, the arbitrator is empowered to require the appointment by Acas of a legal adviser, either on his own initiative or on the application of the parties. If the arbitrator takes the initiative, the parties must be given the opportunity to comment, so as to enable them to object to the proposed appointment.

(6) The arbitrator might decide that on the facts, no issue of EC law applies at all. For example, the employee might allege that the dismissal was for a Transfer of Undertakings (Protection of Employment) Regulations 1981 (TUPE) related reason, but the employer argues and can show that it was for lateness or performance. Although the expert is appointed by Acas, he reports to the arbitrator and the parties and is also subject to the same duty of disclosure as the arbitrator (paras 38, 39 and 91).

(7) The arbitrator can permit the attendance of the expert at the hearing and, under para 92, the arbitrator has the power to order the inevitable adjournment that this will necessitate. Alternatively, the arbitrator can pose questions to the expert in writing or at the hearing.

(8) The role of the expert is to give advice; the arbitrator cannot delegate to the expert the role of decision-maker. In any instance, the parties are to be given the opportunity to comment on any information, opinion or advice given by the expert, consistent with the duty imposed under paras 93 and 48(i).

(9) It must be remembered that although under the terms of the waiver the parties forgo the right to a hearing which might need to be conducted in accordance with the HRA 1998, this does not prevent the employee from arguing, if the employer is a public body, that a potential human rights issue arises in connection with the dismissal. It might be contended that the right to privacy or freedom of expression has been infringed and, in that case, the arbitrator might consider the need to obtain a legal opinion on the issue. Again, it might be better for the arbitrator to determine the facts and then decide whether any issue really exists before adjourning the hearing to obtain legal opinion.

4.16.1 Court determination of preliminary points

Court assistance

The alternative option is to seek court assistance under para 94 of the scheme. As we shall see in Chapter 6, the decision of the arbitrator can be challenged on a point of law under para 164 of the scheme if it is an issue in relation to either

---

39 European Community Treaty 1957 (EC Treaty); Treaty on European Union (TEU) 1992.

EC law or the HRA 1998. If such an issue arises in the course of an arbitration hearing, the parties, or even the arbitrator, might consider that an application to the court for a determination of a preliminary point of law under para 94 of the scheme and s 45 of the Arbitration Act might save time and costs in the long run. The procedure can only be used, however, if first, the court agrees to give a ruling, and secondly, either both parties are in agreement to the application or, if only one party agrees, the arbitrator is in agreement.

The arbitrator's discretion

The arbitrator has discretion on seeking court assistance. Relevant factors to take into account when exercising this discretion are likely to include:

- the importance of the issue to resolution of the dispute;
- the likelihood of delay and disruption and its effect on the arbitration;
- the reasons for the objecting party's objections to the application;
- the expense that might be caused;
- whether a court application would, in fact, be more expeditious or efficient than the appointment of an adviser;
- whether the issue in question substantially affects the rights of either party; and
- whether the court is likely to accept the application.

The court for these purposes is the High Court or the Central London County Court.[40] In contrast to conventional arbitration, the court itself is not required to consider whether determination of the issue will produce substantial savings in costs.[41] Another difference is that unlike in a conventional arbitration, the arbitrator is precluded from continuing the arbitration and making an award pending the court hearing.[42] However, it must be stressed that although the scheme does provide a mechanism to address issues of both EC law and the HRA 1998, the reality is that in practice, it will occur rarely, if at all.

4.17   THE DECISION-MAKING PROCESS

4.17.1 The concept of fairness

The terms of reference require the arbitrator to determine whether the dismissal is fair or unfair. However, the award must go further than that:

- The award on the issue of fairness must identify the reason or, if there is more than one, the principal reason for dismissal. In a redundancy case, the reason for selection for dismissal must be identified.

---

40 Acas Arbitration Scheme (England and Wales) Order 2001 (SI 2001/1185), para 94(2)(a).
41 *Ibid*, para 94(3).
42 *Ibid*, para 94(4).

- Whilst para 97 of the scheme and s 98(2) of the ERA 1996 share similar language, the similarities stop there. If an employer cannot establish the reason for dismissal and determine that it is one of the potentially fair reasons for dismissal identified by the legislation, the employment tribunal is compelled to find that the dismissal was unfair. However, the arbitrator is not operating in the same framework. In particular, there is no obligation when identifying the reason for dismissal to use the statutory categories or language: the task is to make a factual finding, not to attach any form of legal label to the factual reason.

4.17.2 Automatic unfairness

(1) There is one qualification to this in respect of the categories of dismissal identified by the generic description of 'automatic unfairness'. This phrase does not appear in the legislation on unfair dismissal; it is a term of art applied to all the dismissal categories where the tribunal is not required to determine the issue of fairness, but is obliged to find that the dismissal was unfair if it was for any one of those reasons. The most common examples are dismissals for pregnancy, for health and safety reasons, or dismissals in connection with a transfer situation.

(2) These dismissal situations are covered in the scheme at para 95 in two sub-paragraphs:

   (a) any provision of Pt X of the ERA 1996 ... requiring a dismissal for a particular reason to be regarded as unfair; *or* [our emphasis]

   (b) any other legislative provision requiring a dismissal for a particular reason to be regarded as unfair for the purpose of Pt X of the ERA 1996.

(3) It is, however, clear that despite the use of the word 'or', the two sub-paragraphs in para 95 are cumulative and not alternatives.

(4) Although the arbitrator ultimately has to express an opinion on the question of fairness, there may still be a need to resolve contested issues of fact before any such opinion can be given. The employment tribunal is described, with justification, as a fact-finding forum. If required to give extended reasons for its decision, it is obliged to make findings of fact. In return, the appeal courts will not interfere with those findings and will only go behind the decision reached on those facts if the decision was wrong in law on the facts, or was a perverse decision on either the facts or the evidence.[43]

(5) In the case of arbitration, the arbitrator is required not to give reasons, but to state the main considerations which were taken into account in reaching the decision that the dismissal was either fair or unfair. The arbitrator is neither substituting his opinion for that of the employer, nor is he applying legal tests or precedent. He will be considering the Acas Code, applying good industrial relations practice and the norms of the employment sector in question. Most importantly, he will be deciding the outcome on the basis of the representations and evidence presented at the hearing and in the

---

43 See *Yeboah v Crofton* [2002] IRLR 634; *British Telecommunications plc v Sheridan* [1990] IRLR 27.

statements of case. The award will therefore explain, usually in two or three paragraphs and possibly in the language of the parties themselves, why one argument or submission rather than the other succeeded.

4.18   TRIBUNAL VERSUS ARBITRATION

Although we have adopted a heading for this section which suggests that the alternatives are somehow contradictory, it is fair to say that advocates of the Acas scheme, and in particular Acas itself, have stressed that what has been introduced is different, not better. It is an alternative method of dispute resolution, with its own special features, many of which will render it more attractive to applicants and respondents respectively.

4.18.1 The key differences

In this section, we highlight most of the key differences which have been identified by commentators who have compared an adversarial system (the employment tribunals) with an alternative arbitration format for the resolution of employment dismissals. It has to be recognised that the advocates of an alternative arbitration-based format for the resolution of claims for unfair dismissal may not necessarily see the scheme either as ideal or as a model that satisfies the key features of an arbitration format identified by them in their writings.

4.18.2 What is the difference between employment arbitration and a tribunal hearing?

(1) In the pamphlet produced by Acas to accompany the scheme, *Choosing Our Arbitration Scheme*, there is a table, reproduced below with some amendments, summarising the main differences between employment arbitration and an employment tribunal hearing. A similar table is reproduced in Appendix 1 of the Acas Guide to the scheme.[44] Professors Roy Lewis and Jon Clark, the joint authors of the original Institute of Employment Rights pamphlet, in a paper presented to the Industrial Law Society Annual Conference at Oxford in September 2000, prepared another table.[45] It is possible to identify differences other than those set out in the table below.

---

44   Rees, 2000–02.
45   Lewis and Clark, 2000.

Figure 1 – Employment tribunal versus arbitral scheme

Employment tribunal	*Arbitration scheme*
Public hearing at tribunal venue	Private hearing at either an Acas office, a hotel or the employer's premises
Hearing normally completed in a day	Hearing normally completed in half a day
Hearing before a legally qualified chairman and panel of two other members	Hearing before a single Acas-appointed arbitrator experienced in industrial relations
Witnesses cross-examined under oath as in a court	Informal questions through the arbitrator
Legal representation of the parties in a large number of cases	Legal representation permissible but afforded no special status
If dismissal found to be unfair, remedies of reinstatement, re-engagement or compensation	If dismissal found to be unfair, remedies of reinstatement, re-engagement or compensation
Hearing and decision in public	Private hearing and confidentiality of outcome
Appeal on points of law and power to review decisions	Limited power of appeal where there is serious irregularity or lack of jurisdiction

(2) An article by Professor Bill Rees, a barrister and Acas arbitrator, compared the two alternative procedures for the resolution of unfair dismissal applications under seven headings drawn from the original Acas discussion paper:[46]

   (a) informality;

   (b) speed;

   (c) 'value for money';

   (d) user-friendliness;

   (e) flexibility;

   (f) absence of legalism;

   (g) confidentiality.

Some of these, and other perceived differences and advantages claimed for the Acas scheme, need further and closer examination to determine whether the reality justifies the claims made by Acas. As Professor Rees points out in his analysis, Acas has not claimed that the scheme is better, only that it is different and that it offers parties a choice; further, 'in certain respects at least, what one

---

46 Rees, 2000–02.

person would regard as an advantage may possibly be considered a disadvantage by another'.[47]

4.19   VENUE OF THE HEARING

The scheme provides that hearings can be at any venue, although if it is to be at either the employer's premises or another non-neutral venue (such as a trade union's office), then both the parties must agree to this (cl 58). In the Acas guidance, the emphasis is on choosing a venue which is convenient to the parties, and the suggested options are Acas offices or a hotel. Again, the guidance stresses that any other venue, such as a trade union or employer's association office, must be agreed and must not prejudice independence or impartiality. Tribunal hearings take place in the main at regional centres located predominantly in the major cities, although tribunals do sit at other locations, particularly in rural areas.[48]

4.20   PRIVACY VERSUS PUBLICITY

The key differences can be summarised as follows:

- Tribunal hearings are conducted in public and the press attend (though usually only on the first morning of the hearing) and report on the more controversial and entertaining cases, especially if the case has some sort of sexual connotation. Normally, however, only the parties, prospective litigants and students constitute the people sitting in the public seats.
- The tribunal decision will always be published in the register, where it is open to inspection by everyone, and again, there can be press coverage of the more salacious cases. Importantly, the members of the tribunal conduct themselves in full public view.
- In contrast to this, arbitrations are conducted in private with only the parties and their representatives and witnesses present.[49] The press are excluded.
- The arbitrator's award is available only to the parties and Acas.
- Finally, as the hearing is conducted in private, there can be no public scrutiny of the way it is conducted. There will be cases where the employer, sensitive to the risk of unfavourable press comment, will favour the anonymity of arbitration; however, that is the very case where the applicant is likely to favour publicity. As there can be no unilateral recourse to arbitration, it is difficult to contemplate many circumstances in which both parties are likely to favour, all other considerations being equal, both privacy and confidentiality as opposed to publicity.

---

47   Rees, 2000–02.
48   MacMillan, 1999.
49   Acas Arbitration Scheme (England and Wales) Order 2001 (SI 2001/1185), paras 51, 52 and 149.

4.21   STATUS OF THE ADJUDICATING BODY

Tribunals take decisions by a majority; in practice, decisions are usually unanimous. The lay members bring to the tribunal their experience of industrial relations; those on the panel of Acas arbitrators have been appointed for their experience of industrial relations. There are key differences in the decision-making process:

- the employment tribunal, in determining the issue of fairness, must operate within the formula of the 'range of reasonable responses';[50]

- the arbitrator applies the statutory terms of reference, which embrace an industrial relations concept of fairness;[51]

- neither is entitled to substitute his view by determining the issue of fairness by the standard of what he would have done.[52]

4.22   CONDUCT OF THE HEARING

The debate is about whether the essentially adversarial approach of the tribunal, with cross-examination of witnesses irrespective of whether the parties are represented, is a better forum than the inquisitorial nature of arbitration. Is the method whereby an arbitrator is attempting to elicit the relevant facts better suited to resolve a dispute about essentially the same issue – whether the employer was right to dismiss? There are key differences in the two processes, but the employment tribunal procedure is not fixed and inflexible:

- The tribunal rules permit the tribunal to abandon the adversarial approach in favour of a process under which it examines the issues and elicits facts.[53]

- Arbitration practice, where the parties prepare primarily written submissions on their respective cases, might throw up contrasting versions of events which ultimately the arbitrator must resolve, after probing the evidence of witnesses by questions. It will, however, be the arbitrator asking the questions.

- In South Africa, where arbitration is the method of resolving conduct and capability dismissals, the process remains essentially adversarial.[54]

- Arbitrators will be expected to ensure that, consistent with the duty to give the parties the opportunity to put their cases, preliminary statements of case and questions do not become either too lengthy or too much like cross-examination.

---

50   *Iceland Frozen Foods Ltd v Jones* [1982] IRLR 439, EAT; *Post Office v Foley; HSBC Bank v Madden* [2000] IRLR 827, CA.
51   Acas Arbitration Scheme (England and Wales) Order 2001 (SI 2001/1185), para 12.
52   *Ibid; Boys and Girls Welfare Society v McDonald* [1996] IRLR 129.
53   Employment Tribunals (Constitution etc) Regulations 2001 (SI 2001/1171), Sched 1, r 11.
54   See Clark, 1999; for a detailed critique of the New Zealand model, see Corby, 1999.

4.22.1 The reason for dismissal

The tribunal

(1) The ERA 1996 requires the employer to prove the reason or the principal reason for dismissal, and that it is one of the potentially fair reasons for dismissal under s 98. The reasons most frequently relied on are conduct, capability and redundancy.

(2) In the ERA 1996, there are ranges of potential dismissal categories which are automatically unfair – pregnancy, for example. In those instances, the tribunal is required to find the dismissal unfair, irrespective of the procedure followed by the employer, and issues of fairness are irrelevant.

The arbitrator

(3) Beyond the requirement in para 97 of the scheme to identify the reason or principal reason for dismissal or, in the case of redundancy, the reason for selection, there is no such obligation on the arbitrator.

(4) All that the arbitrator is obliged to do, by virtue of para 90 of the scheme, is to 'take account of, but not necessarily follow' the provisions for automatic unfairness in Pt X of the ERA 1996, unless the case involves EC law, in which case, those principles are to be followed. Professor Rees identifies 15 potential situations where EC law is likely to be applicable.

We cannot envisage arbitrators removing protection from employees dismissed in such situations: this would arguably invite judicial intervention because a point of EC law is involved. The more likely outcome is that the parties themselves will decide that cases likely to involve either EC law or questions of automatic unfairness are inappropriate for referral to arbitration.

4.22.2 The issue of fairness

The problems envisaged relate to perceived alternative standards of fairness

The key arguments in this analysis can be summarised as follows:

- The main bone of contention is whether parties will have more confidence in a system where one person decides the issue by a fairly broad industrial relations concept of fairness, or in the tried and trusted system where the decision is taken by three people in accordance with a circumscribed legal concept of fairness.[55]

- There is a danger that employers will not know at the outset of a disciplinary process whether their actions will be judged ultimately by the tribunal standard or the arbitration standard, assuming that they are, in fact,

---

55 See above at note 30.

different. This was a problem identified by a number of commentators when the arbitration alternative was first mooted.[56]

- Professor Rees accepts that having two standards of fair behaviour could undermine good personnel practice; his favoured solution is amendment of the statutory formula in s 98 of the ERA 1996 to substitute the industrial relations standard.

- In any event, there is likely to be the added complication of a third standard of employer behaviour in relation to procedures once the Employment Act, with the abolition of the rule in *Polkey*,[57] comes into force in April 2003.[58]

- In his article in the Industrial Law Journal, John MacMillan, the Regional Chairman of Employment Tribunals in Nottingham, variously described the arbitration test as 'unfettered pragmatism' or the 'unchallengeable whim' of an individual, which carries the risk of confusing 'informality with licence'. After allowing for the fact that the article was published before publication of the scheme, these exaggerated claims ignore the fact that the arbitrator is expressly directed to the Acas Code by the terms of reference set out in para 12 of the scheme (see above at 4.13).

- Tribunals, of course, are also expected to have regard to the provisions of the Acas Code when determining the question of fairness, whilst remaining within the confines of the 'range of reasonable responses' test.[59]

4.23　DELAYS AND FINALITY OF PROCEEDINGS

It is clear from the parliamentary debates in the House of Lords in 1998, when the idea of an alternative arbitration scheme for the resolution of unfair dismissal cases was first debated, that the main justification being advanced was the perception that there was excessive delay and that arbitration offered a speedier process. The key factors in relation to that debate are the following:

- As MacMillan has pointed out, the problem, if there was one at all, existed mainly in London (where most of their Lordships were based) in any event. Figures produced annually by the Employment Tribunals Service (ETS) indicate that more than 85% of standard tribunal cases, of which unfair dismissal cases still represent almost 50%, will be listed for hearing within 26 weeks. The ETS has been meeting that target consistently for the past five years although, significantly, in the year 2000–01, it fell short (the overall figure was 77%).[60] Disguised in that total were Birmingham (57%) and Newcastle (60%), both major centres, where the figures were less than impressive and revealed significant delays in listing for a hearing.

- The ETS does not give statistics for the number of cases that have to be adjourned either close to the hearing date or on the day itself. The ETS Task

---

56　Rees, 2000–02.
57　*Polkey v Dayton Services Ltd* [1988] ICR 142.
58　Employment Act 2002, ss 29 and 34 and Sched 2.
59　*Lock v Cardiff Railway Co Ltd* [1998] IRLR 358; *HSBC Bank v Madden* [2000] IRLR 827, CA.
60　ETS, 2002.

Force has recommended that research be carried out to determine the extent of this problem.[61] There is evidence that this is common in London and Manchester in particular.

- The only time limits specified in the arbitration scheme are that Acas must receive the agreement to submit to arbitration within six weeks of signature by the parties.[62] As parties have only two routes to arbitration – either a compromise agreement or a COT3 drawn up by Acas – it is difficult to determine at present whether access to a hearing will be significantly quicker overall under the arbitration scheme than in the tribunal system. Nevertheless, in some centres, the timescale may have more significant variance. The tables in the ETS report reveal the centres which perform significantly better than the target (Bristol, Exeter, Leeds and Watford).[63]

- Parties will be able to choose the potentially quicker route – namely, arbitration or tribunal. The scheme provides (para 54) that once an arbitrator has been appointed, a hearing shall be arranged 'as soon as reasonably practicable'. This phrase is capable of meaning all things to all people, though Acas did envisage that in practice, hearings would take place within eight weeks. However, with the full co-operation of both parties, this could be reduced to between three and four weeks. Ultimately, the arbitrator can determine venue and date of the hearing if the parties cannot agree, but not until after eight weeks of notification of the arbitration agreement to Acas (para 55). There is, however, a residual power for the arbitrator to expedite a hearing, where either party applies, in two circumstances:

  (a) where an employment tribunal has made an order under the interim relief provisions before the agreement to submit to arbitration; or

  (b) where, in the arbitrator's discretion, other relevant circumstances exist.

This final phrase receives a very brief paragraph in the Acas Guide to the scheme, which does not extend beyond stating that the power exists; obviously, a decision to grant the application will be akin to a judicial decision and not susceptible to challenge or appeal unless perverse. It is subject to the overriding rule that unless the parties agree to expedition, no such order can be made within the eight-week period provided in para 55.

- There is now, though, strong evidence that parties in employment tribunal proceedings will have a hearing date cancelled, often at the last minute, due to the unavailability of a chairman to hear the case.[64] Whereas there is a large pool of members who can be drawn on to hear cases, the process of appointment of both full-time and part-time chairmen takes so long, even assuming that sufficient numbers of suitably qualified candidates apply, that lack of availability of chairmen to hear cases will always be a problem if the number of applications to tribunals continues to increase. Not only that, but in those centres, predominantly London and Manchester, where the practice is to list floating cases which are heard only if earlier cases are settled or

61 See Chapter 7.
62 Acas Arbitration Scheme (England and Wales) Order 2001 (SI 2001/1185), paras 24–27.
63 ETS, 2002.
64 See letter from Yvonne Gallagher in (2002) 9(2) ELA Briefing.

disposed of, there is the added risk that the case will be adjourned, with the inevitable cost that this entails and the inevitable risk of further delay before the hearing can be re-arranged to suit the diaries of the people involved.

• As the arbitrator will only have one matter to dispose of, there is only a remote risk that the hearing will not be completed in the time allowed and on the day; in contrast to the normal practice in the tribunal, the arbitrator will announce the award not at the hearing, but later in writing.

• What the parties will gain from the arbitration process is finality: appeals are only allowed from tribunal decisions on points of law. However, once the appeal process is underway, the likelihood is that the parties will not have the appeal dealt with for at least another 12 months, assuming that it survives the preliminary hearing stage in the EAT. There is then the further prospect of appeal to the Court of Appeal and beyond, and the possibility of the whole case being sent back to the tribunal for a re-hearing, which might not take place until years after the original dismissal.[65] The Acas scheme may also prove attractive when both employers and employees adjust to the shake-up to unfair dismissal law and procedure that will follow the coming into force of both Pts III and IV of the Employment Act 2002.[66]

4.24 REMEDIES

Key questions to consider in relation to the treatment of remedy under the two systems are the following:

(1) In both their original Institute of Employment Rights pamphlet and their paper in 2000, Lewis and Clark envisaged that the arbitrator would not only have a wider range of options in relation to remedy, but that orders for re-employment would be far more common than in tribunal proceedings. Original suggested draft terms of reference for the arbitration scheme would have enabled the arbitrator, for example, to substitute a warning for dismissal. The scheme opted for replication not only of the same remedies as the tribunals, but also of the same principles of compensation.

(2) Only time will tell whether arbitrators are more ready to award re-employment in appropriate cases. The figures produced by the ETS[67] – indicating that in fewer than 1% of cases where the applicant succeeds before the tribunal does the applicant secure re-employment with the dismissing employer – mask the reality that annually, fewer than 20 employees secure this as a remedy. Nothing said or published so far by Acas indicates that an increase in the number of awards of re-employment from the arbitration process is envisaged. In any event, any award by an arbitrator of re-employment which is not complied with by the employer has then to

---

65 See *Bennett v London Borough of Southwark* [2002] IRLR 407.
66 See Chapter 7.
67 ETS, 2002, Table 4: 'Compensation awarded by employment tribunals – unfair dismissal cases.'

be enforced by the employment tribunal in accordance with the statutory formula for additional compensation under s 117 of the ERA 1996.[68]

4.25   ACCESS TO THE SCHEME

What differences are there in relation to access to the dispute resolution process?:

- At present, an applicant not only has the right of unilateral access to the employment tribunal, but can also do so by simple letter, as long as it contains the requisite information.[69] In practice, most applicants use the standard form and its use will be compulsory following the enactment of the Employment Act 2002.

- The scheme, in contrast, will require not only an originating application in most cases, but an arbitration agreement, a completed waiver form and a compromise agreement if the reference to arbitration has not been secured by Acas. It can be argued that this will be an inhibiting factor for respondents as well as applicants and may be one factor which is presently inhibiting take-up of the scheme.

4.26   TIME LIMITS

Although the scheme is informal and differs from tribunal practice and procedure with its adherence to legal tests and rules, there are still time limits which both parties must comply with at various stages in the scheme:

(1) The arbitration agreement must be notified to Acas no later than six weeks from its conclusion (para 24).

(2) The parties have two months from notification of the arbitration agreement to Acas in which to agree between themselves the date and venue of the arbitration hearing. After that period, the arbitrator fixes both (para 54).

(3) Applications for postponement of the hearing date must be made within 14 days of the date of the letter notifying the parties of the hearing date.

(4) Parties must send their statements of case and supporting documentation to the Acas arbitration section no later than 14 days prior to the hearing date (para 68).

(5) Any application to correct an arbitration award must be made to Acas within 28 days of the date of despatch of the award to the parties (para 153). Any amendment must then be made by the arbitrator within 28 days of that application, unless the arbitrator is making the amendment on his own initiative, in which case, he has 28 days from the date of the award (para 154).

---

68   Acas Arbitration Scheme (England and Wales) Order 2001 (SI 2001/1185), para 160.
69   Employment Tribunals (Constitution etc) Regulations 2001 (SI 2001/1171), Sched 1, r 1, on which see MacMillan, 1999, p 37; however, see the Employment Act 2002, s 25 (power to delegate prescription of forms).

(6) In the case of an additional award, the award must be made within 56 days of the date of the original award (para 155).

(7) Unpaid awards attract interest 42 days after the date of despatch of the award to the parties (para 161).

(8) Any legal challenge to the award in the courts has to be made within 28 days of the date of the award (para 165).

(9) It is necessary at this stage to say a little about how time is calculated for these purposes, bearing in mind that different reference dates are used; in some instances it is the date of the award, in others it is the date of posting of either the award or the written notification of the date of a hearing. Paragraph 178 of the scheme provides that time is calculated in accordance with the formula in s 78 of the Arbitration Act 1996: 'When time is being calculated as a specified period of days from a date or an event, the period begins immediately after that date.' The other provisions of the section do not really apply to employment arbitration, as they envisage periods of time not contemplated by the scheme in any event.

(10) It must be stressed that the provisions in the Arbitration Act which enable the court to extend time limits (ss 79 and 80) are not incorporated in the Acas scheme. Until the point is tested, therefore, it has to be assumed that there is no power, at least in the scheme, to extend the strict 28-day time limit in which to challenge the award in the courts. This point is examined more fully in Chapter 5.

CHAPTER 5

SKILLS AND TECHNIQUES

In this chapter, the main features of employment arbitration through its various procedural stages are examined. In particular, we assess its essential features, look at the critical stages in preparing a case for hearing under the scheme and, where appropriate, compare employment arbitration with tribunal practice and procedure. We begin with the speed and informality of the procedure, which is one of the most important aspects to be emphasised.

5.1   SPEED AND INFORMALITY

The Acas Guide to the scheme highlights the following as the key features of employment arbitration. It will be:

- confidential;
- relatively fast;
- cost-efficient;
- non-legalistic; and
- informal.

The issue of legalism is dealt with in 5.2.

5.1.1   Speed and time limits

On the question of speed, Acas, unlike the Employment Tribunals Service (ETS), has avoided setting target times for fixing hearing dates and case disposal from receipt of the arbitration agreement to delivery of the award. However, as we saw in Chapter 4, there are some specific timescales provided in the scheme:

- The parties have six weeks in which to notify Acas of the conclusion of an arbitration agreement; Acas then appoints the arbitrator from its panel.
- The parties then have two months in which to agree the venue and date of the hearing with the arbitrator before the arbitrator can intervene and take the initiative. Failure on the part of the parties to comply with this initial time limit is fatal to the referral to arbitration unless the arbitrator decides, if necessary after a hearing, that the referral should be accepted.
- Requests for adjournments of the hearing date must be made within 14 days of notification. How quickly the overall process can be completed, from acceptance of the agreement to refer the dispute to arbitration by Acas until issue of the award, depends on the stage at which the agreement is concluded and Acas is notified, and then on the diary commitments of the parties and the arbitrator.
- No time limit is set for the arbitrator to write the award and send it to Acas, but Acas is committed, in the Guide, to sending the signed award to the

parties within three weeks of receiving it from the arbitrator. Acas has advised arbitrators that unless there are exceptional circumstances, it expects to receive the draft award no later than a month from the hearing, and preferably sooner.

- As it is likely that the hearing will take place on the date fixed for the hearing, overall, the process from agreement to submit to arbitration to receipt of the award should take between three and six months. However, with full and speedy co-operation from both parties, a shorter process, perhaps as little as eight weeks, might be possible. Based on present projections for take-up of the scheme, there is unlikely to be any difficulty in Acas selecting an arbitrator available to conduct an arbitration hearing. The ETS calculates its 26-week listing target from the date that the notice of appearance is received, which in most cases will be earlier than the agreement to go to arbitration, bearing in mind that the agreement can only be secured after the intervention of an Acas conciliator or through a compromise agreement.

- On balance, therefore, the timescale for completion of the process from dismissal to resolution of the dispute will be similar in both tribunal and arbitration if the comparison is made with the more efficient tribunal centres. At present, with so few completed arbitrations under the scheme, there are no reliable statistics from which conclusions can be drawn about the relative speed of the alternative procedures.

Key factors having a bearing on delay in the tribunal system have been identified to include the following:

- Some tribunal hearing centres encounter considerable delays in listing cases or, more significantly, are open to a high risk of the cancellation of hearing dates due to the non-availability of a chairman.

- Parties in employment tribunals also encounter the problem of listing floating cases to be heard by the first available tribunal, which are then adjourned because no tribunal in fact becomes available in time to hear the case, which is prevalent in the busier hearing centres. It can then be months before another date can be arranged.

- The recruitment and appointment procedure for both part-time and full-time chairmen is slow. Applicants have to apply in writing and complete an extensive application form. Interviews are held, and there may be many candidates to be seen. Even after a candidate is offered the position, there is a delay to enable the necessary checks to be carried out with the Inland Revenue and the relevant professional supervisory bodies. Even then, the successful candidate, in the case of a part-time chairman, has to receive initial training before undertaking sitting duties and, in the case of a full-time appointment, the individual may have to give notice or wind up a practice at the Bar.

- It is not uncommon for the process of appointment of a new full-time chairman to take 12 months, or even longer, from advertisement of the position to occupation of the post.

- There is evidence of institutional delays in the listing of certain centres in the annual reports of the ETS, and anecdotal evidence that there is a high incidence of last-minute cancellations of hearing dates in the employment tribunals. At present, the ETS does not publish any statistics on the prevalence of cancellations of hearing dates in tribunal hearing centres.[1]
- Even with the new regime of allocating a hearing duration to cases and notifying parties that the hearing will deal with remedy if time permits, which has been operating in the employment tribunals since June 2000, it is still not uncommon for there to be a second hearing on the issue of remedy after an initial finding in favour of the applicant. (The arbitration award will deal with all issues, including remedy.)

The formality, or otherwise, of the hearing itself before the single arbitrator will be influenced by other factors, including the following:

- The arbitration hearing will be structured, but it will be more informal than a tribunal hearing. For a start, there is a single arbitrator, not a panel, and in only a few instances will the arbitrator be a lawyer. Fewer than 10% of the arbitrators appointed by Acas are legally qualified, although at least two also sit as part-time chairmen of employment tribunals.
- The hearing will take place in a hotel or an office, rather than in a venue which resembles a court. There are no clerks, as the arbitrator is in charge of the administrative arrangements. The room layout at the hearing will resemble a committee room rather than a courtroom. The arbitrator will be at the head of the table, rather than on a raised dais or platform.
- Evidence is not given on oath. It is unlikely that there will be legal representation. The parties will not be expected to stand up at the commencement of proceedings and when the arbitrator adjourns. Invariably, the individual arbitrator will introduce himself to the parties before the hearing commences. Though this does sometimes happen in the employment tribunal, it will be the norm in arbitration. This is not to say that there will not be a fairly standard procedure to be followed in most instances in arbitration. Acas does, in fact, set out a standard arbitration hearing procedure in Appendix 3 to the Guide, as covered below.

5.2   FLEXIBILITY AND THE AVOIDANCE OF LEGALISM

The charge of legalism is raised in all the criticisms of employment tribunals. In some cases – for example, the law on unfair dismissal for making a protected disclosure, where the statute itself covers a maze of contextual situations – it is hard to see how a legal approach can be ignored. The law on unfair dismissal is contained in legislation which has existed since 1971. Over the years, Parliament has created a number of dismissal situations that are automatically unfair in closely defined situations, most particularly in relation to protected disclosures ('whistle blowing').[2] If there are a lot of lawyers in tribunals, this may be

---

1   See letter from Yvonne Gallagher in (2002) 9(2) ELA Briefing.
2   ERA 1996, ss 43A–L.

because the law is itself complex and requires legal skills to unravel the labyrinths.

What is meant by the avoidance of legalism? When the idea of an alternative arbitration scheme was first mooted, the criticism levelled at employment tribunals was that they had become the victims of excessive 'legalism'. They had become inaccessible, formal, slow and expensive. The authors of that seminal paper[3] illustrated their thesis with a case that had dragged on for years in the employment tribunal and which produced a decision that extended to over 400 pages.[4] Such cases are rare, but some of the newer jurisdictions, particularly in relation to dismissals for making protected disclosures, threaten to throw up ever more complex issues and decisions.[5] Nobody suggests that a system of ADR should be free of rules. When critics refer to legalism in the tribunals, they are usually referring to the following features of a hearing in the tribunals that will not be features of arbitration:

(1) Most commentators are attacking the increasing presence of lawyers in the employment tribunals and the excessive cross-examination of witnesses which make tribunal hearings resemble court hearings.

(2) The 'range of reasonable responses' test is a judicial creation that is not in the legislation. At one stage, there was judicial support for the proposition that it virtually required an employer's decision to be perverse, rather than unfair, before the tribunal could interfere.[6]

(3) Lawyers appear regularly in the employment tribunal. The scheme (para 84) reminds the parties that any person can represent them, but that lawyers will be accorded 'no special status'. It is not entirely clear why this language is used in the scheme, since lawyers enjoy no special status in the employment tribunal. In the main, it is envisaged that representation will be provided by human resources personnel, trade union officials or lay people.

(4) Precedent governs the employment tribunal. As Acas points out in the Guide, arbitrators will apply general principles of fairness and good practice, rather than strict law or legal precedent. The exception to this is the express reference in the scheme to the category of 'automatically unfair dismissals' (para 95), which is covered in Chapter 4.

(5) There will be little justification for the use of lawyers if there is no power to cross-examine witnesses. It is also to be hoped that parties will not use the requirement, under para 69 of the scheme, to prepare a statement of case to present lengthy documents which carry the imprint of lawyers.

(6) The main way in which the arbitration scheme will avoid excessive legalism is by its terms of reference which, in theory, should limit the inquiry to the only issue that has to be determined – the fairness of the dismissal.

---

3   See Chapter 3, note 1.
4   *Port of London Authority v Payne* [1992] IRLR 447.
5   See *Miklaszewicz v Stolt Offshore Ltd* [2002] IRLR 344.
6   *Haddon v Van Den Bergh Foods Ltd* [1999] IRLR 672.

(7) It is the problem areas of EC law and human rights issues which will carry the risk of the introduction of legalism in the arbitration process. The Guide does all it can to discourage parties from using the scheme if it potentially raises issues of EC law or the Human Rights Act (HRA) 1998, but there will still be cases where these issues arise, which the parties could not have foreseen. This subject is covered extensively in Chapter 4, at 4.16.

5.3 CO-OPERATION WITH THE ARBITRATOR AND THE OTHER PARTY

Professor Rees emphasises that parties co-operating both with the arbitrator and with each other assist effective arbitration.[7] There are a number of critical ways in which this can impact:

- Obviously, by agreeing to submit the dispute to arbitration in the first place, either by a compromise agreement or via Acas conciliation.
- By agreeing, with the arbitrator and with each other, the venue and date for the hearing as quickly as possible in the two-month period after appointment of the arbitrator by Acas.
- By complying with the general duty under para 50 at all times (see 4.6).
- By ensuring that if the assistance of an interpreter, signer or communicator is required at the hearing, then Acas is notified well in advance of the hearing (para 60).
- By ensuring that if the date or location of the hearing is inconvenient, then any application for postponement is made in the 14-day time limit specified (para 63).
- By ensuring that all the necessary documents required by Acas are supplied no later than 14 days before the hearing as envisaged (paras 68–71 of the scheme; see 4.4, 4.5 and 4.6).
- By attending the hearing, so as to avoid an unnecessary adjournment (paras 87–88 and below, at 5.9).
- By ensuring that at the hearing, the arbitrator is in a position to deal with remedy if necessary. The arbitrator is required to explore the question of remedy at the hearing, and extensive advice is contained in the Guide to enable the parties to come to the hearing prepared to deal with this aspect of the case (below, at 6.2 and 6.3).

---

7   Rees, 2000–02.

5.4 PREPARATION OF THE STATEMENT OF CASE

The statement of case underpins employment arbitration. The key requirements in relation to preparation by both parties include the following:

- Each party is required to prepare their written statement of case and send it to Acas at least 14 days prior to the hearing (para 68). Both the arbitrator and the other side receive a copy.

- Advice on what the written statement of case should contain is set out in para 69 of the scheme and is amplified by paras 63 and 65 of the Guide. The parties are encouraged to set out briefly the main particulars of the case. In the case of the employer, he ought to put the dismissal in context and explain the background. The disciplinary procedure should be stated, as should the history of the disciplinary proceedings.

- Both the employer and the employee should include an explanation of the events which led up to the dismissal, including an account of the sequence and outcome of any relevant meetings, interviews or discussions.

- Statements from relevant witnesses can be included either in the narrative or attached to the document, which itself ought to extend to no more than three or four typed pages.

Although the parties are allowed to expand it at the hearing, the advantage of a concise but comprehensive statement of case is that it tells the arbitrator what the critical issues are in advance of the hearing, and avoids the arbitrator or either side being taken by surprise. It also complies with the general duty on the parties under para 50 of the scheme. It can be seen that this obligation on both parties – to disclose their case and evidence in advance of the hearing – differs from tribunal practice and procedure, where it is possible for the hearing to proceed solely on the basis of the originating application, the notice of appearance, and the oral evidence of the respective parties. However, the tendency now in the tribunals, and not just in discrimination cases, is increasingly to give directions for the conduct of proceedings to include prior disclosure of witness statements.

5.5 DOCUMENTATION AND DISCLOSURE

Paragraph 68 of the scheme also requires the parties to include all supporting material with the statement of case, and para 70 sets out 10 categories of potential documentation in bullet points. The obvious documents are those that would be required in the employment tribunal:

- contracts of employment and written particulars;
- disciplinary rules and procedures;
- warnings and dismissal letters.

A more brief list covering the same material is at para 65 of the Guide. In respect of the statement of case, witness statements and documentation, parties are expected to be sensible. Arbitrators will not thank parties who arrive at the hearing with bulky lever arch files, as is the case all too frequently in the employment tribunal.

The arbitrator has an obligation under para 48 to avoid unnecessary delay and expense, and is required to adopt procedures suitable to the circumstances. This might involve limiting the paperwork if parties abuse the system. Hopefully, if the use of lawyers is minimised in preparation as well as in representation, this can be achieved. There may be a tendency, however, to err on the side of caution and to include information to ensure that the party in question does not suffer prejudice by virtue of para 74.

There are a number of further principles to be stressed in relation to preparation for the hearing, including the following:

- Materials which have not been supplied cannot be relied on at the hearing without the consent of the arbitrator (para 74). This is designed to prevent parties attempting to secure an unfair advantage, resulting in an unnecessary adjournment.

- Any party can request the other party to produce copies of documents not in their possession. Although the arbitrator has no power under the scheme to compel disclosure of documentation, he is permitted to draw adverse inferences from non-disclosure (para 76). If problems do arise over documents, the arbitrator can either hold a preliminary hearing to sort out the problems or give written directions (see 5.7 below).

5.6   ATTENDANCE OF WITNESSES

So far as witnesses are concerned, the following general rules and principles are likely to be adhered to in the majority of cases:

- The arbitrator has no power to compel the attendance of any person at the hearing. Although the employment tribunal can issue a witness order, the only penalty for non-attendance of the witness is a possible prosecution. In the case of arbitration, the arbitrator is permitted to draw an adverse inference from the failure of an employer to permit the attendance of a worker employed by him.

- The Guide contains more general advice on the use of witnesses at paras 70–72. In particular, the parties should consider having people present who can speak about the events leading up to the dismissal; or their role in the disciplinary procedure; or the organisation's rules, practices and procedures. Where relevant, those operating in the industry or sector concerned should be considered.

- Parties are advised, if possible, to reduce witness statements to writing and to include them with the statement of case.

5.7   PRELIMINARY HEARINGS AND DIRECTIONS

In some cases, there may be differences between the parties over an issue, such as documents or witnesses. In those and other cases, the arbitrator may consider calling the parties to a preliminary hearing to sort out the differences, or give directions in correspondence (para 78). As the aim of the scheme is to avoid unnecessary expense and delay, this will only be resorted to if there is no alternative and the arbitrator considers it essential to facilitate the procedure. The arbitrator can express a view on the desirability of information or evidence being available at the hearing. This is also an opportunity to remind the parties of their obligation to co-operate with the process.

5.8   ORDER OF PROCEEDINGS

Paragraph 80 of the scheme gives the arbitrator a wide general discretion to conduct the hearing in any way he thinks fit, subject to the obligation to comply with the duty under para 48. In practice, the arbitrator will be likely to follow the model procedure set out in Appendix 3 to the Guide.

Among the general principles relating to the conduct of the hearing are the following:

- The arbitrator is responsible for the conduct of the hearing and for ensuring that he obtains all the information necessary to make his award.
- He must also ensure that both parties are enabled to put their case. The scheme refers to a 'reasonable opportunity'; the Guide talks of 'every opportunity'. There is thus a conflict between the wording of the scheme and the Guide, but the scheme's formulation is to be preferred. It is a form of words derived from the Arbitration Act 1996 and is consistent with the aim of employment arbitration – that it should be relatively fast and cost-efficient.
- The arbitrator would be entitled to prevent a party taking too long to present a case. In practice, as the arbitrator is in control and takes the initiative in asking any questions, this ought not to present a problem or, in particular, lead to a challenge in the courts if the arbitrator curtails an unduly lengthy presentation by either party.

The model procedure for the conduct of an employment arbitration envisages the following order of proceedings:

(1) *Introduction*

 (a) The essence of successful employment arbitration is to establish informality and rapport. The parties are called into the room, which is laid out in committee form. The arbitrator will probably have already introduced himself and briefly discussed the arrangements that will be adopted for the hearing.

 (b) When the hearing begins, the arbitrator will introduce himself, then invite the parties to do the same, and identify everyone present. He will then explain how the hearing is to be conducted, and deal with the housekeeping arrangements: the location of toilets and fire escapes. If it is anticipated that the hearing will last longer than the morning, he will inform the parties of the time that the hearing is anticipated to adjourn.

(c) He will remind the parties that unlike in the employment tribunal, the decision (award) will not be given at the end of the hearing, but will be sent in writing to the parties by Acas in due course.

(2) *Oral submission*

Each party is then invited to make an uninterrupted oral submission, in which they can summarise their case, emphasise the main features and deal with the case of the other party:

(a) It will usually be the employer who goes first, as in the employment tribunal, where the dismissal is admitted. This part of the procedure should normally be done without interruption, unless the arbitrator needs to clarify something.

(b) It ought not to consist of either party reading out or repeating what is in the statement of case. In the main, it ought not to last more than 15 minutes. This is the point to make concessions if there are any, to indicate issues of agreement or dispute and to abandon issues if they are either irrelevant or insignificant.

(3) *Discussion of the issues*

The format of this stage of the procedure may vary, depending on the issues raised in the opening submissions:

(a) If there are factual inconsistencies, these can be resolved by calling witnesses to whom questions can be put through the arbitrator.

(b) It might be appropriate to call the individual who was dismissed or the manager who conducted any appeal.

(c) At each stage, whether it is evidence which is being called or points made by either the person presenting the case or someone else on the team, then the other side should be invited to respond. Again, it will usually be the employer who goes first.

(d) The arbitrator will take the initiative in directing questions designed to focus on the critical issues.

(e) At a convenient point, the issue of remedy will have to be canvassed and explored, with evidence if necessary. If the employee is seeking reinstatement or re-engagement, the employer will be expected to deal with the practicability of re-employment. In any event, the employee will have to deal with any attempts that have been made to find alternative employment.

(f) Unlike the practice in tribunal proceedings, an arbitrator has to explore the position in relation to social security benefits, as the recoupment procedure does not apply to arbitration.

(g) Before final submissions are made, the parties should be invited to confirm that they have been able to say everything they wished to say.

(h) At this point, a short adjournment can be offered to enable the parties to prepare final submissions. The arbitrator may recap or summarise the main issues or points raised.

(4) *Closing (final submissions)*

   (a) As with opening submissions, final submissions should be delivered without interruption, usually with the employer going first. This is not the occasion to introduce new points or material, but to summarise the main issues that the parties want the arbitrator to consider.

   (b) In closing the hearing, the arbitrator will seek confirmation that the parties have said all that they wanted. The arbitrator will not announce the decision at the hearing. The format of awards is dealt with in Chapter 6.

5.9   ADDRESSING THE ISSUE OF FAIRNESS

The respective concepts of fairness at the heart of the arbitration scheme and the legislative concept in the ERA 1996 are compared elsewhere. In this section, we consider how it will be dealt with at the arbitration hearing:

- The terms of reference of the arbitrator – to determine the fairness of the dismissal – are set out at para 12 and are at the heart of the scheme. This concept has a statutory meaning in the relevant provisions of the ERA 1996.[8] Notwithstanding the detailed definition in the legislation, it has now acquired a judicial interpretation. The employer must follow a fair procedure. The fairness of the ultimate sanction of dismissal is judged by the judicial litmus test of whether it is within the 'range of reasonable responses' that the employer might have resorted to, irrespective of whether another employer might have dismissed or whether the tribunal might have adopted a different course of action. Further discussion of the debate that has ensued over the judicial formula is contained elsewhere in this book.

- In line with practice in the tribunal, the arbitrator is also required not to substitute his view for that of the employer, but is enjoined, nevertheless, to apply an industrial relations standard of fairness.

- What is this standard and where is it derived from? In the main, this will be determined by the norms of the arbitrator's own experience, and the guidance contained in the Acas Handbook, *Discipline at Work*. Evidence of what happens in the employer's sector of activity is also relevant. Employers in the food industry, for example, are likely to take a strong line on cleanliness and safety; attendance issues are treated very seriously in the transport sector, especially in public transport.

- Employers will be expected to explain to the arbitrator why an individual was dismissed in that particular case; they can demonstrate consistency by evidence of how they have dealt with similar situations in the past. Employers' disciplinary handbooks will remain paramount.

---

8   ERA 1996, s 98(4): 'Where the employer has fulfilled the requirements of sub-s (1), the determination of the question of whether the dismissal is fair or unfair (having regard to the reason shown by the employer) (a) depends on whether in the circumstances (including the size and administrative resources of the employer's undertaking) the employer acted reasonably or unreasonably in treating it as a sufficient reason for dismissing the employee, and (b) shall be determined in accordance with equity and the substantial merits of the case.'

- Two problems arise from this. First, how will employers know what standards arbitrators are applying when hearings take place in private and awards are not published? Secondly, how will the employer know what norms to follow at the dismissal stage? At this stage, he will not know whether the dismissal is to be examined at all and, if so, whether by an employment tribunal or an arbitrator. Moreover, the case may be assessed by two seemingly alternative standards of fairness. In the first instance, although Acas can neither seek to influence an arbitrator nor interfere with the award, the opportunity will arise to meet arbitrators and address particular issues of consistency in the usual way, at conferences and training events.

- Additionally, the main thrust of the Acas publications is directed at procedures rather than outcomes, although they do stress that dismissal should not be the sanction for a first instance of breach of discipline unless it amounts to gross misconduct.

In our considered view, it is likely that the arbitrator will rarely form a different opinion from that of an employment tribunal (had the case followed that route), particularly where the issue is the procedure adopted. The difference is more in the way that the case is disposed of and, in particular, the procedures followed by the two respective dispute resolution procedures. Whether procedural deficiencies in tribunal proceedings will still be as fatal after the enactment of the Employment Act 2002 and the abolition of the rule in *Polkey* must be a moot point.[9] Ultimately, the parties have a choice as to which alternative they wish to pursue.

5.10 THE USE OF LAWYERS

It may not be a case of 'Let's kill all the lawyers',[10] but it is clearly the intention to minimise the role of lawyers in arbitration. The wording of the scheme is curious: 'The parties may be accompanied by any person chosen by them to help them present their case at the hearing, *although no special status will be accorded to legally qualified representatives*' (para 84) (our emphasis). The same wording is adopted in the Guide. In fact, lawyers do not have any special status in the employment tribunal either. They do, however, tend to behave as though the tribunal is adopting a court procedure. Consequently, they tend to insist on adherence to the rules of evidence, expect the procedure adopted to mirror court procedure, and adopt conventional terminology. This factor has probably, over time, led to tribunals tending to adopt a conventional court-based procedure when lawyers are involved, despite the fact that the tribunal rules do not require it and in fact permit a more inquisitorial approach. Admittedly, whichever approach is adopted, evidence will be given and witnesses will be

---

9 An employment tribunal will be able to ignore minor procedural lapses as long as the employer has followed the minimum requirements of the statutory procedure in Sched 2 to the EA 2002: ss 29 and 34, inserting a new s 98A into the ERA 1996.

10 'The first thing we do, let's kill all the lawyers': Shakespeare, *Henry VI Part 2*.

asked questions in the tribunal. The presence of lawyers can in fact not only assist the tribunal in defining the issues, but can also positively facilitate a settlement at the hearing.

Although lawyers may appear in employment arbitration, they should remember these factors:

- Lawyers primarily cross-examine witnesses, and this will not be permitted in employment arbitration. Whether this will enhance or inhibit the process of arbitration, only time will tell.
- It is clear that the absence of an adversarial procedure based primarily on cross-examination of witnesses will probably initially discourage the involvement of lawyers in employment arbitration, particularly at the hearing stage.

5.11 EFFECTIVE QUESTIONS

Cross-examination is a skill which distinguishes lawyers from non-lawyers. It is an essential feature of tribunal litigation as much as of court proceedings. However, when the parties submit their dispute to employment arbitration, they sign a waiver document in which they expressly agree to forgo the right to cross-examine witnesses. When parties appearing without legal representation are invited to ask questions in the employment tribunal, they invariably either give their evidence or repeat what they have already said when giving evidence. The chairman has the task of rephrasing the statement as a question on behalf of the unrepresented party. Problems arise where one party has legal representation (which may be poor) and the unrepresented party receives assistance from the tribunal, which must not trespass into advocacy. Lawyers will be rare visitors to employment arbitration, and the arbitrator will take the initiative in the proceedings. As neither party can ask witnesses direct questions, it is unlikely that questions will arise that have not already been dealt with either in the statement of case or in the arbitrator's own questions. What might be relevant questions? Again, it is difficult to give specific examples, other than to remind ourselves that the arbitrator's primary function is to determine fairness and not, unless it is absolutely vital to disposal of the case, to resolve factual contradictions. It follows that unless the arbitrator has overlooked the point, an employer will seek to secure assurance from the applicant that the employer's procedure was followed (and the converse if it is the employee). After that, from our experience of employment arbitration, the question of consistency of treatment is most likely to arise. The employer will seek to establish that previous cases were dealt with in the same way (and the converse in the case of the employee).

5.12 SETTLEMENT

The initial agreement to submit to arbitration, whether secured by an Acas agreement or through a compromise agreement, is itself a settlement or stay of the tribunal proceedings. Nevertheless, the parties are still free at any time, even after the arbitration hearing has commenced, to resolve the dispute. This is spelled out in brief but unambiguous terms in para 31 of the scheme, and in paras 32–34, there is a procedure for recording any agreement. Where an agreement is reached:

(1) by a request to the arbitrator, or to the Acas arbitration section, the arbitrator (if appointed) or Acas (if not) shall terminate the arbitration proceedings;

(2) the arbitrator (if appointed) may (if requested by the parties) record the settlement in the form of an agreed award;

(3) such an award shall state that it is by consent, and will have the same status and effect as any other award on the merits.

When rendering an agreed award, the arbitrator:

(1) may only record the agreed wording of the parties;

(2) may not approve, vary, transcribe, interpret or ratify a settlement in any way;

(3) cannot, however, record any settlement beyond the scope of the scheme, the arbitration agreement, or the initial reference to the scheme as accepted by Acas. Such matters would have to be recorded either in a separate agreement or in a compromise agreement.

statement or re-engagement. Apart from the fact that this is done during the
ring rather than after a determination on fairness, the scheme mirrors unfair
missal legislation.[1] However, in a number of respects, the arbitrator is neither
mpelled to adopt the same principles as the employment tribunals, nor to
low case law.

Differences, as well as similarities, between the alternative approaches to
medy are likely to include the following:

Tribunals do not usually award remedies of re-employment. For the last year
for which figures are available, only 15 successful cases resulted in the
applicant either getting back his old job or being offered some other job.[2] No
detailed research is available to identify reasons for this statistic, which has
been consistently low since unfair dismissal was introduced in 1971.[3]

• It is unlikely that arbitration awards will be any different, even though the
arbitration process may be quicker than a tribunal route. When the newly
appointed arbitrators were receiving their training on the scheme, it was
pointed out that Acas was not anticipating a greater or lesser likelihood of
re-employment awards.

6.2 THE AVAILABLE REMEDIES

Advocates of an arbitration scheme, or an alternative to the tribunal system,
argued that arbitrators should have more options available than tribunals:
suspension or warnings, for example. The scheme has rejected this option, and
instead replicates (with different terminology) the options of re-employment or
compensation, with two main elements to an award of compensation,
resembling closely the existing statutory basic and compensatory awards.

6.2.1 Factors determining choice of remedy

The approach to remedy is initially dictated by the decision on fairness. If the
arbitrator determines that the dismissal was unfair by the operation of EC law
(pregnancy or TUPE, for example), then he must determine remedy in
accordance with the relevant law on remedies for unfair dismissal. These will be
the relevant provisions of the ERA 1996 and the established case law. It is not
clear how the arbitrator is to discover this case law unless he has already
sought, or then decides to seek, legal advice under para 90 of the scheme. In all
other instances, the arbitrator is obliged to follow the detailed framework of the
scheme (at paras 104–47).

---

1   ERA 1996, ss 112–24.
2   ETS, 2002, Table 3.
3   Industrial Relations Act 1971.

ENFORCING REMEDIES AND CHALLENGING THE AWARD

In this chapter, the way in which remedies are dealt with in e
arbitration is examined. The remedies available to the applicant are
in particular, the differences between remedies in employment arbi
those under the statutory jurisdiction for unfair dismissal. The follow
are then examined: the limited provision that exists for challe
arbitration award; the situations where it exists; the procedure for chal
question of time limits; and the loss of the right to challenge.

6.1 FORM OF THE AWARD

As we saw in Chapter 4, the award must comply with the requireme
para 97 of the scheme. However, there is no 'right' way to write an arbi
award. Nevertheless, Acas has prepared a guidance note for arbitr
suggesting a format for the presentation of an award. Most awards will fol
standard four-section structure, embracing the following:

- Background – the first part of this will be a standard *pro forma* containing
  names of the parties, recording basic information about the employer
  the applicant, followed by a chronological account of the events that led
  the dismissal. It should endeavour to be factual and non-contentious.

- The main arguments – this should contain, in two parts, concise summarie
  of broadly similar length if possible, of the main arguments raised an
  evidence given by the employee and the employer. It will summarise wha
  the parties want the arbitrator to find, not only on whether or not the
  dismissal was fair, but also on remedy.

- Main considerations – conventionally, the parties are to be thanked for their
  presentation. The main points of agreement are indicated, followed by the
  issues which were resolved in relation to the reason for dismissal, the
  procedure followed and the fairness or otherwise of the outcome. Where
  there were disagreements on facts, the nature of how the conflict was
  resolved should be set out, along with the basis of the conclusions drawn.

- The award – this must state whether the dismissal was fair or unfair, the
  degree of any contribution to the dismissal and the remedy awarded. In the
  case of compensation, it will be normal to indicate the approach adopted,
  supported by a worked calculation.

Paragraph 101 of the scheme imposes an obligation on the arbitrator to ensure,
during the arbitration, that the employee is made aware of the alternative
remedies available, so that the employee can indicate a preference for

6.2.2   Awards of reinstatement

Assuming that the applicant expresses a preference at the hearing for reinstatement, the arbitrator must first consider this option. In doing so, he must consider the practicability of reinstatement and the extent to which it would be just to make such an award if the employee contributed to the dismissal. This is the same formula as under the unfair dismissal legislation. Fewer than 1% of successful applicants obtain an order for reinstatement or re-engagement from the employment tribunal. Only time will tell if it is a more attractive remedy to arbitrators. In June 2002, the government was reported as being willing to consider legislating to make the order for reinstatement the norm rather than the exception.[4]

6.2.3   Awards of re-engagement

As with unfair dismissal, the arbitrator must go on to consider the next alternative, that of re-engagement. Re-engagement is the re-employment of the dismissed employee by the same or a different employer – such as a successor or associated employer – in a different capacity. Factors to be taken into account are the same as with reinstatement. Again, the arbitrator follows the same formula and procedure as the employment tribunal. Paragraph 108 of the scheme, in language which is identical to s 116(4) of the ERA 1996, directs the arbitrator to make the terms of an order for re-engagement no less favourable, as far as is reasonably practicable, than an order for reinstatement, unless the employee's conduct has been taken into account.

6.2.4   Permanent replacements

Under the terms of para 108 of the scheme, the arbitrator is required, when deciding whether or not to award reinstatement or re-engagement, to ignore the fact that the employer might have appointed a permanent replacement when determining the issue of practicability. However, this direction can be ignored where the employer can demonstrate either that the employee was critical, and a replacement had to be recruited, or that the employee had not indicated a preference for re-employment, that the replacement employee had been recruited after the lapse of a reasonable period, and that it was reasonable for the employer to recruit a replacement at the time the employee was replaced.[5]

6.2.5   Terms in relation to awards of re-employment

As is made clear in 6.2.3, the terms of any award for reinstatement or re-engagement should be identical, subject to the proviso that in the first instance, it is the same job to which the employee returns, whilst in the latter, it is a different job. Subject to this proviso, the scheme requires that the arbitrator specify the following information in the award.

---

4   (2002) *The Times*, 11 June.
5   Acas Arbitration Scheme (England and Wales) Order 2001 (SI 2001/1185), para 109.

Reinstatement

(1) The award must specify the date for compliance and deal with arrears of pay, sums payable to the employee which would have been paid but for the dismissal, and other rights and privileges (such as seniority and pension rights).

(2) If, but for the dismissal, the employee would have benefited from an improvement to terms and conditions, this must be reflected in the award.

(3) In requiring the employer to pay any arrears of pay, the arbitrator must reduce the sums payable to take into account any sums received by the employee between the date of dismissal and the date of reinstatement, by way of wages from another employer, or pay in lieu of notice or *ex gratia* payments made by the employer.

(4) The arbitrator has a discretion to take into account other benefits received by the employee, but the scheme gives no indication as to what these sums might be. Logically, and as a matter of principle, it ought to include any social security benefits received, such as Job Seekers Allowance, although arguably not Income Support or Housing Benefit.[6] The question of how benefits are to be treated is dealt with as a discrete issue in 6.3.2 below.

Re-engagement

In the case of an award of re-engagement, the award must specify:

(1) the identity of the employer;

(2) the nature of the employment;

(3) the rate of pay;

and must deal with

- any arrears of pay and other benefits it would be appropriate for the employee to receive for the period from the dismissal until the date of the order for re-engagement; and

- any other rights and privileges, as with orders for reinstatement, and specify the date the new employment is to commence. The same rules as are applicable to orders for reinstatement apply in relation to deductions for sums received by the employee in the intervening period.[7]

Continuity of employment

Both awards preserve the continuity of employment of the dismissed employee in the period between dismissal and re-employment.[8]

---

6   *Ibid*, paras 108, 110–12.
7   *Ibid*, paras 113–14.
8   *Ibid*, para 115.

6.2.6 Awards of compensation

Where the arbitrator makes an award of neither reinstatement nor re-engagement, he must make an award of compensation, consisting of a basic amount and a compensatory amount and, if applicable, a supplementary amount. In reality, the concepts and the method of calculation are identical to the rules for calculating the basic award and the compensatory award in the employment tribunal, with some exceptions, which we will deal with below:

(1) *Basic amount*

The rules for calculating the basic amount are set out in detail, at paras 118–34 of the scheme, in identical language to the statutory formula. Arbitrators have been provided with the same Ready Reckoner available to tribunals and are encouraged to use it. The only qualifications are in respect of the method of calculating the period of continuous employment, and the figures to adopt for the purpose of quantifying a week's pay. In both cases, the arbitrator is directed to have regard to, not to apply, the statutory rules in the ERA 1996, as amended from time to time. Whether they will do this in practice must remain a moot point. In every other respect, the arbitrator must apply the rules in relation to age, the maximum period (20 years), reductions for conduct and payments received, and those rules which specify a minimum sum in respect of the award if the reason for dismissal is one of the specified categories.[9]

(2) *Compensatory amount*

In determining the compensatory amount, the arbitrator is required to follow a formula that parallels the statutory framework.

- The sum awarded must therefore be such a sum as is just and equitable having regard to the loss sustained by the employee.
- The employee is expected to mitigate the loss.
- The sum is discounted to take into account the employee's fault leading to the dismissal, and to reflect failure of the employee to use any of the employer's internal appeal procedures.

Arbitrators have been advised of the approach adopted for calculation of the compensatory award by employment tribunals, but they have also been told that it is entirely up to them whether or not they wish to be influenced by that approach. The statutory cap on the maximum does, however, apply.[10] The only exception is if the employee had made a protected disclosure, and this was the reason for dismissal, or had been dismissed for health and safety reasons.[11]

---

9   *Ibid*, paras 118–34.
10 *Ibid*, para 145.
11 *Ibid*, para 145; ERA 1996, Part X, ss 100, 105(3).

(3) *Supplementary amount*

If the arbitrator concludes that the employer had an appeal procedure but prevented the employee from using it, then he can award a supplementary amount if it is just and equitable to do so. The employee's prospects of success in an appeal must be quantified, but in any event the maximum that can be awarded or deducted under the heading is two weeks' wages. Again, the arbitrator is not obliged to follow the statutory rules for calculating this figure.[12]

6.3   DEALING WITH COMPENSATION

As remedy is dealt with at the hearing, the parties will already have been alerted to the need to come to the hearing ready and able to deal with remedy. In relation to the calculation of remedy at the hearing, the following must be observed:

- The employer will have wage details, including details of rate changes and pay awards since the applicant was dismissed.
- The employee will have details of attempts to obtain employment, as well as details of earnings from any new employer.

The arbitrator may already have directed the applicant to prepare a draft calculation of loss, and in any event it may be included in the statement of case. Even if it is not, the arbitrator has power under the scheme to make awards on separate issues, and so is able to deal with the issues of liability and remedy separately. The aim is, however, to deal with all matters at once if possible, and so avoid either the need for a further hearing or the need for two awards. The parties have an obligation to co-operate with the process and the arbitrator, which will require them to supply the requisite financial information to each other and to the arbitrator.

6.3.1   Preventing double recovery

It may be that the employee has argued, in the originating application, that the dismissal is both wrongful and unfair, or that the dismissal is a discriminatory dismissal. Practice in the employment tribunal is to stay the tribunal proceedings pending determination of the arbitration. The arbitrator cannot determine any of these issues, but the tribunal proceedings may, in due course, result in a finding in favour of the applicant and the possibility of the double recovery of compensation. The scheme covers this eventuality, but in practice there may be difficulties. It is likely that the problem will be dealt with in the following way.

---

12   *Ibid*, paras 142–44.

The arbitrator is required to take into account, in any award, the possibility of a potential award by the tribunal, as well as any existing award of compensation. As the practice in the tribunal is to stay proceedings where there is an arbitration agreement, then the arbitrator has two choices:

- either to anticipate the outcome of the other proceedings; or
- to award compensation for the unfair dismissal and leave it to the tribunal to deal with the potential double recovery problem.

The difficulty is that the arbitration award will not be lodged with the tribunal.[13] The employment tribunal, therefore, will have to rely on the parties for an indication of what sums have been awarded by the arbitrator and in respect of what loss. The only alternative is for the applicant to abandon or limit the claimed loss in the arbitration hearing in anticipation of a more favourable award in the tribunal, assuming success in those proceedings. Again, as the arbitration award is confidential, the tribunal is dependent on the parties for reliable information when determining remedy.

6.3.2 Dealing with social security benefits

The statutory scheme for unfair dismissal deals with social security benefits in a particular way. They are not deducted from any compensation award by the tribunal, but are recouped by the Benefits Agency from the employer in accordance with the certificate completed by the tribunal. It is not clear how they ought to be dealt with in arbitration awards. The scheme is silent on the treatment of benefits. We suggest that it is wise to proceed on the following assumptions:

- The most obvious benefit that an applicant will receive is Job Seekers Allowance for the period of unemployment from the date of dismissal until the applicant secures alternative employment, for a maximum of 26 weeks. In some cases, the applicant will also receive Invalidity Benefit, Income Support or Housing Benefit.
- If the reason for dismissal is covered by EC law, the arbitrator will apply the general law on unfair dismissal. The arbitrator will ignore the benefits received, but there will be no mechanism for recoupment and the employer will be required neither to deduct social security benefits received nor to repay the Benefits Agency.
- If the assessment of compensation is made in accordance with the scheme, then the benefits will be taken into account.
- Although there is no reference in the wording of the scheme to deduction of social security benefits, there is a specific reference to the general principle that the sum awarded shall be such a sum as is just and equitable in all the circumstances. We have argued elsewhere that to allow the applicant to recover both loss of wages and benefits would offend this principle, although it has to be recognised that social security benefits are funded in part by the applicant's National Insurance contributions.

---

13   *Ibid*, para 149.

- It is assumed in the Guide issued to arbitrators that State benefits received during any period of absence are to be deducted. It is not apparent whether this advice is applicable to all social security benefits received or merely to Job Seekers Allowance.

6.4   ENFORCEMENT OF THE AWARD

In accordance with the philosophy of the scheme, awards are final and binding on the parties, subject to any right to challenge the award, but there is a procedure for enforcement of awards in the event of non-compliance by the employer:

- Where the employer fails to comply with an order for re-employment, the applicant must apply to the employment tribunal for additional compensation in accordance with s 117 of the ERA 1996, as if the award was that of the tribunal itself.
- The arbitrator is no more able than the employment tribunal to compel an employer to take an employee back, despite the fact that the employer has, in signing the waiver, submitted to the finality of the arbitration process. This is because the law has set its face against compulsion in the employment relationship, and will not force employers to employ a person any more than it will compel an employee to work for an employer.
- Awards of compensation are enforceable in the High Court or county court as if they were judgments of the court.[14] Again, interest is payable in the event of non-payment or late payment by the employer. If the sum awarded, or any part of it, remains unpaid after 42 days from the date that the award is sent to the employer, then it attracts interest on the same basis as a tribunal award.

6.5   CHALLENGING THE AWARD (SITUATIONS, PITFALLS AND TIME LIMITS)

The philosophy of the architects of the arbitration scheme was that the awards should be final, in the sense that they should not be susceptible to legal challenge. This aim has been achieved, but only in part, as there are three potential avenues for challenge to either the process or the outcome. The ambit of the right of challenge and the restrictions on the circumstances in which it can be exercised do, however, mean that the courts will only be able or permitted to interfere in the arbitration process in carefully defined circumstances, as in conventional arbitration. Apart from the issue of EC law, there can be no other challenge on the law or on the facts.

The scheme permits only three types of challenge to the award:

---

14   *Ibid*, para 159, which incorporates the Arbitration Act 1996, s 66.

(1) challenges to the jurisdiction of the arbitrator;

(2) challenges based on a serious irregularity; or

(3) challenges based on an issue of either EC law or the HRA 1998.

6.5.1 Challenges to the jurisdiction of the arbitrator

This ground of challenge, contained in para 162 of the scheme, incorporates and applies s 67 of the Arbitration Act 1996, with certain qualifications. A party can challenge the award if there was a lack of jurisdiction on the part of the arbitrator. Although the challenge is to the award, it is the procedure that is under scrutiny, as with challenges based on an alleged serious irregularity. The likely grounds might include:

- matters relating to the appointment of the arbitrator;
- the issue(s) referred to the arbitrator;
- whether the dispute was within the scope of the scheme; or
- whether the award has purported to deal with something outside the scope of the scheme.

The party challenging the award must give notice to the other side, to the arbitrator and to Acas. The application is made to either the High Court or the Central London County Court, these being the courts with arbitration jurisdiction. It is subject to the rules on time limits, and the appellant may lose the right to object under paras 168 and 165 of the scheme (see 6.5.4 and 6.5.5 below).

6.5.2 Serious irregularity

Again, the formula adopted in the scheme is not to create a specific right of challenge, but to incorporate within it the statutory provisions of the Arbitration Act 1996, with the necessary amendments reflecting the nature of the scheme, and in particular its limited jurisdiction. The grounds are set out in the scheme and in s 68 of the Arbitration Act. The main points to stress are:

- The provisions all relate to an irregularity either in the way the arbitration was conducted or in the award, which the jurisdictional grounds for challenge do not cover.
- There is a potential for overlap between paras 162 and 163 of the scheme of the Act, as s 68(2)(c), for example, extends to a situation where the arbitrator has failed to conduct the arbitration in accordance with the scheme.
- Before the court can interfere, it must be satisfied that the alleged serious irregularity has caused, or will cause, substantial injustice to the party appealing.[15]
- What is a substantial injustice? The Guide quotes the report of the Departmental Advisory Committee on Arbitration Law: 'The test of a

---

15 Arbitration Act 1996, s 68(2).

substantial injustice is intended to be applied by way of support for the arbitral process, not by way of interference with that process. Thus it is only in cases where it can be said that what has happened is so far removed from what could reasonably be expected of the arbitral process that we would expect the court to take action.'

- Both Acas and the arbitrator are to be notified that the award is to be challenged, though they are not parties to any appeal.

6.5.3 Appeals on questions of EC law and the HRA 1998

Both of the previous grounds for challenge relate to the process of the arbitration rather than the outcome, even though the court will normally quash any award if satisfied that the award cannot stand due to any irregularity. Appeals against the substance of the award, whether on the finding of a fair or unfair dismissal or on the remedy awarded, are limited to issues of either EC law or the HRA 1998. Again, this is achieved by incorporating in the scheme the provisions of the Arbitration Act 1996, amended to cover the scheme. The combined effect of para 164 of the scheme, when read with s 69 of the Arbitration Act, is to restrict the right of appeal to these parameters:

- The question must involve an issue of either EC law or the HRA 1998.
- Either the parties must agree that the court should determine the issue of law, or the court must itself grant leave to appeal.
- To grant leave, the court must be satisfied that determination of the issue will substantially affect the rights of either of the parties.
- If the issue is one of EC law, the court must be satisfied that the point is capable of serious argument before granting leave.
- If the issue is not one of EC law, the court must be satisfied either that the award is obviously wrong, or that the issue is one of general public importance and the award is open to serious doubt, before granting leave.
- Finally, in all cases, the court must be satisfied that it is just and proper to determine the issue in all the circumstances before granting leave.

As before, appeals are made to the High Court or the Central London County Court, and both Acas and the arbitrator are to be notified. The time limit for any application to the court for leave is 28 days from the date that the award is sent to the parties by Acas.

The court can confirm the award, vary it, or remit the award to the arbitrator for further consideration, in whole or in part, in the light of the court's determination.

6.5.4 Loss of the right to object

In arbitration law, there are rules which limit the right of a party to take a later objection to the conduct of an arbitration, if that party does not object at the earliest opportunity. The same applies to the scheme:

- Under para 168 of the scheme, a party either taking part in, or continuing to take part in, the arbitration will lose the right to object to an error in relation to jurisdiction, or any other irregularity in the proceedings, if that party does not raise an objection with the court or the arbitrator either immediately or within any time limit provided for by the scheme or the arbitrator.

- This applies to any objection to:
  - o the jurisdiction of the arbitrator;
  - o any improper conduct of the proceedings;
  - o any failure to comply with the arbitration agreement or the scheme; or
  - o any other irregularity affecting the arbitrator or the proceedings.
- The only exception is in relation to a situation where the party in question can show that it did not know, or could not have discovered, the error in question.
- In practice, the arbitrator will ask the parties at the end of the hearing whether they have any reservations or objections to the way the hearing has been conducted. This serves the aim of dealing with the matter there and then if possible, but may prevent the parties raising the matter later.

6.5.5   Time limits and other procedural restrictions

Paragraph 165 of the scheme incorporates into employment arbitration the provisions of s 70 of the Arbitration Act in relation to appeals on all three of the above grounds. For the purposes of this book, it is only necessary to emphasise that the time limit for challenging the award is 28 days, not from the date of the award, as provided for by the legislation, but from the date the award is sent to the parties by Acas. Any application for further time must be made to the court, not to Acas or the arbitrator.

CHAPTER 7

FUTURE STRATEGIES IN
EMPLOYMENT DISPUTE RESOLUTION

This book has demonstrated that ADR offers an alternative to the traditional individual employment dispute resolution route of employment tribunal litigation. Further, it has shown that employment law beyond the Employment Act 2002 offers a new era for revived ADR in employment litigation. In this final chapter, we set out a possible framework for further reform and change, providing some comparative analysis. Overall, we conclude that employment dispute resolution, or EDR, as an alternative to litigation, has a place in modern employment law practice. In addition, since the Employment Tribunal Task Force has now reported, we comment on its recommendations.

7.1   INTERNAL DISCIPLINARY HEARING

The EA 2002 recognises the findings of the 1998 Survey of Employment Tribunal Applications,[1] which noted that despite some 51% of employers and 28% of employees noting the existence of internal procedures, the majority of tribunal proceedings were initiated as a result of presumed procedural failure. Furthermore, some 44% had previous tribunal experience and therefore felt comfortable with litigation. Consequently, if internal disciplinary hearings (IDHs) were more proactive in terms of worker involvement – particularly with regard to the right to accompaniment provided since 1999 under the ERA 1996 – then lower levels of litigation might prevail. If such occurred, then litigation would become largely seen as a means to an end. Therefore, establishing a statutory standard would simultaneously promote EDR rather than litigation and would present a much more coherent method of resolution (that is, pre-tribunal).

The Employment Tribunal Task Force commented in its report that an in-house dispute resolution agreement had been negotiated between the trade union Amicus and the Navy, Army and Air Force Institutes (NAAFI) for the resolution of unfair employment decisions. It is open only to members of the trade union, and then only after the company's internal disciplinary and grievance procedures have been exhausted. Employees complaining of unfair dismissal may still bring tribunal proceedings.[2] Nevertheless, the option of an alternative to litigation is there, and may prevent disputes resulting in a tribunal application if both signatories have confidence in the procedure and its outcomes.

---

1   Employment Market Analysis Report Series, No 13, 2000. See also Earnshaw *et al*, 1998.
2   Report of the Employment Tribunal Task Force, *Moving Forward*, recommendation 7.20.

7.2   WORKPLACE MEDIATION

The Employment Act 2002 emphasises the need for 'amicable and fair' settlement of disputes. Explicitly, it sets out the need for user-friendly internal grievance and disciplinary procedures. However, indirectly, the Act promotes internal mediation. Yet mediation by whom? An independent person – as agreed amongst the parties – and/or an Acas official? Such workplace mediators will need to adopt an EDR approach. Such a mediatory approach will require external persons to provide the necessary independence to satisfy the requirements of Art 6 of the European Convention on Human Rights (the right to a fair hearing). Such a role is also envisaged by the Employment Tribunal Task Force, which recommends that 'mediation pilots should be run by Acas and possibly a commercial organisation'.[3] In a similar vein, the Better Regulation Task Force[4] recommended that Acas should pilot a mediation service for companies with fewer than 50 employees. As with the voluntary arbitration service recommended by the Task Force, presumably the applicant will still be permitted to pursue a tribunal application if mediation fails, and there will need to be safeguards to deal with time limits.

7.3   ARBITRATION

Is an arbitral route applicable to employment law? This text has clearly shown that ADR does apply and that it can resolve disputes as effectively. Moreover, if only from the relatively unsophisticated survey of parties to an employment tribunal unfair dismissal claim, it is clear that there is a prevailing view that arbitration, as opposed to adjudication in the tribunal, could be an attractive option. Of more significance, perhaps, are the results of a survey of Acas collective dispute arbitrations[5] in 1988–89, in which the parties' overall satisfaction with the process was explored.[6] Of the employers and employees surveyed, 87% said that the arbitrator had conducted the hearing to their satisfaction; only 2% expressed positive dissent. In the vast majority of cases, the arbitrator was also held to have acted impartially, enjoyed the parties' trust, sufficiently understood the issues and acted in a courteous and friendly manner. Whilst these results give a clear endorsement of the arbitrators in question, the survey provides no comparative findings as to the relative merits of arbitration versus more traditional methods of dispute resolution, and in fact only 15% of the claims were concerned with discipline and dismissal.[7]

---

3   *Ibid*, recommendation 7.39, p 70.
4   *Employment Regulation: Striking a Balance*, May 2001.
5   That is, voluntary and non-legally binding arbitrations carried out under the auspices of Acas by part-time arbitrators who are specialists in industrial relations and employed on a case by case basis – see Lewis and Clark, 1993.
6   Brown, 1992, cited in Clark, 1999.
7   Over 50% were concerned with general pay and conditions and other pay matters.

According to Lewis and Clark in 1993, 'Arbitration is cheaper, speedier, more informal and more accessible, it avoids the legalism and publicity associated with the tribunal, and offers the possibility of a more flexible range of remedies, including greater likelihood of reinstatement or re-engagement'. It certainly seems indisputable that arbitration proceedings under the new Acas scheme will be less formal, if only to the extent that evidence will not be given under oath and that cross-examination will not be permitted. Informality will no doubt be engendered also by the intention to hold arbitration hearings in Acas premises or hotels, rather than in the more court-like atmosphere of employment tribunal offices. It should be noted, however, that r 9 of Sched 1 to the Employment Tribunals (Constitution and Rules of Procedure) Regulations 1993 (SI 1993/2687) expressly requires a tribunal to 'seek to avoid formality in its proceedings' and enables it 'to conduct the hearing in such a manner as it considers most suitable to the clarification of the issues before it'. Thus, it would appear that whereas the traditional adversarial approach is not to be permitted in arbitration proceedings, tribunals have the flexibility to move from adversarial to inquisitorial mode as and when the nature of the case and the parties' representation require it.

7.4   OTHER ADR SCHEMES?

As observed in Chapter 3, Acas is giving consideration to how to relaunch its low usage arbitral scheme. The Better Regulation Task Force itself recommends that Acas should pilot a voluntary arbitration service and a separate mediation service for small employers (fewer than 50 employees). The arbitration service would be available prior to a tribunal application. Apart from the fact that the service would be available without the need for a tribunal application to have been made, it is difficult to see how this would differ in practice from the existing Acas scheme. In fact, the scheme and Guide (para 7) envisage the possibility of such claims arising. Early indications show that it is lawyer trepidation and user fears of 'being first in the unknown' which may have contributed to the scheme's current low usage. Clearly, a re-education of lawyers, human resource professionals and trade unions alike into the alternatives to litigation, or EDR (as intended by this text), should help to ensure that the relaunched Acas scheme should enjoy greater success than it has had to date. A further boost to the scheme could come following the provision in the EA 2002 for the government to consider asking Acas to include cases under the 'right for parents to work flexible hours', which will be introduced from April 2003.

It is also interesting to note that a fast-track scheme to provide a new dispute resolution culture for unfair dismissal claims in Northern Ireland has recently been positively welcomed. Northern Ireland's Labour Relations Agency

launched its equivalent Acas UK scheme on 11 June 2002.[8] It was endorsed by
Northern Ireland's Minister for Employment and Learning, Carmel Hanna, as
follows: 'It has been introduced as a way for ensuring that parties involved in
an unfair dismissal case can have a faster, less costly, non-legalistic and
confidential means of resolving their dispute.' Eleven arbitrators have been
appointed to bring the system into force. Evidently, such a system sounds
familiar. As the chairman of the Labour Relations Agency, Pat McCartan, puts it:
'The introduction of this scheme provides an opportunity for employers, human
resource professionals and trade union officials to review the means by which
they seek to resolve unfair dismissal disputes. The non-adversarial approach of
arbitration will be conducive to the full involvement of employment relations
practitioners in the process of resolution.'[9]

7.5   EMPLOYMENT DISPUTE RESOLUTION – EDR?

'EDR', as we term it, can be seen as the new 'third way' for employment dispute
resolution. For instance, life beyond the EA 2002 allows for five stages and three
distinct methods of individual dispute resolution in employment law, as
follows.

Figure 2 – The new third way: EDR

Issue/claim	Venue/forum	Dispute resolution method
All issues	Within the organisation	Workplace procedures/ADR
All issues	Intra-organisation mediation	Internal or external mediator/ADR
Breach of contract/wages (simple/small claims)	Fast-track conciliation/ litigation	ADR (thereafter ET)
Unfair dismissal and right to work flexibly	Conciliation/ arbitration/litigation	ADR (thereafter ET)
Discrimination and other issues (technical and complex issues, new rights and precedents, EU law)	Conciliation/litigation	ADR (thereafter ET)

Such a model encourages conciliation/Med-Arb approaches, leaving litigation
as the final stage, but being very much the exception rather than the rule! This is
consistent with many existing EU models, such as those found in Luxembourg,
the Netherlands and Italy, although with less compulsion in favour of ADR.

---

8   See Department for Employment and Learning (NI), Executive Information Service,
     Brief, 10 June 2002.
9   *Ibid.*

Both ideas are consistent with the aims of the government and the Employment Tribunal Task Force to modernise, reduce a rising caseload and manage employment litigation/dispute resolution more effectively.

Above all else, in considering the merits of the new Acas scheme as against the existing system of resolving disputes, it is arguably worth taking into account the views of applicants and respondents in the Hardy research (see Chapter 1, note 23). As expressed at the conclusion of their unfair dismissal hearing, 68% had gone to a tribunal because attempts at mediation/settlement had failed. Such a high percentage seems to indicate that consideration might also be given to the potential for expanding the role of Acas at the pre-tribunal application conciliation stage. In fact, some interesting findings about the role of Acas conciliation emerged from a study carried out in 1997, which canvassed the views of applicants, employers and representatives involved in unfair dismissal claims.[10]

Other models of effective pre-tribunal ADR processes also exist, for example in New Zealand, with its model of mediation.[11] As Corby notes, in 1996–97, 59% of cases lodged with the New Zealand employment tribunal were settled through mediation, though the reasons for this undoubtedly go beyond the effectiveness of the process itself. First, there is an expectation that the parties will undergo mediation, and the New Zealand Employment Contracts Act 1991 itself provides for the establishment of 'appropriate services that will facilitate the mutual resolution by parties to employment contracts of differences that arise between them, it being recognised that, in many cases, such parties are the persons best placed to resolve such differences and should be assisted to do so themselves'.[12]

Furthermore, in Australia, the success rate of conciliation is even higher, at 80–90%, but the parties are *obliged* to attempt to settle the matter via conciliation and, if unsuccessful, the Australian Industrial Relations Commission must issue a certificate indicating its assessment of the merits, and may recommend that the applicant should not pursue a particular ground. This may then be relevant to the later issue of costs in assessing whether a party has acted 'reasonably' in failing to discontinue or to agree to a settlement.[13]

The Employment Tribunal Task Force did include a brief survey of the experience of alternative employment dispute resolution in New Zealand, Australia and Ireland in its report.[14] In particular, the report suggests that there is scope for introducing into the settlement of employment disputes a system similar to that pertaining to mediation in family law.[15] If adopted, there would be an attempt at mediation, possibly by Acas, a private mediator, or even the tribunal, and then, if this fails to secure a settlement, there could be a full hearing. As long as this does not needlessly delay ultimate resolution of the

---

10 Lewis and Legard, 1998.
11 For a fuller discussion of the New Zealand system, see Corby, 1999.
12 See the New Zealand Employment Contracts Act 1991, s 26.
13 Australian Workplace Relations Act 1996, ss 170CF and 170CJ.
14 Report of the Employment Tribunal Task Force, *Moving Forward*, paras 7.22–26.
15 *Ibid*, para 7.25.

dispute, it potentially provides another possible solution not only to the original dispute but also to the problem of the so called 'litigation' or 'compensation culture'.

7.6   CLOSING COMMENTS AND ADVICE

It is now time to act – EDR is here to stay. Lawyers, human resource practitioners, union officials and all in the workplace should prepare themselves for ADR in employment rights matters. As Figure 2 shows, there will be a role for the employment tribunals and the higher courts to hear difficult and complex cases, and to interpret the will of Parliament and the EU as it applies to employment rights issues. However, having laid down the framework, it will be for others to distill the best practice lessons from litigation in such a way that will allow most disputes to be resolved at the EDR stages of the model. This book was written precisely to help with that preparation.

APPENDIX 1

A GUIDE TO THE ACAS ARBITRATION SCHEME

CONTENTS   Paragraphs

A SUMMARY OF THE KEY FEATURES OF THE SCHEME

Arbitration is a method for resolving a dispute in which an arbitrator's decision is binding as a matter of law and has the same effect as a court judgment.

- The Scheme provides an alternative to an employment tribunal hearing in cases of unfair dismissal.

- The arbitration process is confidential, relatively fast, cost-efficient, non-legalistic and informal.

- Entry to the Scheme is entirely voluntary and there must be agreement by both parties to the dispute to go to binding arbitration.

- The employee/s must either have an existing application to the employment tribunal pending or must claim that they have grounds to potentially lodge such an application.

- Entry to the Scheme is via an Arbitration Agreement reached with the assistance of an Acas conciliator or in the format of a compromise agreement drawn up by appropriate representatives.

- Both parties must sign a waiver form which confirms their agreement to go to arbitration and that they understand the process.

- The Arbitration Agreement must be received by the Acas Arbitration Section within six weeks of it being concluded by the parties.

- On receipt of a valid Arbitration Agreement Acas will appoint an arbitrator from its arbitration Panel. Parties will not have a choice of arbitrator.

- Where an employee has a claim(s) in addition to unfair dismissal, any other claim(s) must be pursued separately.

- The Scheme is not designed to deal with complex legal issues.

- In agreeing to go to arbitration the parties waive any jurisdictional issues for example whether the employee had qualifying service, whether any application to the employment tribunal was submitted within time limits, etc.

- The Scheme is not intended to deal with issues of EC law. If such issues arise the arbitrator may appoint a legal adviser to provide guidance.

- Where issues arise under the Human Rights Act 1998 (apart from procedural matters set out in the Scheme) the arbitrator may appoint a legal adviser to provide guidance.

- In addition to the information on the employee's application to the employment tribunal (IT1) and the employer's response (IT3) (where an application to the employment tribunal has been made), the parties will be invited to submit a written statement of their case in advance of the hearing.

- Parties to the dispute must comply with any instruction given by the arbitrator and will be expected to co-operate in the production of relevant documents and the attendance of appropriate witnesses.

- Hearings will be held at a location convenient and accessible to the parties and will not normally last for more than half a day.

- Each party meets their own costs in attending the hearing, however, if a dismissal is found to be unfair the arbitrator can include in the calculation of any compensation a sum to cover the costs incurred by the employee personally in attending the hearing.

- The arbitrator has the power to set dates and locations of hearings if the parties do not co-operate in these arrangements.

- If parties do not attend a hearing without good cause the arbitrator has the power to continue the hearing and decide whether a dismissal was fair or unfair, or where an employee fails to attend without good cause, the case can be treated as dismissed.

- The arbitrator will use an inquisitorial rather than adversarial approach – there will be no cross-examination of witnesses by a party or representative, or swearing of oaths; rather the arbitrator will question the witnesses.

- Instead of applying strict law or legal precedent the arbitrator will take account of general principles of fairness and good practice in the workplace including the principles set out in any relevant Acas Code of Practice *Disciplinary and Grievance Procedures* and Acas *Discipline at Work* Handbook (relevant here means those in existence at the time of the dismissal).

- Exceptions to the non-application of strict law concern EC law or the Human Rights Act 1998 where these are relevant.

- Following the hearing the arbitrator will issue a binding 'Award' summarising each party's case, the arbitrator's main considerations, the decision and, if the dismissal is unfair, the remedy. The award will be confidential to Acas and the parties.

- If a dismissal is found to be unfair an arbitrator can order the same remedies as an employment tribunal. These are reinstatement, re-engagement or compensation.

- There are very limited grounds for challenging an arbitrator's award and parties cannot appeal against an arbitrator's binding award on points of law except in cases where EC law or the Human Rights Act 1998 are relevant.

A GUIDE TO THE ACAS ARBITRATION SCHEME

Copies of the Scheme can be purchased from the Stationery Office. The Scheme is also available on the Acas website www.acas.org.uk.

Introduction

1   The Acas Arbitration Scheme ('the Scheme') has been introduced to provide a voluntary alternative to the employment tribunal for resolution of unfair dismissal disputes. Acas was given the power to introduce the Scheme by the Employment Rights (Dispute Resolution) Act 1998, which inserted a new section, section 212A, into the Trade Union and Labour Relations (Consolidation) Act 1992, making provision for it. The Scheme has been designed to initially operate in England and Wales although it is anticipated that a Scheme to cover Scotland will operate from late 2001. This booklet provides guidance on the Scheme itself, on how to make applications under the Scheme, how to prepare for arbitration hearings, and on the procedure which will be adopted by arbitrators at the hearings.

2   The intention is that the resolution of disputes under the Scheme will be confidential, relatively fast and cost-efficient. Procedures under the Scheme are non-legalistic and far more informal and flexible than the employment tribunal. The process is inquisitorial rather than adversarial with no formal pleadings or cross-examination by parties or representatives. Instead of applying strict law or legal tests (but see paragraphs 12, 85–89)

the arbitrator will have regard to general principles of fairness and good conduct in employment relations including, for example, principles referred to in the Acas Code of Practice *Disciplinary and Grievance Procedures* and the Acas Handbook *Discipline at Work* which were current at the time of the dismissal. In addition, as it is only possible to appeal or otherwise challenge an arbitrator's award (decision) in very limited circumstances, the Scheme should also provide quicker finality of outcome for the parties to an unfair dismissal dispute.

3   This Guide outlines how the Scheme caters for both the informality of alternative dispute resolution as well as the constraints and procedural requirements imposed on it as a matter of law.

4   Acas has established a panel of arbitrators who were recruited through a transparent, accountable and non-discriminatory process. The arbitrators were selected for their knowledge, skills and employment relations experience. They are not employed by Acas, but are appointed on standard terms of appointment, initially for a period of two years, although this might be renewed by Acas at its discretion. It is a condition of their appointment that the arbitrators exercise their duties in accordance with the terms of the Scheme. They are appointed by Acas from the panel on a case by case basis and the parties do not have any choice as to which arbitrator is selected to hear their case. There is however a limited challenge procedure (see paragraphs 122–29). Arbitrators are paid on the basis of time spent in connection with arbitration proceedings. Standard Terms of Appointment are available from Acas.

5   Although it is called the Acas Arbitration Scheme, Acas's role in the Scheme is to recruit the arbitrators, appoint them on a case by case basis and to provide administrative assistance to them. Acas has no role in any case-related decision making which is undertaken exclusively by the arbitrators.

6   Once the parties to an unfair dismissal dispute have concluded an Arbitration Agreement to have the dispute resolved under the Scheme, the unfair dismissal claim can no longer be heard by an employment tribunal.

What types of cases does the Scheme cover?

7   The Scheme is available as an alternative to going to an employment tribunal hearing **only for cases of alleged unfair dismissal**, where either an application has been made to the employment tribunal or where an individual claims that circumstances exist in which they could present such an application. The Scheme is intended for straightforward cases of unfair dismissal for example where an employee has been dismissed because of their conduct/capability, which do not involve jurisdictional or complex legal issues nor raise points of EC law.

Inappropriate cases

8   The Scheme excludes from its scope other kinds of claim which are often related to or raised at the same time as a claim of unfair dismissal, for example, sex/race discrimination cases and claims for unpaid wages. If the claim covers alleged breaches of employment rights other than unfair dismissal, and the parties want to have the unfair dismissal claim heard under the Scheme, the other claim(s) will have to be pursued separately before an employment tribunal or settled. If the non-unfair dismissal claims cannot be settled or withdrawn, the parties should consider whether they really want to

have two hearings, or whether it would be better to have both the unfair dismissal and other claim(s) dealt with by the employment tribunal at a single hearing.

9   If the parties decide that they want the unfair dismissal dispute resolved by arbitration and the other claim(s) resolved in the employment tribunal the arbitrator may decide, where there is an overlap in the cases or if the evidence or findings in one hearing might have a bearing on the other, to postpone the arbitration proceedings pending the outcome of the claim(s) at the employment tribunal. This, however, is a matter for the arbitrator's discretion.

10   Parties should be aware that the normal time limits apply for applications to the employment tribunal and where they wish the employment tribunal to consider other claims they must ensure that these have been made within the time limits. If they have not, although the employment tribunal has discretion to extend time limits in certain circumstances, it is not possible to guarantee in any particular case that it will do so.

11   The Scheme is not intended for cases which raise questions of EC law such as unfair dismissal claims which are based on an EC right. It is strongly recommended that parties who have cases which raise such questions consider applying for their dispute(s) to be heard at the employment tribunal. Examples of such cases could include those where an employee is claiming that the reason for their dismissal is sex discrimination; dismissals relating to the transfer of an undertaking; and claims that the dismissal was related to exercising a right under the Working Time Regulations.

12   If cases are referred where EC law is relevant or where such issues are identified during an arbitration hearing, any of the parties may apply to the arbitrator or the arbitrator may decide of his or her own volition, that a legal adviser be appointed by Acas to report to the arbitrator and the parties on the question of EC law (see paragraphs 85–89).

13   Additionally, if the dispute raises complex legal issues, the Scheme should not be used. If parties are unclear as to whether a dispute involves such issues, they should seek advice.

14   Nor should it be used where there is a dispute between the parties over whether or not the employment tribunal has jurisdiction to hear the unfair dismissal case. Examples of jurisdictional disputes include whether the applicant was an employee of the employer; whether the employee had the necessary period of service to bring a claim; whether a dismissal actually took place; or, whether the claim was made within the specified time limits. **When agreeing to go to arbitration under the Scheme, both parties waive their ability to have such issues considered and are accepting as a condition of the Scheme that no such jurisdictional issue is in dispute between them. The arbitrator will not therefore deal with such matters and will make the assumption that all jurisdictional issues have been resolved prior to the hearing, even if they are raised by the parties during the arbitration process.**

15   Acas will accept cases of alleged constructive dismissal for hearing under the Scheme where both parties request this but with the following proviso. In such cases, employees are attempting to argue that certain conduct of their employer amounted to a fundamental breach of their contract of employment, and that they were therefore entitled to resign. In such circumstances there will normally be a dispute between the parties as to whether or not a dismissal took place, and an employment tribunal and not arbitration will be the route for having the case heard. **However, if both parties agree that the events which took place amounted to a dismissal**, then the case could, if the parties wish, go to arbitration under the Scheme for an arbitrator to decide whether the dismissal was fair or unfair. Indeed, in agreeing to use the Scheme the parties will be taken to have agreed that a dismissal has taken place.

16   Where the parties decide not to use the Scheme, the services of an Acas conciliator will remain available to the parties if they wish to attempt to reach a settlement which will resolve the matter without the need for an employment tribunal hearing.

Where parties or their representatives are in any doubt as to whether to use the Scheme they should contact the Arbitration Section at Acas Head Office (see details in paragraph 132).

When to consider using the Scheme

17   Generally it is better if the parties, or their representatives, can resolve the dispute between them through internal procedures (where these exist), by negotiating directly with each other, or with the help of an Acas conciliator. When it is clear that none of these ways is likely to resolve an unfair dismissal claim, the parties may wish to consider using arbitration as an alternative to going to an employment tribunal hearing. Each of these methods has different features, and neither one is 'better' than the other. Each party should make themselves aware of the features of each method, so that they can decide which one they would prefer to use. However, as arbitration is voluntary, both parties have to agree to go to arbitration before the Scheme can be used. A comparison of the areas where there are significant differences between the approach adopted by employment tribunals and the one used in arbitration is at Appendix 1.

Legal aid

18   Legal aid might be available for limited initial advice on an employee's case and for preparation for the arbitration hearing. However, legal aid is not available for representation at the hearing. For further information contact a solicitor, a Citizen's Advice Bureau or the Community Legal Service Directory line 0845 608 1122 (calls charged at local rate) or minicom 0845 609 6677. Also the Community Legal Service's website may be contacted on www.legalservices.gov.uk.

Entry into the Scheme

Arbitration Agreement

19   **Entry to the Scheme is entirely voluntary. Once both parties have concluded an agreement to go to arbitration (the Arbitration Agreement), the unfair dismissal claim can no longer be pursued in an employment tribunal. It is important therefore that all the parties involved are fully aware of the effect of referring their dispute to arbitration, and that they understand clearly how the arbitration process works. If the agreement to go to arbitration is subsequently not accepted by Acas because it does not satisfy the requirements set out in the Scheme, the parties will have to resolve their dispute by other means or if available, have recourse to an employment tribunal. Employees will, of course, wish to bear in mind the time limits (normally three months from the effective date of termination) for presenting a claim of unfair dismissal to an employment tribunal.**

20   To ensure that parties are fully informed on the implications of referring their dispute to arbitration, an Arbitration Agreement can only be reached either through an Acas Conciliated Agreement or a Compromise Agreement following advice to the former employee from a relevant independent adviser. Both types of Agreement **must be in**

writing, and any Compromise Agreement must conform to the statutory requirements for example at section 203 of the Employment Rights Act 1996.

21 **In submitting the dispute to arbitration the parties are accepting that the arbitrator's decision is final and binding. They are also agreeing to do everything necessary for the arbitration process to proceed smoothly, including co-operating in the arrangement of any hearing and complying with any order or direction of the arbitrator. They are accepting the way in which the arbitration process is conducted, as outlined in the Scheme and explained in this Guide, including the procedure at the hearing itself.** They will therefore be expected to co-operate fully with the process by fulfilling the duties placed on parties by it (see paragraphs 47–48).

22 The suggested wording for inclusion in Arbitration Agreements is at Appendix 2. However it should be noted that there are other statutory requirements for compromise agreements which must be met. The employee's relevant independent adviser will advise on these requirements.

23 Parties may use their own wording for other parts of a conciliated agreement if they are settling other issues in dispute or reaching agreement on other matters which are outside the scope of the Scheme. However, it is recommended that the agreement to go to arbitration be on a separate document.

Although parties can vary the words of the agreement to go to arbitration and not use those suggested in Appendix 2, no provision of the Scheme can be varied.

Waiver

24 Given its informal nature, parties agreeing to refer a dispute to the Scheme are taken to have agreed to waive certain rights that they would otherwise have if the matter had been heard by an employment tribunal. Such rights include: the right to a public hearing; the cross-examination of witnesses; compelling the attendance of witnesses; the production of documents to be ordered; the right to a published and fully reasoned decision and the right to have the dispute resolved in accordance with strict law (except in cases involving points of EC law or issues under the Human Rights Act 1998, other than procedural matters within the Scheme). In order to confirm this waiver, a Waiver Form (a copy is included in this Guide) must be completed by each party in all cases and must accompany either the Conciliated Agreement or Compromise Agreement in order for the Arbitration Agreement to be valid. Employees must personally sign their Form although a representative may sign the employer's waiver on their behalf and the signature on the Waiver Form must be witnessed in all cases. The witness can be anyone selected by the party but please note that an Acas conciliator cannot act in this capacity.

Parties are advised to keep a copy of their own Waiver Form, however, the Acas Arbitration Section will send a copy of each party's waiver to the other party/ies.

Terms of reference

25 Every Arbitration Agreement under the Scheme will be taken as an agreement that the arbitrator should decide whether the dismissal was fair or unfair and also the appropriate remedy.

26   The terms of reference which will be used by the arbitrator in each case are:

'In deciding whether the dismissal was fair or unfair, the arbitrator shall:

- have regard to general principles of fairness and good conduct in employment relations (including, for example, principles referred to in any relevant Acas *Disciplinary and Grievance Procedures* Code of Practice or *Discipline at Work* Handbook), instead of applying legal tests or rules (for example court decisions or legislation);

- apply EC law.

The arbitrator shall not decide the case by substituting what he or she would have done for the actions taken by the Employer.

If the arbitrator finds the dismissal unfair, he or she shall determine the appropriate remedy under the terms of this Scheme.'

Nothing in these Terms of Reference affects the operation of the Human Rights Act 1998 insofar as this is applicable and relevant and (with respect to procedural matters) has not been waived by virtue of the provisions of the Scheme.

27   Parties are not able to require an arbitrator to hear a case which would require him or her to depart from the provisions of the Scheme. If an Arbitration Agreement seeks to vary any provision of the Scheme, the dispute will not be eligible for arbitration under the Scheme.

Existing dispute

28   The Arbitration Agreement must relate to an existing dispute. There should be no automatic references to the Scheme in an individual's contract of employment or company procedures as this would compromise the voluntary nature of entry to the Scheme.

29   *Checklist for a valid Arbitration Agreement*

---

i   The Agreement must be in writing.

ii   The Agreement must concern an existing dispute.

iii The Agreement must not seek to vary or alter any provision of the Scheme (including the Terms of Reference).

iv   The Agreement must have been reached either with the assistance of an Acas conciliator (a 'Conciliated Agreement') or through a compromise agreement conforming to the requirements of the Employment Rights Act 1996 (a 'Compromise Agreement').

v   The Agreement must be accompanied by completed Waiver Forms (one from each party). There is a copy of the form in this Guide.

vi   The Agreement must be received by the Acas Arbitration Section (address at paragraph 132 of this Guide) within six weeks of its conclusion by the parties.

---

30   In cases where the Arbitration Agreement is reached through a Compromise Agreement it will be the responsibility of the parties' representatives to ensure that a valid Arbitration Agreement for the Scheme is concluded. Where there is any doubt on this issue the Acas Arbitration Section should be contacted (see paragraph 132). In cases where the Arbitration Agreement is brokered via an Acas conciliator, the conciliator will inform the parties or their representatives of the requirements of a valid Arbitration Agreement.

Notification to Acas of an agreement to go to arbitration under the Scheme

31 In all cases the concluded Arbitration Agreement should be forwarded to the Acas Arbitration Section at Acas Head Office (see paragraph 132) as soon as possible but within the six week time limit after both parties have signed the agreement to go to arbitration and each party has signed a Waiver Form.

32 Where the parties have agreed to opt for arbitration under the Scheme through an Agreement reached with the assistance of an Acas conciliator, either the conciliator or the parties/representatives must send the Conciliated Agreement and Waiver Forms to the Acas Arbitration Section at Acas Head Office (see paragraph 132) within the six week time limit. Where IT1 and IT3 forms have been completed, copies of these should also be sent. Where an Originating Application to the employment tribunal has not been submitted the parties should advise the Acas Arbitration Section of the circumstances of the dispute. This notification should be in writing or recorded by any means so as to be usable for subsequent reference for example e-mail/facsimile. Although the Acas conciliator may assist the parties by sending documentation, responsibility for ensuring that the appropriate documentation is sent to the Acas Arbitration Section remains with the parties/representatives.

33 Where the parties have opted for arbitration under the Scheme by means of a Compromise Agreement, the parties or their independent adviser or representative(s) must notify the Acas Arbitration Section (see paragraph 132) by sending them a copy of the Compromise Agreement and the Waiver Form within the six week time limit. Where IT1 and IT3 forms have been completed, copies of these should also be sent. Where an Originating Application to the employment tribunal has not been submitted the parties should advise the Acas Arbitration Section of the circumstances of the dispute. This notification should be in writing or recorded by any means so as to be usable for subsequent reference for example e-mail/facsimile.

34 On receipt of the Arbitration Agreement the Arbitration Section at Acas Head Office will check that all requirements of the Scheme have been met and will then notify the parties accordingly.

Invalid Arbitration Agreements

35 Where an Arbitration Agreement is received which is invalid the case will not be eligible to be heard under the Scheme. Where this situation arises, the Acas Arbitration Section will contact the parties or their representatives to establish whether this situation can be rectified. If it cannot and no valid Arbitration Agreement is reached, the parties will have to resolve their dispute by other means or apply/re-apply to the employment tribunal if they are able to do so.

Time limit for notification of Arbitration Agreements

36 **In order to avoid delays parties are advised to send Arbitration Agreements to the Acas Arbitration Section as soon as possible after they have been concluded.** Acas will not provide a hearing under the Scheme if the Arbitration Agreement is notified to the Acas Arbitration Section more than **six weeks** after the conclusion of the Agreement by the parties unless it was not reasonably practicable to notify Acas within this time limit. 'Notified' here means the date the Arbitration Agreement is received by the Acas Arbitration Section. The Arbitration Agreement is treated as 'concluded' on the date it is

signed, or if signed by different people at different times, on the date of the last signature. If it was not reasonably practicable for the Agreement to be notified to Acas within the six week period, any party notifying an Agreement outside this period should explain the reason for the delay in writing, and send this explanation to the Acas Arbitration Section. Acas will ask an arbitrator to consider the explanation, and the arbitrator may seek the views of the other party and may call both parties to a hearing to discuss the reasons for the delay. The arbitrator will then issue an award on whether or not the Agreement can be accepted for hearing under the Scheme.

Withdrawal or settlement of cases before or during arbitration hearings

Withdrawal

37 Once the Arbitration Agreement has been concluded and forwarded to Acas, the individual who brought the claim of unfair dismissal is free to withdraw from the arbitration process at any time provided that the withdrawal is in writing or recorded by any means so as to be usable for subsequent reference for example e-mail/facsimile, and sent either to the Acas Arbitration Section or to the arbitrator (via the Acas Arbitration Section) (see paragraph 132). This withdrawal will constitute a dismissal of the claim. **In withdrawing the claim the individual must understand that they have no right to re-open the original claim to the employment tribunal.** The employer cannot unilaterally withdraw from the agreement to go to arbitration.

Settlement

38 Parties are free to reach private agreements to settle the dispute which was the subject of arbitration at any time before the end of the hearing. Having done so the parties may ask the Acas Arbitration Section or the arbitrator (if one has been appointed) to terminate the arbitration proceedings. They can also request the arbitrator (if appointed) to record this agreement as their 'agreed' award which would then be enforceable in the same way as any other award. The arbitrator has the power only to record such agreements, and will not approve, vary, transcribe, interpret or ratify them in any way. In order for the arbitrator to do this, the parties will first have to agree the wording of the agreement which they wish the arbitrator to record.

39 The arbitrator does not have the power to record agreements which are outside his or her remit, for example in respect of a personal injury claim associated with the dismissal, or which contain a remedy which it is beyond the power of the arbitrator to award, for example the retention by the employee of a company car. If parties wish to settle disputes which are wider than the issue being determined by arbitration, but they wish the appropriate part of their agreement to be endorsed by the arbitrator, the agreement must clearly identify the part of the settlement which relates to the issue before the arbitrator. **Any other parts of the agreement will not be recorded by the arbitrator as being included in their award.**

40 Alternatively, parties may agree terms privately between themselves, usually in writing, on the basis of which they wish to withdraw from arbitration but, in doing so, they must accept that the terms do not constitute an award by the arbitrator. In this case confirmation in writing, or recorded by any means so as to be usable for subsequent reference for example e-mail/facsimile, that the employee wishes to withdraw from arbitration must be sent to the Acas Arbitration Section or given to the arbitrator.

The Scheme in outline

Arrangements for the hearing

The following description is by way of general guidance only. It is to be noted that all procedural and evidential matters are within the arbitrator's discretion, subject to certain provisions of the Scheme.

Appointment of an arbitrator

41   Once Acas has accepted an Agreement for arbitration under the Scheme, an arbitrator will be appointed by Acas from its arbitration Panel and the parties will be notified of the arbitrator's name.

42   Before being appointed and until the arbitration is concluded, the arbitrator has a duty to disclose to Acas in writing any circumstances, in a particular case, likely to give rise to any justifiable doubts as to his or her impartiality. This information will be disclosed to the parties.

43   Parties will not normally have a choice about a particular arbitrator to hear their case, although there may be exceptional circumstances when a party feels that the appointed arbitrator might not be able to be impartial, for example because they have a connection with one of the parties. That party should then contact the Acas Arbitration Section as soon as possible.

Removal of an arbitrator

44   Arbitrators may only be removed by Acas or by order of the Court. A party to an arbitration can apply to remove an arbitrator where circumstances exist that give rise to justifiable doubts as to his or her impartiality or where he or she is physically/mentally incapable of conducting the proceedings or there are justifiable doubts as to his or her capacity to do so. Where a party has such doubts about the arbitrator they should apply in the first instance to Acas. If Acas refuses the application the party may then apply to the Court. The Court will only exercise its discretion with respect to removal if the party has already applied to and been refused by Acas. The arbitrator may continue the proceedings and make an award while an application to Acas or the Court is pending.

Death and replacement of an arbitrator

45   The authority of an arbitrator is personal and ceases on his or her death. In the event of an arbitrator dying or becoming incapacitated after being appointed to conduct an arbitration under the Scheme, but before an award has been signed by the arbitrator, a new arbitrator will be appointed. If, for any reason, including death or incapacity, an arbitrator ceases to hold office, Acas will appoint a replacement arbitrator who will decide whether, and to what extent, any previous proceedings should stand.

General duty of the arbitrator

46   The arbitrator has a general duty to act fairly and impartially as between the parties, giving each party a reasonable opportunity of putting his or her case and dealing with that of his or her opponent, and also to adopt procedures suitable to the circumstances of

the particular case, avoiding unnecessary delay or expense so as to provide a fair means for resolution of the dispute.

General duty of the parties

47   The parties to an arbitration have a duty to do everything necessary to ensure that the proceedings progress smoothly and are not delayed. They must comply with any direction made by the arbitrator.

48   If either party fails to comply with any aspect of the procedure set out in the Scheme or any direction by the arbitrator, the arbitrator may adjourn a hearing if in his or her view it would be unfair to either party to proceed or may draw an adverse inference from the act of non-compliance. In drawing such an adverse inference an arbitrator may assume that a party has failed to comply in an attempt to conceal a weakness in the merits of their case.

Consolidation of cases/combined proceedings

49   Acas has the power, with the agreement of the parties, to consolidate cases which are brought against the same employer and are based on common facts.

Agreeing the hearing date and venue

50   Once appointed, the arbitrator, with the administrative assistance of the Acas Arbitration Section, will arrange a hearing as soon as is reasonably practicable. **The Scheme does not allow a decision to be made on written evidence alone even if both parties wish it.** The Acas Arbitration Section will contact the parties with details of the date and venue for the hearing.

51   The hearings will be held as far as possible at a location convenient for both parties, usually at a neutral venue such as Acas premises or a hotel. However, where the parties agree, the hearing can be held at the employee's former workplace, or at a representative's premises, such as the offices of a trade union or an employers' association where this does not prejudice independence or impartiality. Where premises have to be hired, Acas will meet reasonable costs in doing so.

52   Parties will be expected to co-operate by agreeing a date and venue with the arbitrator for a hearing to take place within two months of the Acas Arbitration Section being notified of the Agreement. The appointed arbitrator has the power to decide:

a   when and where the hearing should be if the parties are unable to agree on a mutually acceptable date and

b   on the merits of any applications by either or both parties for postponements.

Expedited hearings

53   If, before the parties opt to have their unfair dismissal dispute decided by arbitration, an employment tribunal makes an order under the interim relief provisions, and the parties wish to have an arbitrator hear the case quickly, Acas will, once it is informed that an interim relief order exists, and once it has accepted the Agreement into the Scheme, appoint an arbitrator who will attempt to arrange a hearing as soon as is reasonably practicable. Interim relief is a remedy available to employees who have alleged that their dismissal was for an 'inadmissible reason'. Examples of these include dismissal for being

For arbitrations in Wales either a Welsh-speaking arbitrator or translation will be
[provide]d where either of the parties or any witnesses indicate that they would like to
[use W]elsh at the hearing.

[Travelling] expenses/loss of earnings

[It is] a provision of the Scheme that each party will meet their own travelling expenses and
[tho]se of others assisting them, whether representatives or witnesses. In addition, no loss
[of] earnings are payable by Acas to anyone involved in the arbitration. However, where an
[ar]bitrator rules that a dismissal was unfair, he or she may include in the calculation of any
[c]ompensation a sum to cover reasonable travelling costs and loss of earnings incurred by
[t]he employee personally in attending the hearing.

[Ou]tline of procedure before the hearing

[62] Arbitration is most effective as a method of resolving disputes when each party, and the
arbitrator, has the fullest possible opportunity to consider the arguments of both parties
before the hearing takes place. Once a date has been agreed for the hearing, the parties
should bear in mind the need to allow enough time for the preparation of their case, and
for sending via the Acas Arbitration Section to the other party, and to the arbitrator,
written evidence such as copies of documents that they will be making use of and
statements from others who they will be calling to speak at the hearing. To help them in
preparing their case, parties should read the Acas Code of Practice *Disciplinary and
Grievance Procedure* and the Acas Handbook *Discipline at Work*, which the arbitrator will
have regard to in reaching a decision. Copies of these documents can be obtained from the
Acas Reader service, the address of which is at the back of this Guide.

63 The parties should send written statements of case (see paragraph 65) and any supporting
documentation or other material which they wish to rely on at the hearing to the Acas
Arbitration Section (see paragraph 132) so that they are received by Acas at least 14 days
prior to the hearing. These will be in addition to the IT1 and IT3 forms. All written
submissions received will be sent to the arbitrator and copied to the other party. If for
some reason a party is unable to produce a written statement before the hearing, the fact
that they have not done so will not count against them when the arbitrator makes their
decision. Written statements of case which have not been provided prior to a hearing may
only be relied upon at the hearing with the arbitrator's permission.

64 Exceptionally, arbitrators at their discretion may permit additional papers to be
introduced at the hearing itself, although these should never seek to introduce completely
new points or arguments, and will need to be made available to the other party as well as
to the arbitrator. **It is not consistent with the spirit of arbitration for one side to seek
advantage over the other through the last-minute submission of papers. Attempts to do
so may only result in adjournments or undue delays whilst the other party is given
time to study the papers.**

65 Written statements of case should briefly set out the main particulars of the case as the
party sees it, and which can then be expanded upon, if necessary, at the hearing. It is
helpful for statements to be written (typed if possible) on one side of the paper. It is also
helpful if the pages and paragraphs are numbered. The statement should include an
explanation of the events which led up to the dismissal, including an account of the
sequence and outcome of any relevant meetings, interviews or discussions.

a member of, or taking part in the activities of, an in
join or remain a member of a trade union. An a
provisional or interim relief.

54 An arbitrator has the discretion to expedite a hearing
either of his or her own volition or at the request of the par.

Applications for postponements of, or different venues for initial, ana

55 Once the arbitrator has set a date and venue for the initial heai
postponement of, or a different venue for, a hearing may be ma
writing, via the Acas Arbitration Section (see paragraph 132), settii
party feels that the arbitrator should review the decision to hold the i
or at that venue. This should be done within **14 days** of the date of the .
hearing arrangements. The parties will be given reasonable opportunit\
the application following which the arbitrator, without an oral hearin\
decision as to whether the application should be allowed. If the application
original arrangements will stand.

56 Applications for postponements or change of venue of the hearing received a
days specified above will be considered at the arbitrator's discretion.

57 As well as this specific power to postpone initial hearings the arbitrator has a \
discretion with respect to subsequent postponements.

Non-attendance at the hearing

58 If a party fails to attend the hearing without providing an acceptable explanation, the
arbitrator may continue the hearing in that party's absence, taking account of any written
submissions and documents which have been submitted by that party. Where it is the
employee who fails to attend the hearing without providing an acceptable explanation,
the arbitrator also has the option of writing to them asking for an explanation for their
non-attendance. If the employee does not demonstrate reasonable cause why they did not
attend, the arbitrator may rule in an award that the claim is deemed to have been
dismissed.

Assistance at the hearing

59 Where a party will need any assistance at the hearing, such as the services of an
interpreter, signer or communicator, they should let the Acas Arbitration Section know at
the earliest opportunity in order that appropriate arrangements can be made. Where the
arbitrator agrees that such help is required, Acas will meet the reasonable cost of
providing it. Parties should also let the Acas Arbitration Section know if they have any
special requirements which might affect arrangements for the hearing.

Use of the Welsh language

60 The proceedings will generally be in English, however, where the provisions of the Welsh
Language Act 1993 apply, Acas will offer a choice of language for the proceedings and
arrangements will be made to correspond with parties in the Welsh language should they

110

wish it.
provid
speak

Travellin

61 It is
th
of
a

Copies of relevant documents/supporting documentation may include:

- Letters of appointment.
- Contracts of employment.
- Written statement of particulars of employment.
- Company handbooks, rules and procedures.
- Time sheets and attendance records.
- Performance appraisal reports.
- Warning letters/dismissal letters/written reasons for dismissal.
- Evidence of, either attempts to seek new employment or, of earnings in new employment and social security payments (where applicable).

66   In addition, information which will help the arbitrator to assess compensation, if it is awarded, should be sent (see paragraph 83).

Requests for documents

67   Before the hearing either party may request from the other party access to, and/or copies of, documents which are not in the requesting party's possession, but which they feel could be important to their case. Where such documents are copied direct to the other party, a copy should also be sent to the Acas Arbitration Section to forward to the arbitrator. In responding to reasonable requests for copies of documents, parties should normally bear the cost of reproducing them, and of sending them to both the requesting party and to Acas.

68   Although arbitrators have no power to compel either party to comply with the requirement to exchange information, they can take failure to do so into account in reaching their decision. An arbitrator may draw an adverse inference and it could therefore count against a party if they have refused to co-operate by exchanging documents and other information before the hearing.

69   Documents, other than copies of the IT1 and IT3, which may have been supplied to an Acas conciliator before an agreement to go to arbitration was reached, will not be copied to the arbitrator or the other party by Acas from its own records. In addition, the Acas conciliator will not provide the arbitrator with any details of the conciliation process.

Calling others to speak at the hearing

70   At least 14 days prior to the hearing the parties should also provide the Acas Arbitration Section with a list of names and title/role of all those people who will accompany them to the hearing or be called as a witness. In deciding this issue each party should consider whether they wish to have present at the hearing others who, for example, can support from their personal experience statements made about events leading up to the dismissal; speak about their role in the disciplinary proceedings; or, inform the arbitrator about the operation of the organisation's rules, practices and procedures, and where relevant, those operating in the industry or sector concerned. Parties should bear in mind, however, that unlike at an employment tribunal hearing, the arbitrator will not ask such people to swear

an oath or an affirmation, nor allow a process of cross-examination. However, it is very likely that such witnesses will be questioned directly by the arbitrator. Parties may consider it sufficient to submit a signed statement from the witness containing their account of events instead of calling the witness to the hearing, although this would mean that the witness could not add to their statement during the hearing or be questioned on it and it is therefore possible that the evidence will not carry as much weight. Any such statements should be sent to the Acas Arbitration Section to be copied to the arbitrator and to the other party. Even where people are to appear in person, details of what they are going to say should be sent to Acas for copying to the arbitrator and the other party.

71   All those people who are on the list(s) of those accompanying each party should be present at the start of the hearing. Any witnesses whose details have not been provided in advance of the hearing may only be called with the arbitrator's permission.

Requests for attendance of witnesses

72   The arbitrator has no power to compel anybody's attendance at the hearing, whichever party has asked them to come. However, employers who are parties to arbitration hearings should co-operate by allowing current employees time off from work should the dismissed employee wish to call them to attend the hearing. Such employees should only be those who are in a position to provide relevant information to the arbitrator. The arbitrator may draw an adverse inference and it may count against the employer when the arbitrator is reaching a decision if they have unreasonably refused time off in these circumstances to a current employee who has relevant evidence to give.

Preliminary hearings and directions

73   In cases where the arbitrator believes that there are likely to be considerable differences between the parties in respect of procedural points, for example over the availability or exchange of documents, or whether or not certain employees will be allowed time off to attend the hearing, the arbitrator has the power to call the parties to a preliminary hearing to attempt to resolve their differences. Alternatively the arbitrator may give procedural directions in correspondence. The arbitrator may express views on the desirability of information and/or evidence being available at the hearing, and remind the parties of their duty to act co-operatively in order to progress the arbitration hearing.

Conduct of the hearing

74   In conducting the arbitration hearing (as with every other part of the proceedings) the arbitrator has a responsibility to act fairly and impartially, giving each party a reasonable opportunity of putting their case and dealing with that of the other party. The arbitrator must adopt procedures suitable to the circumstances of the particular case, avoiding unnecessary delay or expense and providing a fair way of resolving the dispute.

75   The arbitrator is responsible, within general principles contained in the Scheme, for the conduct of the hearing and all matters relating to procedures and evidence. Given this discretion the arbitrator is free to conduct the proceedings in a way which is very different from the employment tribunal (see Appendix 3). The arbitrator also has the power to adjourn a hearing.

76 The language of the proceedings will be English, unless the Welsh language provisions apply (see paragraph 60).

77 The purpose of the hearing is to allow both parties to explain their case in full to the arbitrator, and also to comment on the case being put by the other party. It also allows the arbitrator to put questions directly to either party or anybody else attending the hearing in order to ascertain the facts and clarify any points being made, and to attempt to resolve any inconsistencies or conflicts in the two accounts being presented by the parties before making a decision. The arbitrator will adopt an inquisitorial approach and encourage both parties, and anyone whom they have called to be present at the hearing, to speak freely in order that as full a picture as possible of what happened can emerge. At the hearing the arbitrator will also consider documents submitted by the parties, and question them about these.

78 Parties may bring, if they wish, someone to help them present their case at the hearing, although no special status will be accorded to legally qualified representatives. The parties are liable for any fees or expenses incurred by any representative they appoint. The arbitrator will have the right to address questions direct to either party and to anybody else who is attending the hearing to speak on their behalf. However, nobody will be required to swear oaths or affirmations and no party or witness will be cross-examined by any other party or representative.

79 Hearings will be informal, and normally completed in less than a day. The rules of evidence which apply in the courts will not apply in the arbitration hearing. **The hearing will be held in private, generally with only the arbitrator, the parties and sometimes, with the consent of the parties, an Acas official or arbitrator in training present. In the case of EC law or Human Rights Act 1998 being relevant a legal adviser may also attend the hearing (see paragraphs 85–87).** The arbitrator will normally open the hearing by explaining his or her role and then confirm that he or she will be deciding whether the dismissal was fair or unfair and if unfair then what the remedy should be.

80 The arbitrator will then conduct the hearing in accordance with his or her general discretion using, as a broad guide, the standard arbitration hearing procedure (see Appendix 3). The arbitrator retains a full discretion, however, to depart from this suggested order of procedure. The arbitrator will be able to assist any party having difficulties in fully explaining their case. Before the hearing is closed the arbitrator will normally obtain an assurance from each party that everything that they wished to say has been said, and that they have had sufficient opportunity to comment on or attempt to rebut what has been said by the other party.

81 Towards the end of the hearing and before the arbitrator has decided whether the dismissal was fair or unfair, he or she will explain to the employee what orders for reinstatement/re-engagement may be made and in what circumstances and ask the employee whether he or she is seeking such a remedy.

82 If the employer believes that it would not be practicable to re-employ the former employee, he or she must be prepared to produce evidence to support that argument. Likewise, if the employee argues that it is practicable for them to be re-employed, they should be prepared to provide supporting evidence.

83 The parties will also be asked to agree the details provided concerning the employee's income which will be used to calculate any award of compensation, should the dismissal be found to have been unfair. The parties should attend the hearing able to provide the arbitrator with information relevant to the calculation of compensation, if appropriate,

which may include documents showing: the employee's date of birth, the date employment began, the date from which the dismissal took effect, gross weekly pay, weekly take home pay, pay slips, P60s or wage records, notice entitlement, termination payments (redundancy, pay in lieu of notice, *ex gratia* awards), details of benefits paid to the employee such as company car, pension, travelling expenses and free or subsidised accommodation, and guidance about, and if available actuarial assessments of pension entitlements. This information should refer both to the job from which the employee was dismissed, and any jobs they have had since. Details should also be provided concerning any net earnings or welfare benefits received since the dismissal by the employee, and of attempts that they have made to find work and if they have been unable to find work, what they consider their job prospects to be. Where a party requires the assistance of an expert witness, for example to deal with pension issues, all costs for that witness must be met by the relevant party.

84 No further evidence will be accepted after the end of a substantive hearing, without the arbitrator's permission, although the arbitrator may occasionally request that a party sends further documentation. Where this happens, the documentation should be sent to the Acas Arbitration Section (see paragraph 132) for copying to the arbitrator and to the other party who will be able to comment, if necessary, before the arbitrator reaches a decision.

Appointment of legal advisers for points of EC law and the Human Rights Act 1998

85 The Scheme is not intended for cases which involve issues of EC law. Parties who have such cases are strongly recommended to have them heard in the employment tribunal. However, where such cases are referred to be heard under the Scheme or cases are referred which involve matters under the Human Rights Act 1998, the arbitrator has the power, either at his or her own discretion or at the request of either party (and with his or her agreement) to require the appointment of a legal adviser. On request from the arbitrator Acas will appoint a legal adviser to report to the arbitrator and the parties. The legal adviser is under the same duty of disclosure as the arbitrator (see paragraph 42) and must disclose in writing to Acas any circumstances likely to give rise to any justifiable doubts as to his or her impartiality in any particular case to which they are appointed.

86 Where such issues of EC law or the Human Rights Act 1998 are not identified prior to the hearing but arise once the hearing is underway, the arbitrator may identify the need for a legal adviser to be involved and will inform Acas, who will then make the appointment. In these cases there may need to be an adjournment of the hearing pending appointment of the legal adviser.

87 The legal adviser may attend the hearing or be consulted in correspondence. He or she will advise the arbitrator but will not take over responsibility for the arbitration proceedings and will not ultimately decide the dispute. The parties will be given a reasonable opportunity to comment on any information, opinion or advice offered by the legal adviser. Following this the arbitrator will take the legal adviser's information, opinion or advice into account when determining the dispute. The proceedings will remain informal and the arbitrator will continue to adopt an inquisitorial approach.

Court determination of preliminary points

88   In cases where EC law and/or the Human Rights Act 1998 are relevant a party may apply to the High Court or Central London County Court for the determination of a preliminary point of law. Any such application must identify the question of law to be determined. The application may only be made with the agreement of all other parties to the arbitration or with the permission of the arbitrator and must state the grounds on which the question is to be decided by the Court. The party making the application must notify the other party/ies and the Court must be satisfied that the determination of this point substantially affects the rights of one or more of the parties to the arbitration.

How the arbitrator reaches a decision

89   Each case will be decided in accordance with the Terms of Reference. Having listened to the arguments put forward by the parties and any others whom they have asked to speak, and taken into account any documentation tabled during the arbitration process, the arbitrator will come to a decision. In doing so the arbitrator will have regard to the guidance given in the Acas Code of Practice *Disciplinary and Grievance Procedures* and the Acas Handbook *Discipline at Work* and make use of their own experience of accepted standards in the workplace. Where an arbitrator uses specific experience in determining a case he or she will afford the parties the opportunity to comment upon it. The arbitrator will **not** base any decision on legal tests or precedent except in cases where EC law and/or the Human Rights Act 1998 are relevant, even if these have been referred to by the parties during the hearing. Nor will the arbitrator substitute what he or she would have done for the actions taken by the employer. **The arbitrator will not decide or announce the outcome of the case at the hearing.**

Remedies available under the Scheme

Where the arbitrator is determining the remedy in a case which does not involve points of EC law he or she will apply the provisions of the Scheme. However, where an arbitrator is determining a remedy in a case in which the dismissal was unfair by reason of the operation of EC law, he or she will apply the provisions of the relevant statute(s) and case law.

Automatic unfairness

90   In deciding whether a dismissal is fair or unfair in a case which does not involve EC law, the arbitrator will take account of, but not necessarily follow, the provisions for automatic unfairness in Part X (Unfair Dismissal) of the Employment Rights Act 1996. However, where they are deciding a case where EC law applies, the arbitrator must apply the relevant statutory provisions for automatic unfairness.

Reinstatement/re-engagement

91   In all cases where the arbitrator decides that a dismissal is unfair, if the employee so wishes, the arbitrator may order reinstatement or re-engagement. The arbitrator will first consider reinstatement. An order for reinstatement is an order that the employer shall treat the employee in all respects as if he or she had not been dismissed. In deciding whether to make such an order, the arbitrator will take into consideration the employee's

wishes; the practicability of complying with an order for reinstatement; and, in cases where the employee was partly to blame for the dismissal, whether or not it would be just to make such an award.

92 If the arbitrator awards reinstatement the order for reinstatement will specify any compensation due to the employee for arrears of pay (or other benefit) for the period between the date of dismissal and the date of reinstatement, any rights such as seniority/ pension rights which must be restored to the employee and the date by which these must be complied with. The employee must also benefit from any improvements to their terms and conditions during the period following dismissal for example a pay increase/increased holiday allowance. When assessing the compensation due to the employee the arbitrator will deduct any wages in lieu of notice or *ex gratia* payments received from the employer, any payments received in respect of employment with another employer since their dismissal and any other benefits which the arbitrator considers appropriate.

93 If the arbitrator decides not to award reinstatement he or she will consider awarding re-engagement and, if so, on what terms this should be. An order for re-engagement, which like any other remedy, must be made in the form of an award, is an order that the employee be re-engaged by the employer, a successor of the employer or an associated employer, in employment comparable to that from which he or she was dismissed (or other suitable employment).

94 Again, in doing so the arbitrator will take into consideration the employee's wishes; the practicability of the employee returning to work for the employer, or a successor or associated employer; and, in cases where the employee was partly to blame for the dismissal, whether or not it would be just to make such an award. If ordering re-engagement the arbitrator will, so far as is reasonably practicable, do so on terms which are as favourable as an order for reinstatement, unless the employee was partly or wholly to blame for the dismissal, where the arbitrator will take this factor into account.

95 An order for re-engagement will specify the terms on which it is to take place, including: the identity of the employer, the nature of the employment, the remuneration for the employment, any compensation due to the employee for arrears of pay (or other benefit) which the employee might reasonably be expected to have had for the period between the date of dismissal and the date of re-engagement, any rights such as seniority/pension rights which must be restored to the employee and the date by which these must be complied with. When assessing the compensation due to the employee the arbitrator will deduct any wages in lieu of notice or *ex gratia* payments received from the employer, any payments received in respect of employment with another employer since the dismissal and any other benefits which the arbitrator considers appropriate.

Permanent replacement

96 If the employer has replaced the dismissed employee with a permanent replacement the arbitrator can only take account of this when considering ordering reinstatement/re-engagement if (a) it was not practicable for the employer to arrange for the employee's work to be done without engaging the replacement, or (b) a reasonable period of time had elapsed before the employee had indicated that they were seeking to be re-employed and by the time the replacement was engaged it was no longer reasonable for the employee's work to be done except by a permanent replacement.

Continuity of employment

97 Where the arbitrator does award reinstatement or re-engagement the employee's continuity of employment will be preserved in the same way as it would be under an employment tribunal award.

Awards of compensation

98 Where reinstatement or re-engagement are not sought by the former employee, or are not considered appropriate by the arbitrator, he or she can award compensation to be paid by the employer to the employee.

99 Where compensation is awarded it will consist of a basic amount, a compensatory amount and, in some circumstances, a supplementary amount. These largely reflect the basic award, compensatory award and supplementary award which employment tribunals may order.

The basic amount

100 The basic amount will be based on the employee's age, length of service and weekly pay. The way in which the arbitrator will make this calculation is set out in the Scheme and summarised in Appendix 4 to this Guide.

Minimum basic amounts

101 Minimum basic amounts, subject to the same criteria and limits as those awarded by employment tribunals, will be awarded in cases where the arbitrator has found the dismissal unfair and the reason or principal reason for the dismissal or selection for redundancy was one of the following: being a designated health and safety representative, an employee representative or a candidate for election as such for the purposes of consultation on redundancy or transfers of undertakings, workforce representatives/ candidates in an election under the Working Time Regulations, employee trustees of occupational pension Schemes and dismissals related to trade union membership or activities.

102 Before any reductions to the basic amount can be taken into account (see Appendix 4) the minimum basic amount in such cases shall not be less than the amount specified in the relevant statute.

Basic amount of two weeks' pay in certain circumstances (Sections 138 and 141 Employment Rights Act 1996)

103 If an employee has been dismissed because of redundancy and he or she is not entitled to a redundancy payment by virtue of section 141 of the Employment Rights Act 1996 or is not regarded as dismissed by virtue of section 138 of that Act, the basic amount will be limited to two weeks' pay.

Limits on the basic amount

104 The arbitrator is required to have regard to the statutory maximum limits on a 'week's pay' used for the calculation of the basic amount (see sections 220–29 of the Employment Rights Act 1996). This is subject to a statutory limit which is reviewed each year.

Reductions to the basic amount

105 The ways in which the arbitrator may reduce the basic amount are set out in the Scheme and summarised in Appendix 4.

Compensatory amount

106 The compensatory amount will be calculated to reflect what the arbitrator considers is just and equitable in all the circumstances and will take account of the employee's financial loss insofar as it is attributable to the action taken by the employer. Employees are however under a duty to reduce this loss by, for example, seeking suitable new employment.

Reductions to the compensatory amount

107 Once the calculation has been made, the arbitrator may reduce the amount by a proportion that he or she finds just and equitable if the dismissal was found to any extent to be caused, or contributed to, by any conduct of the employee.

Limits on the compensatory amount

108 The compensatory amount cannot exceed the employment tribunal statutory limit, which is reviewed from time to time, except in certain health and safety cases and in cases where the employee made a protected disclosure (whistleblowers).

Internal appeals procedures

109 Where an employee has failed to use an internal appeals procedure provided by the employer to appeal against a dismissal, the Scheme provides for the arbitrator to reduce the compensatory amount by an amount he or she considers just and equitable, up to a maximum of two weeks' pay. The Scheme provides for a supplementary amount, which will be an amount the arbitrator considers to be just and equitable up to a maximum of two weeks' pay to be payable in certain circumstances where the employer prevented an employee from appealing against dismissal under the organisation's appeals procedure.

Double recovery

110 The parties must supply details of any relevant awards of compensation that may have been made by any tribunal or court in connection with the matters which are the subject of the claim before the arbitrator. Where an employee relies on the same act by the employer in a claim of unfair dismissal as he or she relies on in a claim before an employment tribunal under the Sex Discrimination 1975 and/or the Race Relations Act 1976 and/or the Disability Discrimination Act 1995, the arbitrator cannot award

compensation in respect of any loss which has already been taken into account by the tribunal.

Insolvency of employer

111 In cases where the employer has become insolvent, the basic amount may be paid by the Secretary of State for Trade and Industry on the same basis as employment tribunal awards.

The form of the arbitrator's award (decision)

112 The arbitrator's decision is called an 'award'. The arbitrator will send to the parties, or their nominated representatives, through Acas, a final and binding award stating the reason for the dismissal and whether it was fair or unfair. The arbitrator's award will be in writing and will include reference to the main considerations which were taken into account in reaching the decision that the dismissal was fair or unfair. If the arbitrator has decided that the dismissal was unfair, the award will also contain details of the remedy which the arbitrator has awarded. The award will be signed and dated by the arbitrator.

113 The arbitrator may make more than one award at different times on different aspects of the matters to be determined in the case. For example he or she may make an award relating to whether or not the dismissal was unfair but due to lack of information available at the hearing on the employee's losses may subsequently issue an award on compensation.

Correction of awards

(NOTE – Correction of award in this context refers *only* to the removal of any clerical or computational mistake, or error arising from an accidental slip or omission, or to clarify or remove any ambiguity in the award and does not imply the ability to overturn the arbitrator's award through an appeal or challenge.)

114 The arbitrator's award will be issued simultaneously by Acas to both parties. This will be done within three weeks of the award having been signed and dated by the arbitrator. Before the award is circulated the Acas Arbitration Section may check it for any clerical or other errors and may refer the award back to the arbitrator to establish whether he or she wishes to rectify these before the award is issued to the parties. Acas does not however interfere with the decision itself. The arbitrator may, either on his or her own initiative or on application of a party or Acas, correct the award or clarify any ambiguity. Any correction of the award shall be made within **28 days** of the date the application was received by the arbitrator, or where the correction is made at the arbitrator's initiative, within **28 days** of the date of the award. Any correction of the award will form part of the award.

115 If the arbitrator decides that it is necessary he or she may make an additional award in respect of any claim which was argued before him or her but not dealt with in the original award. If a new issue has arisen the arbitrator will afford the parties the opportunity to comment before issuing an additional award. It should be noted however, that an additional award cannot revisit any issue that has already been dealt with in a previous award. Any additional award will be made within **56 days** of the date of the original award. Any application for an additional award must be made to the Acas Arbitration

Section within **28 days** of the date the award was despatched to the applying party by Acas.

Confidentiality of awards

116 Arbitrators' awards are confidential to Acas, the parties and their representatives and will not be published by Acas. However, Acas maintains confidential records of cases, decisions and awards for monitoring and evaluation purposes and may publish general summary information concerning cases heard under the Scheme as it sees fit, without identifying individual cases or parties. Awards will not be lodged with the employment tribunal by Acas. However, an award may be lodged at an employment tribunal by a party who is enforcing an award of reinstatement or re-engagement which has not been honoured by the other party.

Effect of awards

117 The arbitrator's award is final and binding both on the parties and on any persons claiming through or under them.

Enforcing awards

118 Awards will be enforceable in the High Court or County Court.

119 Where an arbitration award for reinstatement or re-engagement has been made and not complied with, the employee in the original unfair dismissal case should refer the matter to an employment tribunal for appropriate compensation to be awarded as if the decision had been made by the tribunal itself.

Interest

120 Where an employer does not pay any compensation awarded by the arbitrator within 42 days of the date of despatch of the award by Acas to the employer, interest will be payable on the same basis as for employment tribunal awards.

Appeals

121 There will be no right of appeal on a point of law or fact in respect of the arbitrator's award, which will be final and binding on the parties. The only exception to this is a narrow exception with respect to points of EC law and the Human Rights Act 1998 (see paragraphs 128–29).

Challenging the arbitrator's award

122 Challenges to the arbitrator's award can only be made in the very limited circumstances which are outlined below.

Challenges on grounds of substantive jurisdiction

123 A party to an arbitration may challenge an arbitrator's award on the grounds of substantive jurisdiction. Such a challenge could be to the validity of the arbitration and whether the dispute was within the scope of the Scheme, the way in which the arbitrator was appointed and/or which matters were submitted to arbitration in accordance with the Arbitration Agreement.

124 Challenges should be made to the High Court or Central London County Court within 28 days of the date the award was despatched to the party by Acas and notice of the challenge should be sent to Acas, the arbitrator (via Acas) and to the other party/ies. However, parties may lose their right to make a challenge if they did not raise the points at issue at the time with the arbitrator or otherwise raise the issue within the provisions of the Scheme and if they continued to take part in the proceedings without objection. If the Court upholds a challenge on the grounds of substantive jurisdiction, it may confirm the award, vary the award or set the award aside either in whole or part.

Challenges on grounds of serious irregularity

125 Challenges in respect of the conduct of the arbitrator, the proceedings or the award may only be made on the grounds of serious irregularity which has caused or will cause substantial injustice to the party making the challenge. Such challenges concern the way in which the dispute was determined rather than the end result itself.

126 Challenges should be made to the High Court or Central London County Court **within 28 days** of the date the award was despatched to the party by Acas and notice of the challenge should be sent to Acas and to the other party/ies. However, parties may lose their right to make a challenge if they did not raise the point(s) at issue at the time with the arbitrator or otherwise raise the issue within the provisions of the Scheme and continued to take part in the proceedings without objection. If the Court upholds a challenge on the grounds of serious irregularity, it may remit the award to the arbitrator for reconsideration, set the award aside, or declare the award to be of no effect. It may do any of these in respect of the award as a whole, or only in respect of part of it.

127 The limited categories of serious irregularity on which a challenge may be brought are set out in the Scheme. The test of 'Substantial Injustice' has been very narrowly defined in the Report of the Departmental Advisory Committee (DAC) on Arbitration Law – the official guide to the Arbitration Act 1996. It states that 'The test of a "substantial injustice" is intended to be applied by way of support for the arbitral process, not by way of interference with that process. Thus it is only in those cases where it can be said that what has happened is so far removed from what could reasonably be expected of the arbitral process that we would expect the court to take action'. It continues 'Having chosen arbitration the parties cannot validly complain of substantial injustice unless what has happened simply cannot on any view be defended as an acceptable consequence of that choice'.

Appeals on questions of EC law and the Human Rights Act 1998

128 Where a point of EC law or a matter under the Human Rights Act 1998 has been considered by the arbitrator, a party may appeal to the High Court or Central London

County Court on a question of law arising out of an arbitrator's award. The appeal must be made **within 28 days** of the date the award was despatched to the party by Acas and notice of the appeal should be sent to Acas and to the other party/ies. The Court will only consider the appeal with either the agreement of the other party or if it grants permission itself to hear it. It will only grant permission on the basis that the determination of the question will substantially affect the rights of one or more of the parties; if the appeal raises a point of EC law, that the point is capable of serious argument; or in other cases the decision of the arbitrator is obviously wrong or the question is one of public importance and the arbitrator's decision is open to serious doubt and that despite the agreement of the parties to have the matter determined by arbitration, it is just in the circumstances for the Court to determine the question. As with other challenges this form of review is extremely narrow.

129 If the Court upholds an appeal on a question of EC law or a matter under the Human Rights Act 1998 it may by order confirm the award, vary the award, remit the award to arbitration, in whole or part, for reconsideration in the light of the Court's determination or set aside the award in whole or part.

Immunity

130 An arbitrator will not be liable for anything done or omitted in the discharge of his or her functions as an arbitrator, unless the act or omission is shown to have been in bad faith. This applies also to a legal adviser appointed by Acas.

131 Acas, by reason of having appointed an arbitrator or a legal adviser, will not be liable for anything done or omitted by the arbitrator or a legal adviser in the discharge of his or her function as an arbitrator.

Service of documents and notices on the Acas Arbitration Section

132 All documents relating to the Scheme which are for the attention of Acas should be sent by pre-paid post to:

Acas Arbitration Section
Acas Head Office
Brandon House
180 Borough High Street
London SE1 1LW

Tel No: 020 7210 3742

or transmitted by facsimile to the Acas Arbitration Section at the following number:

Fax No: 020 7210 3691

Or sent by e-mail to: arbitration@acas.org.uk.

Territorial operation of the Scheme

133 The Scheme is to operate throughout England and Wales.

Further information

134 If parties to an arbitration under the Scheme require any further information about the arbitration process, they should contact the Arbitration Section at Acas Head Office (see paragraph 132) rather than the appointed arbitrator for their case or the Acas conciliator who had previously dealt with the employment tribunal claim.

Address of Acas Reader

Copies of all Acas publications can be obtained from the Acas mailing house at:

Acas Reader Ltd
PO Box 16
Earl Shilton
Leicester LE9 8ZZ

Tel No: 01455 852225

APPENDIX 1: EMPLOYMENT TRIBUNALS AND ACAS ARBITRATION: A COMPARISON

Unfair dismissal/key process areas	Employment tribunal	Arbitration
Decision (fair or unfair dismissal) based on	Statute and case law/ 'test of reasonableness'	Acas Code of Practice and Handbook and general principles of fairness and good conduct
Those hearing the case	Legally qualified chairman and side members	Acas arbitrator with knowledge/experience of employment relations, sitting alone
Location of hearing	ET office	By agreement at a hotel/ Acas office/the workplace/ representatives' premises or other
Length of hearing	Normally at least one day	Normally half a day
Presentation of evidence	Cross-examination of 'witnesses' on oath	Informal presentation, no oaths or cross-examination by parties but questioning by arbitrator
Availability of 'witnesses' and documents	Witness orders, orders for discovery/inspection or production by witnesses of documents	No powers in Scheme to make orders, but failure of parties to co-operate can count against them when decision is made
Expenses to attend hearing/loss of earnings	Tribunal can reimburse expenses and losses for parties, witnesses and some representatives	No expenses paid by Acas, but compensation for unfair dismissals may include a sum for cost of attending hearing
Remedies/awards	Statutory provisions/ interim relief available	Acas Scheme/interim relief not available
Publicity	Public hearing and award	Private hearing/ confidential award
Appeal/challenge	Can be made to EAT and appellate courts	No appeal on point of law or fact (other than EC law or Human Rights Act issues); challenge only for jurisdiction and serious irregularity

Adapted from an original table by Jon Clark and Roy Lewis, first published in Personnel Management, *June 1992*

APPENDIX 2: SUGGESTED WORDING FOR INCLUSION IN AN ARBITRATION AGREEMENT

'The parties hereby agree to submit the dispute concerning the alleged unfair dismissal of [name of employee] to arbitration in accordance with the Acas Arbitration Scheme having effect by virtue of the Acas Arbitration Scheme (England and Wales) Order 2001 (SI 2001 No 1185).'

APPENDIX 3: STANDARD ARBITRATION HEARING PROCEDURE

(The following is a guideline only: procedures are flexible and an arbitrator may structure the procedure in any way that is appropriate in accordance with his or her general duty.)

The arbitrator is responsible for the conduct of the hearing, for ensuring that he or she obtains all the information needed to make his or her award and that the parties are given every opportunity to present their evidence and arguments. Although the arbitrator will decide the way in which the hearing is to be conducted, the following paragraphs broadly describe the procedure that an arbitrator would normally adopt.

Stage 1: Introduction

The arbitrator will introduce him or herself and ask the parties to introduce all those present at the hearing. He or she will explain the way in which the hearing is to be conducted and any domestic arrangements applicable to the location, for example, fire instructions.

Stage 2: Oral presentations

Each party will be asked to make an opening statement that draws attention to the main points of their respective cases, and which may include comments on the other party's written submission. The employer would normally make their statement first. These statements would usually be made without interruption unless the arbitrator or the other party, through the arbitrator, wished to clarify any factual information.

Stage 3: Discussion of the issues

The next stage is that the arbitrator will discuss the issues with the parties. This normally starts with the arbitrator asking questions of the parties. One party may also suggest questions which the arbitrator might put to the other party. The party to whom the question is directed may respond themselves or call upon anyone accompanying them to respond. The person answering the question may call upon another member of the team to make a supporting statement. If one party responds to a question, the other party will be given the opportunity to comment on the response. Again, the party may comment themselves or invite someone accompanying them to do so instead or as well.

The arbitrator will, where appropriate, seek views from the parties on whether, should the dismissal be found to have been unfair, reinstatement or re-engagement of the employee would be a suitable award. In addition, the arbitrator will seek information which will help to inform the calculation of compensation should it be awarded.

Finally, the arbitrator will ask the parties if they feel that they have had an opportunity to say everything that they wished to say and sufficient opportunity to respond to what the other party had to say. The arbitrator may suggest a short adjournment to allow the parties to prepare for their final submissions.

Stage 4: Closing statements

The parties will be offered the opportunity to make a final statement to the arbitrator; the employer would usually make their statement first.

The final statements should be a summary of the main points the parties wish the arbitrator to take into account in reaching his or her decision and should contain no new material.

In closing the hearing the arbitrator will seek a final confirmation from each party that they have nothing further to add.

The arbitrator will not announce his or her decision at the hearing.

APPENDIX 4: MATTERS AN ARBITRATOR CONSIDERS WHEN CALCULATING BASIC AMOUNTS

Basic amount

1 Calculations

The basic amount is calculated by first determining the length of the employee's continuous employment, ending with the effective date of termination of employment. Up to 20 years can count. The arbitrator then calculates the following for each of those years and adds them together:

1.5 week's gross pay for each year between ages 41–64;

1.0 week's gross pay for each year between ages 22–40;

0.5 week's gross pay for each year up to and including age 21.

(There is a reduction by one-twelfth for each complete month of service following the 64th birthday.)

The maximum number of weeks' pay that the basic amount can comprise is 30.

The Scheme directs the arbitrator to have regard to a number of statutory definitions when determining the basic amount including the statutory maximum on a week's pay.

2 Reduction of basic amount

The Scheme provides for reductions in the basic amount to take account of:

• unreasonable refusal of reinstatement (the arbitrator can reduce the amount by such proportion as they consider just and equitable);

• conduct prior to dismissal (the arbitrator can reduce the award by such proportion as they consider just and equitable). The arbitrator will not/cannot reduce a basic amount due to the employee's conduct in a redundancy case unless the reason for selecting the employee for dismissal was one referred to in paragraph 103 and in such circumstances can only apply the reduction to the minimum basic amount. In assessing conduct which might reduce the basic amount, the arbitrator will not take account (if relevant) of those matters set out in section 155 of the Trade Union and Labour Relations (Consolidation) Act 1992 – relating to trade union membership and activities;

- an award to an employee under a dismissal procedures agreement;
- a redundancy payment having been made to the employee.

WAIVER OF RIGHTS

The Acas Arbitration Scheme ('the Scheme') is entirely voluntary. In agreeing to refer a dispute to arbitration under the Scheme, both parties agree to waive rights that they would otherwise have if, for example, they had referred their dispute to the employment tribunal. This follows from the informal nature of the Scheme, which is designed to be a confidential, relatively fast, cost-efficient and non-legalistic process.

As required by section VI of the Scheme, as a confirmation of the parties' agreement to waive their rights, this form must be completed by each party and submitted to Acas together with the agreement to arbitration.

A detailed description of the informal nature of arbitration under the Scheme, and the important differences between this and the employment tribunal, is contained in the Acas Guide to the Scheme ('the Acas Guide'), which should be read by each party before completing this form.

The Scheme is not intended for disputes involving complex legal issues, or questions of EC law. Parties to such disputes are strongly advised to consider applying to the employment tribunal, or settling their dispute by other means.

This form does not list all the differences between the Scheme and the employment tribunal, or all of the features of the Scheme to which each party agrees in referring their dispute to arbitration.

I, ...,

the Applicant/Respondent/Respondent's duly authorised representative [delete as appropriate] confirm my agreement to each of the following points:

1   Unlike proceedings in the employment tribunal, all proceedings under the Scheme, including all hearings, are conducted in private. There are no public hearings, and the final award will be confidential.

2   All arbitrators under the Scheme are appointed by Acas from the Acas arbitration Panel (which is a panel of impartial, mainly non-lawyer, arbitrators appointed by Acas on fixed, but renewable, terms). The appointment process and the Acas arbitration Panel is described in the Scheme and the Acas Guide. Neither party will have any choice of arbitrator.

3   Proceedings under the Scheme are conducted differently from the employment tribunal. In particular:

- arbitrators will conduct proceedings in an informal manner in all cases;

- the attendance of witnesses and the production of documents cannot be compelled (although failure to co-operate may be taken into account by the arbitrator);

- there will be no oaths or affirmations, and no cross-examination of witnesses by parties or their representatives;

- the arbitrator will take the initiative in asking questions and ascertaining the facts (with the aim of ensuring that all relevant issues are considered), as well as hearing each side's arguments;

- the arbitrator's decision will only contain the main considerations that have led to the result; it will not contain full or detailed reasons;

- the arbitrator has no power to order interim relief.

4   Once parties have agreed to refer their dispute to arbitration in accordance with the Scheme, the parties cannot then return to the employment tribunal.

5   In deciding whether or not the dismissal was fair or unfair, the arbitrator shall have regard to general principles of fairness and good conduct in employment relations (including, for example, principles referred to in any relevant Acas *Disciplinary and Grievance Procedures* Code of Practice or *Discipline at Work* Handbook). Unlike the employment tribunal, the arbitrator will not apply strict legal tests or rules (for example court decisions or legislation), with certain limited exceptions set out in the Scheme (see for example paragraph 12).

Similarly, in cases that do not involve EC law, the arbitrator will calculate compensation or award any other remedy in accordance with the terms of the Scheme, instead of applying strict legal tests or rules.

6   Unlike the employment tribunal, there is no right of appeal from awards of arbitrators under the Scheme (except for a limited right to appeal questions of EC law and, aside from procedural matters set out in the Scheme, questions concerning the Human Rights Act 1998).

7   Unlike the employment tribunal, in agreeing to arbitration under the Scheme, parties agree that there is no jurisdictional argument, ie no reason why the claim cannot be heard and determined by the arbitrator. In particular, the arbitrator will assume that a dismissal has taken place, and will only consider whether or not this was unfair. This is explained further in the Scheme and in the Acas Guide.

Signed..

Dated...

In the presence of:

Signature ....

Full name..

Position...

Address..

APPENDIX 2

ACAS ARBITRATION SCHEME

I   INTRODUCTION

1   The Acas Arbitration Scheme ('the Scheme') is implemented pursuant to section 212A of the Trade Union and Labour Relations (Consolidation) Act 1992 ('the 1992 Act').

2   The Scheme provides a voluntary alternative to the employment tribunal for the resolution of unfair dismissal disputes, in the form of arbitration.

3   Resolution of disputes under the Scheme is intended to be confidential, informal, relatively fast and cost-efficient. Procedures under the Scheme are non-legalistic, and far more flexible than the traditional model of the employment tribunal and the courts. For example (as explained in more detail below), the Scheme avoids the use of formal pleadings and formal witness and documentary procedures. Strict rules of evidence will not apply, and, as far as possible, instead of applying strict law or legal precedent, general principles of fairness and good conduct will be taken into account (including, for example, principles referred to in any relevant Acas *Disciplinary and Grievance Procedures* Code of Practice or *Discipline at Work* Handbook). Arbitral decisions ('awards') will be final, with very limited opportunities for parties to appeal or otherwise challenge the result.

4   The Scheme also caters for requirements imposed as a matter of law (for example the Human Rights Act 1998, existing law in the field of arbitration and EC law).

II   THE ROLE OF ACAS

5   As more fully explained below, cases enter the Scheme by reference to Acas, which appoints an arbitrator from a panel (see paragraphs 35–37 below) to determine the dispute. Acas provides administrative assistance during the proceedings, and may scrutinise awards and refer any clerical or other similar errors back to the arbitrator. Disputes are determined, however, by arbitrators and not by Acas.

Routing of communications

6   Unless in the course of a hearing, all communications between either party and the arbitrator shall be sent via the Acas Arbitration Section.

7   Paragraph 172 below sets out the manner in which any document, notice or communication must be served on, or transmitted to, Acas or the Acas Arbitration Section.

III   TERMS AND ABBREVIATIONS

8   The term 'Employee' is used to denote the claimant (ie the former employee), including any person entitled to pursue a claim arising out of a contravention, or alleged contravention, of Part X of the Employment Rights Act 1996.

9   The term 'Employer' is used to denote the respondent.

10   The term 'EC law' means:

  i   any enactment in the domestic legislation of England and Wales giving effect to rights, powers, liabilities, obligations and restrictions from time to time created or arising by or under the Community Treaties, and

  ii   any such rights, powers, liabilities, obligations and restrictions which are not given effect by any such enactment.

11   With the exception of paragraph 21 i below ('Requirements for entry into the Scheme'), references to anything being written or in writing include its being recorded by any means so as to be usable for subsequent reference.

IV   ARBITRATOR'S TERMS OF REFERENCE

12   Every agreement to refer a dispute to arbitration under this Scheme shall be taken to be an agreement that the arbitrator decide the dispute according to the following Terms of Reference:

Nothing in the Terms of Reference affects the operation of the Human Rights Act 1998 in so far as this is applicable and relevant and (with respect to procedural matters) has not been waived by virtue of the provisions of this Scheme.

In deciding whether the dismissal was fair or unfair, the arbitrator shall:

i   have regard to general principles of fairness and good conduct in employment relations (including, for example, principles referred to in any relevant Acas *Disciplinary and Grievance Procedures* Code of Practice or *Discipline at Work* Handbook), instead of applying legal tests or rules (eg court decisions or legislation);

ii   apply EC law.

The arbitrator shall not decide the case by substituting what he or she would have done for the actions taken by the Employer.

If the arbitrator finds the dismissal unfair, he or she shall determine the appropriate remedy under the terms of this Scheme.

V   SCOPE OF THE SCHEME

Cases that are covered by the Scheme

13   This Scheme only applies to cases of alleged unfair dismissal (ie disputes involving proceedings, or claims which could be the subject of proceedings, before an employment tribunal arising out of a contravention, or alleged contravention, of Part X of the Employment Rights Act 1996).

14   The Scheme does not extend to other kinds of claim which are often related to, or raised at the same time as, a claim of unfair dismissal. For example, sex discrimination cases, and claims for unpaid wages are not covered by the Scheme.

15   If a claim of unfair dismissal has been referred for resolution under the Scheme, any other claim, even if part of the same dispute, must be settled separately, or referred to the employment tribunal, or withdrawn. In the event that different aspects of the same dispute are being heard in the employment tribunal as well as under the Scheme, the

arbitrator may decide, if appropriate or convenient, to postpone the arbitration proceedings pending a determination by the employment tribunal.

Waiver of jurisdictional issues

16 Because of its informal nature, the Scheme is not designed for disputes raising jurisdictional issues, such as for example:

- whether or not the Employee was employed by the Employer;
- whether or not the Employee had the necessary period of continuous service to bring the claim;
- whether or not time limits have expired and/or should be extended.

17 Accordingly, when agreeing to refer a dispute to arbitration under the Scheme, both parties will be taken to have accepted as a condition of the Scheme that no jurisdictional issue is in dispute between them. The arbitrator will not therefore deal with such issues during the arbitration process, even if they are raised by the parties, and the parties will be taken to have waived any rights in that regard.

18 In particular, in agreeing to arbitration under the Scheme, the parties will be treated as having agreed that a dismissal has taken place.

Inappropriate cases

19 The Scheme is not intended for disputes involving complex legal issues. Whilst such cases will be accepted for determination (subject to the Terms of Reference), parties are advised, where appropriate, to consider applying to the employment tribunal or settling their dispute by other means.

VI   ACCESS TO THE SCHEME

20 The Scheme is an entirely voluntary system of dispute resolution: it will only apply if parties have so agreed.

Requirements for entry into the Scheme

21 Any agreement to submit a dispute to arbitration under the Scheme must satisfy the following requirements (an 'Arbitration Agreement'):

i   the agreement must be in writing;

ii   the agreement must concern an existing dispute;

iii the agreement must not seek to alter or vary any provision of the Scheme;

iv   the agreement must have been reached either:

   (a) where a conciliation officer has taken action under section 18 of the Employment Tribunals Act 1996 (a 'Conciliated Agreement') or

   (b) through a compromise agreement, where the conditions regulating such agreements under the Employment Rights Act 1996 are satisfied (a 'Compromise Agreement');

v   the agreement must be accompanied by a completed Waiver Form for each party, in the form of Appendix A.

22 Where an agreement fails to satisfy any one of these requirements, no valid reference to the Scheme will have been made, and the parties will have to settle their dispute by other means or have recourse to the employment tribunal.

23 Where:

i   a dispute concerning unfair dismissal claims as well as other claims has been referred to the employment tribunal, and

ii the parties have agreed to settle the other claims and refer the unfair dismissal claim to arbitration under the Scheme, a separate settlement must be reached referring the unfair dismissal claim to arbitration which satisfies all the requirements listed above (although it may form part of one overall settlement document).

Notification to Acas of an Arbitration Agreement

24 All Arbitration Agreements must be notified to Acas within six weeks of their conclusion, by either of the parties or their independent advisers or representatives, or an Acas conciliator, sending a copy of the agreement and Waiver Forms, together with IT1 and IT3 forms if these have been completed, to the Acas Arbitration Section.

25 For the purposes of the previous paragraph, an Arbitration Agreement is treated as 'concluded' on the date it is signed, or if signed by different people at different times, on the date of the last signature.

26 Where an Arbitration Agreement is not notified to Acas within six weeks, Acas will not arrange for the appointment of an arbitrator under the Scheme, unless notification within that time was not reasonably practicable. Any party seeking to notify Acas of an Arbitration Agreement outside this period must explain in writing to the Acas Arbitration Section the reason for the delay. Acas shall appoint an arbitrator, in accordance with the appointment provisions below, to consider the explanation, and that arbitrator may seek the views of the other party, and may call both parties to a hearing to establish the reasons for the delay. The arbitrator shall then rule in an award on whether or not the agreement can be accepted for hearing under the Scheme.

27 Any such hearing and award will be governed by the provisions of this Scheme.

Consolidation of proceedings

28 Where all parties so agree in writing, Acas may consolidate different arbitral proceedings under the Scheme.

VII   SETTLEMENT AND WITHDRAWAL FROM THE SCHEME

Withdrawal by the Employee

29 At any stage of the arbitration process, once an Arbitration Agreement has been concluded and the reference has been accepted by Acas, the party bringing the unfair dismissal claim may withdraw from the Scheme, provided that any such withdrawal is in writing. Such a withdrawal shall constitute a dismissal of the claim.

Withdrawal by the Employer

30 Once an Arbitration Agreement has been concluded and the reference has been accepted by Acas, the party against whom a claim is brought cannot unilaterally withdraw from the Scheme.

Settlement

31 Parties are free to reach an agreement settling the dispute at any stage.

32 If such an agreement is reached:

i upon the joint written request of the parties to the arbitrator or the Acas Arbitration Section, the arbitrator (if appointed) or the Acas Arbitration Section (if no arbitrator has been appointed) shall terminate the arbitration proceedings;

ii if so requested by the parties, the arbitrator (if appointed) may record the settlement in the form of an agreed award (on a covering *pro forma*).

33 An agreed award shall state that it is an award of the arbitrator by consent and shall have the same status and effect as any other award on the merits of the case.

34 In rendering an agreed award, the arbitrator:

i may only record the parties' agreed wording;

ii may not approve, vary, transcribe, interpret or ratify a settlement in any way;

iii may not record any settlement beyond the scope of the Scheme, the Arbitration Agreement or the reference to the Scheme as initially accepted by Acas.

VIII APPOINTMENT OF AN ARBITRATOR

The Acas Arbitration Panel

35 Arbitrators are selected to serve on the Acas Arbitration Panel on the basis of their practical knowledge and experience of discipline and dismissal issues in the workplace. They are recruited through an open recruitment exercise, and appointed to the Panel on the basis of standard terms of appointment. It is a condition of their appointment that they exercise their duties in accordance with the terms of this Scheme. Each appointment is initially for a period of two years, although it may be renewed by Acas, at the latter's discretion. Payment is made by Acas on the basis of time spent in connection with arbitral proceedings.

Appointment to a case

36 Arbitral appointments are made exclusively by Acas from the Acas Arbitration Panel. Parties will have no choice of arbitrator.

37 Once Acas has been notified of a valid Arbitration Agreement, it will select and appoint an arbitrator, and notify all parties of the name of the arbitrator so appointed.

Arbitrator's duty of disclosure

38 Immediately following selection (and before an appointment is confirmed by Acas), every arbitrator shall disclose in writing to Acas (to be forwarded to the parties) any circumstances known to him or her likely to give rise to any justifiable doubts as to his or her impartiality, or confirm in writing that there are no such circumstances.

39 Once appointed, and until the arbitration is concluded, every arbitrator shall be under a continuing duty forthwith to disclose to Acas (to be forwarded to the parties) any such circumstances which may have arisen since appointment.

Removal of arbitrators

40 Arbitrators may only be removed by Acas or the court (under the provisions in paragraphs 41 to 43 below).

41 Applications under the Scheme to remove an arbitrator on any of the grounds set out in sections 24(1)(a) and (c) of the Arbitration Act 1996 shall be made in the first instance to Acas (addressed to the Acas Arbitration Section).

42 If Acas refuses such an application, a party may thereafter apply to the court.

43 (1) *Sections 24(1)(a) and (c), 24(2), 24(3), 24(5) and 24(6) of the Arbitration Act 1996[a] shall apply to arbitrations conducted in accordance with the Scheme, subject to the following modifications.*

    (2) *In subsection (1) for '(upon notice to the other parties, to the arbitrator concerned and to any other arbitrator) apply to the court' substitute '(upon notice to the other party, to the arbitrator concerned and to the Advisory, Conciliation and Arbitration Service ("Acas")) apply to the High Court or Central London County Court'.*

(a) 1996 c23.

Sections 24(1)(a) and (c), (2), (3), (5) and (6) of the Arbitration Act 1996 provide as follows:

24(1) A party to arbitral proceedings may (upon notice to the other parties, to the arbitrator concerned and to any other arbitrator) apply to the court to remove an arbitrator on any of the following grounds –

    (a) that circumstances exist that give rise to justifiable doubts as to his impartiality;

    ...

    (c) that he is physically or mentally incapable of conducting the proceedings or there are justifiable doubts as to his capacity to do so;

  ...

    (2) If there is an arbitral or other institution or person vested by the parties with power to remove an arbitrator, the court shall not exercise its power of removal unless satisfied that the applicant has first exhausted any available recourse to that institution or person.

    (3) The arbitral tribunal may continue the arbitral proceedings and make an award while an application to the court under this section is pending.

  ...

    (5) The arbitrator concerned is entitled to appear and be heard by the court before it makes any order under this section.

    (6) The leave of the court is required for any appeal from a decision of the court under this section.

(3) *In subsection (2) –*

    (a) *omit 'If there is an arbitral or other institution or person vested by the parties with power to remove an arbitrator';*

    (b) *for 'that institution or person' substitute 'Acas'.*

44 The arbitrator may continue the proceedings and make an award while an application to Acas (as well as the court) to remove him or her is pending.

Death of an arbitrator

45 The authority of an arbitrator is personal and ceases on his or her death.

Replacement of arbitrators

46 Where an arbitrator ceases to hold office for any reason, he or she shall be replaced by Acas in accordance with the appointment provisions above.

47 Once appointed, the replacement arbitrator shall determine whether and, if so, to what extent the previous proceedings should stand.

IX   GENERAL DUTY OF THE ARBITRATOR

48 The arbitrator shall:

    i   act fairly and impartially as between the parties, giving each party a reasonable opportunity of putting his or her case and dealing with that of his or her opponent, and

    ii   adopt procedures suitable to the circumstances of the particular case, avoiding unnecessary delay or expense, so as to provide a fair means for the resolution of the matters falling to be determined.

49 The arbitrator shall comply with the general duty (see paragraph 48 above) in conducting the arbitral proceedings, in his or her decisions on matters of procedure and evidence and in the exercise of all other powers conferred on him or her.

X   GENERAL DUTY OF THE PARTIES

50 The parties shall do all things necessary for the proper and expeditious conduct of the arbitral proceedings. This includes (without limitation) complying without delay with any determination of the arbitrator as to procedural or evidential matters, or with any order or directions of the arbitrator, and co-operating in the arrangement of any hearing.

XI   CONFIDENTIALITY AND PRIVACY

51 Arbitrations, and all associated procedures under the Scheme, are strictly private and confidential.

52 Hearings may only be attended by the arbitrator, the parties, their representatives, any interpreters, witnesses and a legal adviser if appointed. If the parties so agree, an Acas official or arbitrator in training may also attend.

XII   ARRANGEMENTS FOR THE HEARING

Initial arrangements

53 A hearing must be held in every case, notwithstanding any agreement between the parties to a purely written procedure.

54 Once an arbitrator has been appointed by Acas, a hearing shall be arranged as soon as reasonably practicable by him or her, with the administrative assistance of the Acas Arbitration Section.

55 The arbitrator shall decide the date and venue for the hearing, insofar as an agreement cannot be reached with all parties within two months of the initial notification to Acas of the Arbitration Agreement.

56 The Acas Arbitration Section shall contact all parties with details of the date and venue for the hearing.

Expedited hearings

57 If:

i   before the parties have agreed to refer a dispute to arbitration under the Scheme, an employment tribunal makes an order under interim relief provisions, or

ii   in the arbitrator's discretion, other relevant circumstances exist, the arbitrator may expedite the hearing, on the application of any party.

Venue

58 Hearings may be held in any venue, provided that the hearing will only be held at the Employee's former workplace, or a similarly non-neutral venue, if all parties so agree.

59 Where premises have to be hired for a hearing, Acas shall meet the reasonable costs of so doing.

Assistance

60 Where a party needs the services of an interpreter, signer or communicator at the hearing, Acas should be so informed well in advance of the hearing. Where an arbitrator agrees that such assistance is required, Acas shall meet the reasonable costs of providing this.

Travelling expenses/loss of earnings

61 Every party shall meet their own travelling expenses and those of their representatives and witnesses.

62 No loss of earnings are payable by Acas to anyone involved in the arbitration. However, where an arbitrator rules that a dismissal was unfair, he or she may include in the calculation of any compensation a sum to cover reasonable travelling expenses and loss of earnings incurred by the Employee personally in attending the hearing.

Applications for postponements of, or different venues for, initial hearings

63 Any application for a postponement of, or a different venue for, an initial hearing must be made in writing, with reasons, to the arbitrator via the Acas Arbitration Section within 14 days of the date of the letter notifying the hearing arrangements. Such applications will be determined by the arbitrator without an oral hearing after all parties have received a copy of the application and been given a reasonable opportunity to respond.

64 If the application is rejected, the initial hearing will be held on the original date and/or in the original venue.

65 This provision does not affect the arbitrator's general discretion (set out below) with respect to postponements after an initial hearing has been fixed, or with respect to other aspects of the procedure. In particular, procedural applications may be made to the arbitrator at the hearing itself.

XIII   NON-COMPLIANCE WITH PROCEDURE

66 If a party fails to comply with any aspect of the procedure set out in this Scheme, or any order or direction by the arbitrator, or fails to comply with the general duty in section X above, the arbitrator may (in addition to any other power set out in this Scheme):

i   adjourn any hearing, where it would be unfair on any party to proceed; and/or

ii   draw such adverse inferences from the act of non-compliance as the circumstances justify.

XIV   OUTLINE OF PROCEDURE BEFORE THE HEARING

67 Once a hearing has been fixed, the following procedure shall apply, subject to any direction by the arbitrator.

Written materials

68 At least 14 days before the date of the hearing, each party shall send to the Acas Arbitration Section (for forwarding to the arbitrator and the other party) one copy of a written statement of case, together with:

i   any supporting documentation or other material to be relied upon at the hearing; and where appropriate

ii   a list of the names and title/role of all those people who will accompany each party to the hearing or be called as a witness.

69 Written statements of case should briefly set out the main particulars of each party's case, which can then be expanded upon if necessary at the hearing itself. The statement should include an explanation of the events which led up to the dismissal, including an account of the sequence and outcome of any relevant meetings, interviews or discussions. The parties should come to the hearing prepared to address the practicability of reinstatement or re-engagement, insofar as the Employee seeks such remedies.

70 Supporting documentation or other material may include (without limitation) copies of:

i   contracts of employment;

ii   letters of appointment;

iii written statement of particulars of employment;

iv time sheets and attendance records;

v performance appraisal reports;

vi warning and dismissal letters;

vii written reasons for dismissal, where these have been given;

viii company handbooks, rules and procedures;

ix any information which will help the arbitrator to assess compensation, including (without limitation):

    (a) pay slips, P60s or wage records;

    (b) details of benefits paid to the Employee such as travelling expenses and free or subsidised accommodation;

    (c) guidance about, and (if available) actuarial assessments of, pension entitlements;

    (d) details of any welfare benefits received;

    (e) evidence of attempts to find other work, or otherwise mitigate the loss arising from the dismissal;

x signed statements of any witnesses or outlines of evidence to be given by witnesses at the hearing.

71 The parties must also supply details of any relevant awards of compensation that may have been made by any other tribunal or court in connection with the subject matter of the claim.

72 Legible copies of documents must be supplied to Acas even if they have already been supplied to an Acas conciliator before the Arbitration Agreement was concluded.

73 No information on the conciliation process, if any, shall be disclosed by an Acas conciliator to the arbitrator.

Submissions, evidence and witnesses not previously notified

74 Written statements of case and documentary or other material that have not been provided to the Acas Arbitration Section prior to the hearing (in accordance with paragraph 68 above) may only be relied upon at the hearing with the arbitrator's permission.

75 All representatives and witnesses who have been listed as accompanying a party at the hearing should be present at the start of the hearing. Witnesses who have not been included in a list submitted to the Acas Arbitration Section prior to the hearing may only be called with the arbitrator's permission.

Requests for documents

76 Any party may request the other party to produce copies of relevant documents which are not in the requesting party's possession, custody or control. Although the arbitrator has no power to compel a party to comply, the arbitrator may draw an adverse inference from a party's failure to comply with a reasonable request.

Requests for attendance of witnesses

77 Although the arbitrator has no power to compel the attendance of anybody at the hearing, the arbitrator may draw an adverse inference if an employer who is a party to the

arbitration fails or refuses to allow current employees or other workers (who have relevant evidence to give) time off from work to attend the hearing, should such an employer be so requested.

Preliminary hearings and directions

78 Where the arbitrator believes that there may be considerable differences between the parties over any issue, including the availability or exchange of documents, or the availability of witnesses, the arbitrator may call the parties to a preliminary hearing to address such issues, or he or she may give procedural directions in correspondence.

79 In the course of a preliminary hearing or in correspondence, the arbitrator may express views on the desirability of information and/or evidence being available at the hearing.

XV   OUTLINE OF PROCEDURE AT THE HEARING

Arbitrator's overall discretion

80 Subject to the arbitrator's general duty (Section IX above), and subject to the points set out below, the conduct of the hearing and all procedural and evidential matters (including applications for adjournments and changes in venue) shall be for the arbitrator to decide.

Language

81 The language of the proceedings shall be English, unless the Welsh language is applicable by virtue of the Welsh Language Act 1993 (as amended from time to time). Reference should be made to paragraph 60 above if the Welsh language is to be used.

Witnesses

82 No party or witness shall be cross-examined by a party or representative, or examined on oath or affirmation.

Examination by the arbitrator

83 The arbitrator shall have the right to address questions directly to either party or to anybody else attending the hearing, and to take the initiative in ascertaining the facts and (where applicable) the law.

Representatives

84 The parties may be accompanied by any person chosen by them to help them to present their case at the hearing, although no special status will be accorded to legally qualified representatives. Each party is liable for any fees or expenses incurred by any representatives they appoint.

Strict rules of evidence

85 The arbitrator will not apply strict rules of evidence (or any other rules) as to the admissibility, relevance or weight of any material (oral, written or other) sought to be tendered on any matters of fact or opinion.

Interim relief

86 The arbitrator shall have no power to order provisional or interim relief, but may expedite the proceedings where appropriate.

Non-attendance at the hearing

87 If, without showing sufficient cause, a party fails to attend or be represented at a hearing, the arbitrator may:

   i   continue the hearing in that party's absence, and in such a case shall take into account any written submissions and documents that have already been submitted by that party; or

   ii adjourn the hearing.

88 In the case of the non-attendance of the Employee, if the arbitrator decides to adjourn the hearing, he or she may write to the Employee to request an explanation for the non-attendance. If the arbitrator decides that the Employee has not demonstrated sufficient cause for the non-attendance, he or she may rule in an award that the claim be treated as dismissed.

Post-hearing written materials

89 No further submissions or evidence will be accepted after the end of the substantive hearing without the arbitrator's permission, which will only be granted in exceptional circumstances. Where permission is granted, any material is to be sent to the Acas Arbitration Section, to be forwarded to the arbitrator and all other parties.

XVI   QUESTIONS OF EC LAW AND THE HUMAN RIGHTS ACT 1998

Appointment of legal adviser

90 The arbitrator shall have the power, on the application of any party or of his or her own motion, to require the appointment of a legal adviser to assist with respect to any issue of EC law or the Human Rights Act 1998 that, in the arbitrator's view and subject to paragraph 12 above (Arbitrator's Terms of Reference), might be involved and relevant to the resolution of the dispute.

91 The legal adviser will be appointed by Acas, to report to the arbitrator and the parties, and shall be subject to the duty of disclosure set out in paragraphs 38 and 39 above.

92 The arbitrator shall allow the legal adviser to attend the proceedings, and may order an adjournment and/or change in venue to facilitate this.

93 The parties shall be given a reasonable opportunity to comment on any information, opinion or advice offered by the legal adviser, following which the arbitrator shall take such information, opinion or advice into account in determining the dispute.

Court determination of preliminary points

94 (1) *Section 45 of the Arbitration Act 1996[a] shall apply to arbitrations conducted in accordance with the Scheme, subject to the following modifications.*

(2) *In subsection (1) –*

(a) *for 'Unless otherwise agreed by the parties, the court' substitute 'The High Court or Central London County Court';*

(b) *for 'any question of law' substitute 'any question (a) of EC law, or (b) concerning the application of the Human Rights Act 1998';*

(c) *omit 'An agreement to dispense with reasons for the tribunal's award shall be considered an agreement to exclude the court's jurisdiction under this section'.*

(3) *In subsection (2)(b) omit sub-paragraph (i).*

(4) *Omit subsection (4).*

(5) *After subsection (6), insert –*

'(7) In this section, 'EC law' means –

(a) *any enactment in the domestic legislation of England and Wales giving effect to rights, powers, liabilities, obligations and restrictions from time to time created or arising by or under the Community Treaties, and*

(b) *any such rights, powers, liabilities, obligations and restrictions which are not given effect by any such enactment.'*

(a) 1996 c23.

Section 45 of the Arbitration Act 1996 provides as follows:

(1) Unless otherwise agreed by the parties, the court may on the application of a party to arbitral proceedings (upon notice to the other parties) determine any question of law arising in the course of the proceedings which the court is satisfied substantially affects the rights of one or more of the parties. An agreement to dispense with reasons for the tribunal's award shall be considered an agreement to exclude the court's jurisdiction under this section.

(2) An application under this section shall not be considered unless –

(a) it is made with the agreement of all the other parties to the proceedings, or

(b) it is made with the permission of the tribunal and the court is satisfied –

(i) that the determination of the question is likely to produce substantial savings in costs, and

(ii) that the application was made without delay.

(3) The application shall identify the question of law to be determined and, unless made with the agreement of all the other parties to the proceedings, shall state the grounds on which it is said that the question should be decided by the court.

(4) Unless otherwise agreed by the parties, the arbitral tribunal may continue the arbitral proceedings and make an award while an application to the court under this section is pending.

(5) Unless the court gives leave, no appeal lies from a decision of the court whether the conditions specified in subsection (2) are met.

(6) The decision of the court on the question of law shall be treated as a judgment of the court for the purposes of an appeal.

But no appeal lies without the leave of the court which shall not be given unless the court considers that the question is one of general importance, or is one which for some other special reason should be considered by the Court of Appeal.

XVII AUTOMATIC UNFAIRNESS

95 In deciding whether the dismissal was fair or unfair, subject to paragraph 12 above (Arbitrator's Terms of Reference), the arbitrator shall have regard to

   i   any provision of Part X of the Employment Rights Act 1996 (as amended from time to time) requiring a dismissal for a particular reason to be regarded as unfair, or

   ii   any other legislative provision requiring a dismissal for a particular reason to be regarded as unfair for the purpose of Part X of the Employment Rights Act 1996.

XVIII AWARDS

Form of the award

96 The award shall be in writing, signed by the arbitrator.

97 The award (unless it is an agreed award) shall:

   i   identify the reason (or, if more than one, the principal reason) for the dismissal (or, in a redundancy case, the reason for which the employee was selected for dismissal);

   ii   contain the main considerations which were taken into account in reaching the decision that the dismissal was fair or unfair;

   iii state the decision(s) of the arbitrator;

   iv   state the remedy awarded, together with an explanation;

   v   state the date when it was made.

Awards on different issues

98 The arbitrator may make more than one award at different times on different aspects of the matters to be determined.

99 The arbitrator may, in particular, make an award relating:

   i   to an issue affecting the whole claim, or

   ii   to a part only of the claim submitted to him or her for decision.

100 If the arbitrator does so, he or she shall specify in his or her award the issue, or the claim or part of a claim, which is the subject matter of the award.

Remedies

101 In every case, the arbitrator shall:

   i   explain to the Employee what orders for reinstatement or re-engagement may be made in an award and under what circumstances these may be granted; and

   ii   ask the Employee whether he or she wishes the arbitrator to make such an award.

102 In the event that the arbitrator finds that the dismissal was unfair:

   i   if the Employee expresses such a wish, the arbitrator may make, in an award, an order for reinstatement or re-engagement (in accordance with the provisions below); or

   ii   if no such order for reinstatement or re-engagement is made, the arbitrator shall make an award of compensation (calculated in accordance with the provisions below) to be paid by the Employer to the Employee.

103 In cases where the arbitrator finds that the dismissal was unfair by reason of the operation of EC law, the arbitrator shall apply the relevant provisions of English law with respect to remedies for unfair dismissal, insofar as these may differ from sections XIX and XX of the Scheme.

XIX   AWARDS OF REINSTATEMENT OR RE-ENGAGEMENT

Definitions

104 An order for reinstatement (which must be in the form of an award) is an order that the Employer shall treat the Employee in all respects as if he or she had not been dismissed.

105 An order for re-engagement (which must be in the form of an award) is an order, on such terms as the arbitrator may decide, that the Employee be engaged by the Employer, or by a successor of the Employer or by an associated Employer, in employment comparable to that from which he or she was dismissed or in other suitable employment.

Choice of remedy

106 In exercising his or her discretion with respect to the remedy to be awarded under paragraph 102 i above, the arbitrator shall first consider whether to make an order for reinstatement, and in so doing shall take into account:

i   whether the Employee wishes to be reinstated;

ii   whether it is practicable for the Employer to comply with an order for reinstatement; and

iii where the Employee caused or contributed to some extent to the dismissal, whether it would be just to order his or her reinstatement.

107 If the arbitrator decides not to make an order for reinstatement, he or she shall then consider whether to make an order for re-engagement and, if so, on what terms. In so doing, the arbitrator shall take into account:

i   any wish expressed by the Employee as to the nature of the order to be made;

ii   whether it is practicable for the Employer (or a successor or an associated employer) to comply with an order for re-engagement; and

iii where the Employee caused or contributed to some extent to the dismissal, whether it would be just to order his or her re-engagement and (if so) on what terms.

108 If ordering re-engagement, the arbitrator shall do so on terms which are, so far as is reasonably practicable, as favourable as an order for reinstatement (with the exception of cases where contributory fault has been taken into account under paragraph 107 iii above).

Permanent replacements

109 Where in any case an Employer has engaged a permanent replacement for a dismissed Employee, the arbitrator shall not take that fact into account in determining, for the purposes of paragraphs 106 ii and 107 ii above, whether it is practicable to comply with an order for reinstatement or re-engagement. This does not apply, however, where the Employer shows:

i   that it was not practicable for him or her to arrange for the dismissed Employee's work to be done without engaging a permanent replacement, or

ii   that:

(a) he or she engaged the replacement after the lapse of a reasonable period, without having heard from the dismissed Employee that he or she wished to be reinstated or re-engaged, and

(b) when the Employer engaged the replacement it was no longer reasonable for him or her to arrange for the dismissed Employee's work to be done except by a permanent replacement.

Reinstatement

110 On making an order for reinstatement, the arbitrator shall specify:

i   any amount payable by the Employer in respect of any benefit which the Employee might reasonably be expected to have had but for the dismissal (including arrears of pay) for the period between the date of termination of employment and the date of reinstatement,

ii   any rights and privileges (including seniority and pension rights) which must be restored to the Employee, and

iii the date by which the order must be complied with.

111 If the Employee would have benefited from an improvement in his or her terms and conditions of employment had he or she not been dismissed, an order for reinstatement shall require him or her to be treated as if he or she had benefited from that improvement from the date on which he or she would have done so but for being dismissed.

112 In calculating for the purposes of paragraph 110 i above any amount payable by the Employer, the arbitrator shall take into account, so as to reduce the Employer's liability, any sums received by the Employee in respect of the period between the date of termination of employment and the date of reinstatement by way of:

i   wages in lieu of notice or *ex gratia* payments paid by the Employer, or

ii   remuneration paid in respect of employment with another employer, and such other benefits as the arbitrator thinks appropriate in the circumstances.

Re-engagement

113 On making an order for re-engagement the arbitrator shall specify the terms on which reengagement is to take place, including:

i   the identity of the employer,

ii   the nature of the employment,

iii the remuneration for the employment,

iv   any amount payable by the employer in respect of any benefit which the Employee might reasonably be expected to have had but for the dismissal (including arrears of pay) for the period between the date of termination of employment and the date of re-engagement,

    v   any rights and privileges (including seniority and pension rights) which must be restored to the Employee, and

    vi   the date by which the order must be complied with.

114 In calculating, for the purposes of paragraph 113 iv above, any amount payable by the employer, the arbitrator shall take into account, so as to reduce the Employer's liability, any sums received by the Employee in respect of the period between the date of termination of employment and the date of re-engagement by way of:

    i   wages in lieu of notice or *ex gratia* payments paid by the employer, or

    ii   remuneration paid in respect of employment with another employer, and such other benefits as the arbitrator thinks appropriate in the circumstances.

Continuity of employment

115 The Employee's continuity of employment will be preserved in the same way as it would be under an award of the employment tribunal.

XX   AWARDS OF COMPENSATION

116 When an arbitrator makes an award of compensation, instead of an award for reinstatement or re-engagement, such compensation shall consist of a *basic amount* and a *compensatory amount*.

117 Where paragraph 142 below applies, an award of compensation shall also include a *supplementary amount*.

The basic amount

118 (Subject to the following provisions) the basic amount shall be calculated by:

    i   determining the period, ending with the effective date of termination (see paragraph 119 below), during which the Employee has been continuously employed (see paragraph 120 below),

    ii   reckoning backwards from the end of that period the number of years of employment falling within that period, and

    iii allowing the appropriate amount (see paragraph 121 below) for each of those years of employment.

119 As to the 'effective date of termination':

    i   the 'effective date of termination' means:

        (a) in relation to an Employee whose contract of employment is terminated by notice, whether given by his or her Employer or by the Employee, the date on which the notice expires;

        (b) in relation to an Employee whose contract of employment is terminated without notice, the date on which the termination takes effect; and

        (c) in relation to an Employee who is employed under a contract for a fixed term which expires without being renewed under the same contract, the date on which the term expires.

ii   Where:

   (a) the contract of employment is terminated by the Employer, and

   (b) the notice required by section 86 of the Employment Rights Act 1996 (as amended from time to time) to be given by an Employer would, if duly given on the material date, expire on a date later than the effective date of termination (as defined in paragraph 119 i above),

   the later date is the effective date of termination.

iii In paragraph 119 ii (b) above, 'the material date' means:

   (a) the date when notice of termination was given by the Employer, or

   (b) where no notice was given, the date when the contract of employment was terminated by the Employer.

iv   Where:

   (a) the contract of employment is terminated by the Employee, and

   (b) the material date does not fall during a period of notice given by the Employer to terminate that contract, and

   (c) had the contract been terminated not by the Employee but by notice given on the material date by the Employer, that notice would have been required by section 86 of the Employment Rights Act 1996 (as amended from time to time) to expire on a date later than the effective date of termination (as defined in paragraph 119 i above), the later date is the effective date of termination.

v   In paragraph 119 iv above, 'the material date' means:

   (a) the date when notice of termination was given by the Employee, or

   (b) where no notice was given, the date when the contract of employment was terminated by the Employee.

120 In determining 'continuous employment', the arbitrator shall have regard to Chapter I of Part XIV of the Employment Rights Act 1996 (as amended from time to time).

121 The 'appropriate amount' means:

i   one and a half weeks' pay for a year of employment in which the Employee was not below the age of 41,

ii   one week's pay for a year of employment (not within sub-paragraph i above) in which he or she was not below the age of 22, and

iii half a week's pay for a year of employment not within sub-paragraphs i or ii above.

122 In calculating the amount of a week's pay of an Employee, the arbitrator shall have regard to Chapter II of Part XIV of the Employment Rights Act 1996, as amended from time to time, or any other relevant statutory provision applicable to the calculation of a week's pay.

123 Where 20 years of employment have been reckoned under paragraph 118 above, no account shall be taken under that paragraph of any year of employment earlier than those 20 years.

124 Where the effective date of termination is after the 64th anniversary of the day of the Employee's birth, the amount arrived at under paragraphs 118, 121 and 123 above shall be reduced by the 'appropriate fraction' (see paragraph 125 below).

125 The 'appropriate fraction' means the fraction of which:

i   the numerator is the number of whole months reckoned from the 64th anniversary of the day of the Employee's birth in the period beginning with that anniversary and ending with the effective date of termination (see paragraph 119 above), and

ii   the denominator is 12.

Minimum basic amounts in certain cases

126 A 'minimum basic amount' shall apply where the arbitrator has found that the dismissal was unfair, and where the reason (or, if more than one, the principal reason):

* in a redundancy case (see paragraph 129 i below), for selecting the Employee for dismissal, or

* otherwise, for the dismissal was one of the following:

Health and safety cases

i   Having been designated by the Employer to carry out activities in connection with preventing or reducing risks to health and safety at work, the Employee carried out (or proposed to carry out) any such activities;

ii   being a representative of workers on matters of health and safety at work or member of a safety committee:

(a) in accordance with arrangements established under or by virtue of any enactment, or

(b) by reason of being acknowledged as such by the Employer,

the Employee performed (or proposed to perform) any functions as such a representative or a member of such a committee.

Working time cases

iii Being:

(a) a representative of members of the workforce for the purposes of Schedule 1 to the Working Time Regulations 1998 (as amended from time to time), or

(b) a candidate in an election in which any person elected will, on being elected, be such a representative,

performed (or proposed to perform) any functions or activities as such a representative or candidate.

Trustees of occupational pension schemes

iv   Being a trustee of a relevant occupational pension scheme which relates to his or her employment, the Employee performed (or proposed to perform) any functions as such a trustee.

Employee representatives

v   Being:

(a) an employee representative for the purposes of Chapter II of Part IV of the Trade Union and Labour Relations (Consolidation) Act 1992 (redundancies) or Regulations 10 and 11 of the Transfer of Undertakings (Protection of Employment) Regulations 1981 (as amended from time to time), or

(b) a candidate in an election in which any person elected will, on being elected, be such an employee representative, performed (or proposed to perform) any functions or activities as such an employee representative or candidate;

vi the Employee took part in an election of employee representatives for the purposes of Chapter II of Part IV of the Trade Union and Labour Relations (Consolidation) Act 1992 (redundancies) or Regulations 10 and 11 of the Transfer of Undertakings (Protection of Employment) Regulations 1981 (as amended from time to time).

Union membership or activities

vii The Employee:

(a) was, or proposed to become, a member of an independent trade union, or

(b) had taken part, or proposed to take part, in the activities of an independent trade union at an appropriate time, or

(c) was not a member of any trade union, or of a particular trade union, or of one of a number of particular trade unions, or had refused, or proposed to refuse, to become or remain a member.

viii For the purposes of paragraphs vii above to xi below, in defining the terms 'trade union' and 'independent trade union', the arbitrator shall have regard to sections 1 and 5 of the Trade Union and Labour Relations (Consolidation) Act 1992, as amended from time to time.

ix For the purposes of paragraph vii (b) above, an 'appropriate time' means:

(a) a time outside the employee's working hours, or

(b) a time within his or her working hours at which, in accordance with arrangements agreed with or consent given by his or her employer, it is permissible for him or her to take part in the activities of a trade union;

and for this purpose 'working hours', in relation to an Employee, means any time when, in accordance with his or her contract of employment, he or she is required to be at work.

x Where the reason, or one of the reasons, for the dismissal was:

(a) the employee's refusal, or proposed refusal, to comply with a requirement (whether or not imposed by his or her contract of employment or in writing) that, in the event of his or her not being a member of any trade union, or of a particular trade union, or of one of a number of particular trade unions, he or she must make one or more payments, or

(b) his or her objection, or proposed objection, (however expressed) to the operation of a provision (whether or not forming part of his or her contract of employment or in writing) under which, in the event mentioned in paragraph x (a) above, his or her employer is entitled to deduct one or more sums from the remuneration payable to him or her in respect of his or her employment,

the reason shall be treated as falling within paragraph vii (c) above.

xi References in paragraphs vii to x above to being, becoming or ceasing to remain a member of a trade union include references to being, becoming or ceasing to remain a member of a particular branch or section of that union or of one of a number of particular branches or sections of that trade union; and references to taking part in the activities of a trade union shall be similarly construed.

Other categories

xii Where the reason or principal reason for the dismissal of the Employee qualifies under any other applicable legislative provision for a minimum basic award.

127 Before any reductions are taken into account under paragraphs 130–34 below ('Reductions to the basic amount'), the 'minimum basic amount' shall not be less than:

i   in cases within paragraph 126 i, ii, iii, iv, v and vi above, the amount provided for in section 120(1) of the Employment Rights Act 1996, as amended from time to time;

ii   in cases within paragraph 126 vii above, the amount provided for in section 156 of the Trade Union and Labour Relations (Consolidation) Act 1992, as amended from time to time;

iii in cases within paragraph 126 xii above, the amount provided for in the relevant legislation.

Basic amount of two weeks' pay in certain cases

128 Where:

i   the arbitrator finds that the reason (or, where there is more than one, the principal reason) for the dismissal of the Employee is that he or she was redundant and

ii   the Employee:

(a) by virtue of section 138 of the Employment Rights Act 1996, as amended from time to time, is not regarded as dismissed for the purposes of Part XI of that Act, or

(b) by virtue of section 141 of that Act, as amended from time to time, is not, or (if he or she were otherwise entitled) would not be, entitled to a redundancy payment, the basic amount shall be two weeks' pay (for the definition of 'week's pay', see paragraph 122 above).

129 For the purposes of this Scheme:

i   for the definition of 'redundancy', the arbitrator shall have regard to section 139 of the Employment Rights Act 1996, as amended from time to time;

ii   for the definition of 'redundancy payment', the arbitrator shall have regard to Part XI of the Employment Rights Act 1996, as amended from time to time.

Reductions to the basic amount

130 Where the arbitrator finds that the Employee has unreasonably refused an offer by the Employee which (if accepted) would have the effect of reinstating the Employee in his or her employment in all respects as if he or she had not been dismissed, the arbitrator shall reduce or further reduce the basic amount to such extent as he or she considers just and equitable having regard to that finding.

131 Where the arbitrator considers that any conduct of the Employee before the dismissal (or, where the dismissal was with notice, before the notice was given) was such that it would be just and equitable to reduce or further reduce the basic amount to any extent, the arbitrator shall reduce or further reduce that amount accordingly. In assessing such conduct, the arbitrator shall disregard (if relevant) those matters set out in section 155 of the Trade Union and Labour Relations (Consolidation) Act 1992, as amended from time to time.

132 The preceding paragraph does not apply in a redundancy case (see paragraph 129 i above) unless the reason for selecting the Employee for dismissal was one of those specified in paragraph 126 above ('Minimum basic amounts in certain cases'), and in such a case, the preceding paragraph applies only to so much of the basic amount as is payable because of paragraph 126 above.

133 Where the Employee has been awarded any amount in respect of the dismissal under a dismissal procedures agreement designated under section 110 of the Employment Rights Act 1996 (as amended from time to time), the arbitrator shall reduce or further reduce the amount of the basic award to such extent as he or she considers just and equitable having regard to that award.

134 The basic amount shall be reduced or further reduced by the amount of any payment made by the Employer to the Employee on the ground that the dismissal was by reason of redundancy (whether in pursuance of Part XI of the Employment Rights Act 1996, as amended from time to time, or otherwise).

The compensatory amount

135 (Subject to the following provisions) the compensatory amount shall be such as the arbitrator considers just and equitable in all the circumstances having regard to the loss sustained by the Employee in consequence of the dismissal – insofar as that loss is attributable to action taken by the Employer.

136 The loss referred to in paragraph 135 above shall be taken to include:

i any expenses reasonably incurred by the Employee in consequence of the dismissal, and

ii (subject to iii below) loss of any benefit which he or she might reasonably be expected to have had but for the dismissal.

iii In respect of any loss of:

– any entitlement or potential entitlement to a payment on account of dismissal by reason of redundancy (whether in pursuance of Part XI of the Employment Rights Act 1996, as amended from time to time, or otherwise) or

– any expectation of such a payment,

only the loss referable to the amount (if any) by which such a payment would have exceeded the basic amount in respect of the same dismissal (as calculated under the provisions set out above – but excluding any reductions under paragraphs 130–34 above ('Reductions to the basic amount')).

137 In ascertaining the loss referred to in paragraph 135 above, the arbitrator shall apply the principle that a person has a duty to mitigate his or her loss.

138 In determining, for the purposes of paragraph 135 above, how far any loss sustained by the Employee was attributable to action taken by the Employer, no account shall be taken of any pressure which by:

i calling, organising, procuring or financing a strike or other industrial action, or

ii threatening to do so, was exercised on the Employer to dismiss the Employee; and that question shall be determined as if no such pressure had been exercised.

Reductions to the compensatory amount

139 Where the arbitrator finds that the dismissal was to any extent caused or contributed to by any conduct of the Employee, he or she shall reduce the compensatory amount by such proportion as he or she considers just and equitable having regard to that finding. In assessing such conduct, the arbitrator shall disregard (if relevant) those matters set out in section 155 of the Trade Union and Labour Relations (Consolidation) Act 1992, as amended from time to time.

140 If:

i   any payment was made by the Employer to the Employee on the ground that the dismissal was by reason of redundancy (whether in pursuance of Part XI of the Employment Rights Act 1996, as amended from time to time, or otherwise); and

ii   the amount of such a payment exceeds the basic amount that would have been payable (under the provisions set out above – excluding for this purpose reductions on account of redundancy payments (see paragraph 129 above)),

that excess goes to reduce the compensatory amount.

Internal appeal procedures

141 Where an award of compensation is to be made, and the arbitrator finds that:

i   the Employer provided a procedure for appealing against dismissal, and

ii   the Employee was, at the time of the dismissal or within a reasonable period afterwards, given written notice stating that the Employer provided the procedure and including details of it, but

iii the Employee did not appeal against the dismissal under the procedure (otherwise than because the Employer prevented him or her from doing so), the arbitrator shall reduce the compensatory amount included in an award of compensation by such amount (if any) as he or she considers just and equitable.

142 Where an award of compensation is to be made, and the arbitrator finds that:

i   the Employer provided a procedure for appealing against dismissal, but

ii   the Employer prevented the Employee from appealing against the dismissal under the procedure, the award of compensation shall include a supplementary amount, being such amount (if any) as the arbitrator considers just and equitable.

143 In determining the amount of a reduction under paragraph 141 above or a supplementary amount under paragraph 142 above, the arbitrator shall have regard to all the circumstances of the case, including in particular the chances that an appeal under the procedure provided by the Employer would have been successful.

144 The amount of such a reduction or supplementary amount shall not exceed the amount of two weeks' pay (for the definition of 'week's pay', see paragraph 122 above).

Limits on the compensatory amount

145 With the exception of:

i   cases falling within sections 100 or 105(3), of the Employment Rights Act 1996, as amended from time to time (health and safety cases), and

ii   cases where the reason (or, if more than one, the principal reason):

(a) in a redundancy case, for selecting the Employee for dismissal, or

(b) otherwise for the dismissal,

was that the Employee made a protected disclosure (within the meaning of Part IVA of the Employment Rights Act 1996, as amended from time to time); and

iii   cases falling within any other exception to the statutory limit,

no compensatory amount awarded by an arbitrator shall exceed the statutory limit provided for in section 124(1) of the Employment Rights Act 1996, as amended from time to time.

146 The limit referred to above applies to the amount which the arbitrator would award (apart from paragraph 145 above) in respect of the subject matter of the complaint, after taking into account:

i   any payment made by the Employer to the Employee in respect of that matter, and

ii   any reduction in the amount of the award required by any enactment or rule of law.

Double recovery

147 Where the same acts of the Employer are relied upon by the Employee:

i   to ground a claim for unfair dismissal in arbitration as well as

ii   to ground a claim in the employment tribunal for discrimination (under the Sex Discrimination Act 1975 and/or the Race Relations Act 1976 and/or the Disability Discrimination Act 1995, or any other relevant statute),

the arbitrator shall not award compensation in respect of any loss or other matter which is to be or has been taken into account by the employment tribunal in awarding compensation with respect to the discrimination claim.

In this regard, the arbitrator shall have regard to any information supplied by the parties under paragraph 71 above.

XXI   ISSUE OF AWARDS AND CONFIDENTIALITY

148 The arbitrator's award shall be sent by Acas to both parties.

149 The award shall be confidential, and shall only be issued to the parties or to their nominated advisers or representatives. Awards will not be published by Acas, or lodged with the employment tribunal by Acas, although awards may be retained by Acas for monitoring and evaluation purposes, and, from time to time, Acas may publish general summary information concerning cases heard under the Scheme, without identifying any individual cases.

XXII   CORRECTION OF AWARDS

Scrutiny of awards by Acas

150 Before being sent to the parties, awards may be scrutinised by Acas to check for clerical or computational mistakes, errors arising from accidental slips or omissions, ambiguities, or errors of form. Without affecting the arbitrator's liberty of decision, Acas may refer the award back to the arbitrator (under the provisions below) in order to draw his or her attention to any such point.

Correction by the arbitrator

151 The arbitrator may, on his or her own initiative or on the application of a party or Acas:

   i   correct the award so as to remove any clerical or computational mistake, or error arising from an accidental slip or omission, or to clarify or remove any ambiguity in the award, or

   ii   make an additional award in respect of any part of the claim which was presented to the arbitrator but was not dealt with in the award.

152 Insofar as any such correction or additional award involves a new issue that was not previously before the parties, this power shall not be exercised without first affording the parties a reasonable opportunity to make written representations to the arbitrator.

153 Any application by a party for the exercise of this power must be made via the Acas Arbitration Section within 28 days of the date the award was despatched to the applying party by Acas.

154 Any correction of the award shall be made within 28 days of the date the application was received by the arbitrator or, where the correction is made by the arbitrator on his or her own initiative, within 28 days of the date of the award.

155 Any additional award shall be made within 56 days of the date of the original award.

156 Any correction of the award shall form part of the award.

XXIII   EFFECT OF AWARDS, ENFORCEMENT AND INTEREST

Effect of awards

157 Awards made by arbitrators under this Scheme are final and binding both on the parties and on any persons claiming through or under them.

158 This does not affect the right of a person to challenge an award under the provisions of the Arbitration Act 1996 as applied to this Scheme.

Enforcement

159 (1) *Section 66 of the Arbitration Act 1996*[a] *shall apply to arbitrations conducted in accordance with the Scheme, subject to the following modifications:*

(2) *In subsection (1) for 'tribunal pursuant to an arbitration agreement' substitute 'arbitrator pursuant to the Scheme (except for an award of reinstatement or re-engagement)'.*

(3) *In subsection (3) for '(see section 73)' substitute '(see section XXV of the Scheme)'.*

(4) *After subsection (4) insert –*

'(5) *In this section –*

"*the court" means the High Court or a county court; and*

"*the Scheme" means the arbitration scheme set out in the Schedule to the Acas Arbitration Scheme (England and Wales) Order 2001.'*

160 Awards of reinstatement or re-engagement will be enforced by the employment tribunal in accordance with section 117 of the Employment Rights Act 1996 (enforcement by award of compensation).

Interest

161 Awards of compensation that are not paid within 42 days of the date on which the award was despatched by Acas to the Employer will attract interest on the same basis as for employment tribunal awards.

(a) 1996 c23.

Section 66 of the Arbitration Act 1996 provides as follows:

(1) An award made by the tribunal pursuant to an arbitration agreement may, by leave of the court, be enforced in the same manner as a judgment or order of the court to the same effect.

(2) Where leave is so given, judgment may be entered in terms of the award.

(3) Leave to enforce an award shall not be given where, or to the extent that, the person against whom it is sought to be enforced shows that the tribunal lacked substantive jurisdiction to make the award.

The right to raise such an objection may have been lost (see section 73).

(4) Nothing in this section affects the recognition or enforcement of an award under any other enactment or rule of law, in particular under Part II of the Arbitration Act 1950 (enforcement of awards under Geneva Convention) or the provisions of Part III of this Act relating to the recognition and enforcement of awards under the New York Convention or by an action on the award.

XXIV CHALLENGING THE AWARD

Challenges on grounds of substantive jurisdiction

162 (1) *Section 67 of the Arbitration Act 1996[a] shall apply to arbitrations conducted in accordance with the Scheme, subject to the following modifications.*

(2) *In subsection (1) –*

(a) *for '(upon notice to the other parties and to the tribunal) apply to the court' substitute '(upon notice to the other party, to the arbitrator and to Acas) apply to the High Court or the Central London County Court';*

(b) *for '(see section 73)' substitute '(see section XXV of the Scheme)';*

(c) *after 'section 70(2) and (3)' insert 'as modified for the purposes of the Scheme'.*

(3) *After subsection (1) insert –*

'*(1A) In this section –*

"Arbitration Agreement" means an agreement to refer a dispute to arbitration in accordance with, and satisfying the requirements of, the Scheme;

"the Scheme" means the arbitration scheme set out in the Schedule to the Acas Arbitration Scheme (England and Wales) Order 2001; and

"substantive jurisdiction" means any issue as to –

(a) *the validity of the Arbitration Agreement and the application of the Scheme to the dispute or difference in question;*

(b) *the constitution of the arbitral tribunal; or*

(c) *the matters which have been submitted to arbitration in accordance with the Arbitration Agreement.'*

(a) Section 67 of the Arbitration Act 1996 provides as follows:
(1) A party to arbitral proceedings may (upon notice to the other parties and to the tribunal) apply to the court –
   (a) challenging any award of the arbitral tribunal as to its substantive jurisdiction; or
   (b) for an order declaring an award made by the tribunal on the merits to be of no effect, in whole or in part, because the tribunal did not have substantive jurisdiction.
   A party may lose the right to object (see section 73) and the right to apply is subject to the restrictions in section 70(2) and (3).
(2) The arbitral tribunal may continue the arbitral proceedings and make a further award while an application to the court under this section is pending in relation to an award as to jurisdiction.
(3) On an application under this section challenging an award of the arbitral tribunal as to its substantive jurisdiction, the court may by order –
   (a) confirm the award,
   (b) vary the award, or
   (c) set aside the award in whole or in part.
(4) The leave of the court is required for any appeal from a decision of the court under this section.

Challenges for serious irregularity

163 (1) *Section 68 of the Arbitration Act 1996[a] shall apply to arbitrations conducted in accordance with the Scheme, subject to the following modifications.*

  (2) *In subsection (1) –*

    (a) *for '(upon notice to the other parties and to the tribunal) apply to the court' substitute '(upon notice to the other party, to the arbitrator and to Acas) apply to the High Court or Central London County Court';*

    (b) *for '(see section 73)' substitute '(see Part XXV of the Scheme)';*

    (c) *after 'section 70(2) and (3)' insert 'as modified for the purposes of the Scheme'.*

  (3) *In subsection (2) –*

    (a) *in paragraph (a) for 'section 33 (general duty of tribunal)' substitute 'Part IX of the Scheme (General Duty of the Arbitrator)';*

    (b) *in paragraph (b) after 'see section 67' insert 'as modified for the purposes of the Scheme';*

(a) 1996 c23.

Section 68 of the Arbitration Act 1996 provides as follows:

(1) A party to arbitral proceedings may (upon notice to the other parties and to the tribunal) apply to the court challenging an award in the proceedings on the ground of serious irregularity affecting the tribunal, the proceedings or the award.

A party may lose the right to object (see section 73) and the right to apply is subject to the restrictions in section 70(2) and (3).

(2) Serious irregularity means an irregularity of one or more of the following kinds which the court considers has caused or will cause substantial injustice to the applicant –

  (a) failure by the tribunal to comply with section 33 (general duty of tribunal);

  (b) the tribunal exceeding its powers (otherwise than by exceeding its substantive jurisdiction: see section 67);

  (c) failure by the tribunal to conduct the proceedings in accordance with the procedure agreed by the parties;

  (d) failure by the tribunal to deal with all the issues that were put to it;

  (e) any arbitral or other institution or person vested by the parties with powers in relation to the proceedings or the award exceeding its powers;

  (f) uncertainty or ambiguity as to the effect of the award;

  (g) the award being obtained by fraud or the award or the way in which it was procured being contrary to public policy;

  (h) failure to comply with the requirements as to the form of the award; or

  (i) any irregularity in the conduct of the proceedings or in the award which is admitted by the tribunal or by any arbitral or other institution or person vested by the parties with powers.

(3) If there is shown to be serious irregularity affecting the tribunal, the proceedings or the award, the court may –

  (a) remit the award to the tribunal, in whole or in part, for reconsideration,

  (b) set the award aside in whole or in part, or

(continued ...)

    (c) *in paragraph (c) for 'agreed by the parties' substitute 'as set out in the Scheme';*

    (d) *in paragraph (e) for 'any arbitral or other institution or person vested by the parties with powers in relation to the proceedings or the award' substitute 'Acas';*

    (e) *omit paragraph (h);*

    (f) *in paragraph (i) for 'any arbitral or other institution or person vested by the parties with powers in relation to the proceedings or the award' substitute 'Acas'.*

(4) *In subsection (3) –*

    (a) *in paragraph (b) insert 'vary the award or' before 'set the award aside';*

    (b) *omit 'The court shall not exercise its power to set aside or to declare an award to be of no effect, in whole or in part, unless it is satisfied that it would be inappropriate to remit the matters in question to the tribunal for reconsideration.'*

(5) *After subsection (4) insert –*

'(5) In this section, "the Scheme" means the arbitration scheme set out in the Schedule to the Acas Arbitration Scheme (England and Wales) Order 2001.'

Appeals on questions of EC law and the Human Rights Act 1998

164 (1) *Section 69 of the Arbitration Act 1996[a] shall apply to arbitrations conducted in accordance with the Scheme, subject to the following modifications.*

    (2) *In subsection (1) –*

        (a) *omit 'Unless otherwise agreed by the parties';*

        (b) *for '(upon notice to the other parties and to the tribunal) appeal to the court' substitute '(upon notice to the other party, to the arbitrator and to Acas) appeal to the High Court or Central London County Court';*

(continued ...)

    (c) declare the award to be of no effect, in whole or in part.

The court shall not exercise its power to set aside or to declare an award to be of no effect, in whole or in part, unless it is satisfied that it would be inappropriate to remit the matters in question to the tribunal for reconsideration.

(4) The leave of the court is required for any appeal from a decision of the court under this section.

(a) 1996 c23.

Section 69 of the Arbitration Act 1996 provides as follows:

(1) Unless otherwise agreed by the parties, a party to arbitral proceedings may (upon notice to the other parties and to the tribunal) appeal to the court on a question of law arising out of an award made in the proceedings.

An agreement to dispense with reasons for the tribunal's award shall be considered an agreement to exclude the court's jurisdiction under this section.

(2) An appeal shall not be brought under this section except –

    (a) with the agreement of all the other parties to the proceedings, or

    (b) with the leave of the court.

The right to appeal is also subject to the restrictions in section 70(2) and (3).

(continued ...)

(c) for 'a question of law' substitute 'a question (a) of EC law, or (b) concerning the application of the Human Rights Act 1998';

(d) omit 'An agreement to dispense with reasons for the tribunal's award shall be considered an agreement to exclude the court's jurisdiction under this section.'

(3) In subsection (2) after 'section 70(2) and (3)' insert 'as modified for the purposes of the Scheme'.

(4) In subsection (3) –

(a) omit paragraph (b);

(b) in paragraph (c) after the words 'on the basis of the findings of fact in the award' insert 'insofar as the question for appeal raises a point of EC law, the point is capable of serious argument, and insofar as the question for appeal does not raise a point of EC law'.

(5) In subsection (7) omit 'The court shall not exercise its power to set aside an award, in whole or in part, unless it is satisfied that it would be inappropriate to remit the matters in question to the tribunal for reconsideration.'

(continued ...)

(3) Leave to appeal shall be given only if the court is satisfied –
   (a) that the determination of the question will substantially affect the rights of one or more of the parties,
   (b) that the question is one which the tribunal was asked to determine,
   (c) that, on the basis of the findings of fact in the award –
      (i) the decision of the tribunal on the question is obviously wrong, or
      (ii) the question is one of general public importance and the decision of the tribunal is at least open to serious doubt, and
   (d) that, despite the agreement of the parties to resolve the matter by arbitration, it is just and proper in all the circumstances for the court to determine the question.
(4) An application for leave to appeal under this section shall identify the question of law to be determined and state the grounds on which it is alleged that leave to appeal should be granted.
(5) The court shall determine an application for leave to appeal under this section without a hearing unless it appears to the court that a hearing is required.
(6) The leave of the court is required for any appeal from a decision of the court under this section to grant or refuse leave to appeal.
(7) On an appeal under this section the court may by order –
   (a) confirm the award,
   (b) vary the award,
   (c) remit the award to the tribunal, in whole or in part, for reconsideration in the light of the court's determination, or
   (d) set aside the award in whole or in part.
   The court shall not exercise its power to set aside an award, in whole or in part, unless it is satisfied that it would be inappropriate to remit the matters in question to the tribunal for reconsideration.
(8) The decision of the court on an appeal under this section shall be treated as a judgment of the court for the purposes of a further appeal.
   But no such appeal lies without the leave of the court which shall not be given unless the court considers that the question is one of general importance or is one which for some other special reason should be considered by the Court of Appeal.

(6) *After subsection (8) insert –*

    '(9) In this section –

        "EC law" means –

            (a) any enactment in the domestic legislation of England and Wales giving effect to rights, powers, liabilities, obligations and restrictions from time to time created or arising by or under the Community Treaties, and

            (b) any such rights, powers, liabilities, obligations and restrictions which are not given effect by any such enactment; and

        "the Scheme" means the arbitration scheme set out in the Schedule to the Acas Arbitration Scheme (England and Wales) Order 2001.'

Time limits and other procedural restrictions on challenges to awards

165 (1) *Section 70 of the Arbitration Act 1996*[a] *shall apply to arbitrations conducted in accordance with the Scheme, subject to the following modifications.*

(a) 1996 c23.

Section 70 of the Arbitration Act 1996 provides as follows:

(1) The following provisions apply to an application or appeal under section 67, 68 or 69.

(2) An application or appeal may not be brought if the applicant or appellant has not first exhausted –

(a) any available arbitral process of appeal or review, and

(b) any available recourse under section 57 (correction of award or additional award).

(3) Any application or appeal must be brought within 28 days of the date of the award or, if there has been any arbitral process of appeal or review, of the date when the applicant or appellant was notified of the result of that process.

(4) If on an application or appeal it appears to the court that the award –

(a) does not contain the tribunal's reasons, or

(b) does not set out the tribunal's reasons in sufficient detail to enable the court properly to consider the application or appeal, the court may order the tribunal to state the reasons for its award in sufficient detail for that purpose.

(5) Where the court makes an order under subsection (4), it may make such further order as it thinks fit with respect to any additional costs of the arbitration resulting from its order.

(6) The court may order the applicant or appellant to provide security for the costs of the application or appeal, and may direct that the application or appeal be dismissed if the order is not complied with.

The power to order security for costs shall not be exercised on the ground that the applicant or appellant is –

(a) an individual ordinarily resident outside the United Kingdom, or

(b) a corporation or association incorporated or formed under the law of a country outside the United Kingdom, or whose central management and control is exercised outside the United Kingdom.

(7) The court may order that any money payable under the award shall be brought into court or otherwise secured pending the determination of the application or appeal, and may direct that the application or appeal be dismissed if the order is not complied with.

(8) The court may grant leave to appeal subject to conditions to the same or similar effect as an order under subsection (6) or (7).

This does not affect the general discretion of the court to grant leave subject to conditions.

(2) In subsection (1) after 'section 67, 68 or 69' insert '(as modified for the purposes of the Scheme)'.

(3) In subsection (2) –

   (a) omit paragraph (a);

   (b) in paragraph (b) for 'section 57 (correction of award or additional award)' substitute 'section XXII of the Scheme (Correction of Awards)'.

(4) In subsection (3) for 'of the award or, if there has been any arbitral process of appeal or review, of the date when the applicant or appellant was notified of the result of that process' substitute 'the award was despatched to the applicant or appellant by Acas'.

(5) Omit subsection (5).

(6) After subsection (8) insert –

   '(9) In this section, "the Scheme" means the arbitration scheme set out in the Schedule to the Acas Arbitration Scheme (England and Wales) Order 2001.'

Common law challenges and saving

166 Sections 81(1)(c) and 81(2) of the Arbitration Act 1996[a] shall apply to arbitrations conducted in accordance with the Scheme.

Challenge or appeal: effect of order of the court

167(1) Section 71 of the Arbitration Act 1996[b] shall apply to arbitrations conducted in accordance with the Scheme, subject to the following modifications:

(2) In subsection (1) after 'section 67, 68 and 69' insert '(as modified for the purposes of the Scheme)'.

(a) 1996 c23.

Sections 81(1)(c) and 81(2) of the Arbitration Act 1996 provide as follows:

(1) Nothing in this Part shall be construed as excluding the operation of any rule of law consistent with the provisions of this Part, in particular, any rule of law as to –

   ...

   (c) the refusal of recognition or enforcement of an arbitral award on grounds of public policy.

(2) Nothing in this Act shall be construed as reviving any jurisdiction of the court to set aside or remit an award on the ground of errors of fact or law on the face of the award.

(b) 1996 c23.

Section 71 of the Arbitration Act 1996 provides as follows:

(1) The following provisions have effect where the court makes an order under section 67, 68 or 69 with respect to an award.

(2) Where the award is varied, the variation has effect as part of the tribunal's award.

(3) Where the award is remitted to the tribunal, in whole or in part, for reconsideration, the tribunal shall make a fresh award in respect of the matters remitted within three months of the date of the order for remission or such longer or shorter period as the court may direct.

(4) Where the award is set aside or declared to be of no effect, in whole or in part, the court may also order that any provision that an award is a condition precedent to the bringing of legal proceedings in respect of a matter to which the arbitration agreement applies, is of no effect as regards the subject matter of the award or, as the case may be, the relevant part of the award.

(3) *After subsection (3) insert –*

  '(3A) In this section, "the Scheme" means the arbitration scheme set out in the Schedule to the Acas Arbitration Scheme (England and Wales) Order 2001.'

(4) *Omit subsection (4).*

XXV LOSS OF RIGHT TO OBJECT

168 If a party to arbitral proceedings under this Scheme takes part, or continues to take part, in the proceedings without making, either forthwith or within such time as is allowed by the arbitrator or by any provision in this Scheme, any objection:

i that the arbitrator lacks substantive jurisdiction (as defined in paragraph 162 above), aside from any jurisdictional objection with respect to the circumstances of the dismissal, which will be waived in any event, as set out in paragraphs 16–18 above,

ii that the proceedings have been improperly conducted,

iii that there has been a failure to comply with the Arbitration Agreement or any provision of this Scheme, or

iv that there has been any other irregularity affecting the arbitrator or the proceedings,

he or she may not raise that objection later, before the arbitrator or the court, unless he or she shows that, at the time he or she took part or continued to take part in the proceedings, he or she did not know and could not with reasonable diligence have discovered the grounds for the objection.

XXVI IMMUNITY

169 An arbitrator under this Scheme is not liable for anything done or omitted in the discharge or purported discharge of his or her functions as arbitrator unless the act or omission is shown to have been in bad faith. This applies to a legal adviser appointed by Acas as it applies to the arbitrator himself or herself.

170 Acas, by reason of having appointed an arbitrator or nominated a legal adviser, is not liable for anything done or omitted by the arbitrator or legal adviser in the discharge or purported discharge of his or her functions.

XXVII MISCELLANEOUS PROVISIONS

Requirements in connection with legal proceedings

171 (1) *Sections 80(1), (2), (4), (5), (6) and (7) of the Arbitration Act 1996*[u] *shall apply to arbitrations conducted in accordance with the Scheme, subject to the following modification:*

(2) *In subsection (1) for 'to the other parties to the arbitral proceedings, or to the tribunal' substitute 'to the other party to the arbitral proceedings, or to the arbitrator, or to Acas'.*

Service of documents and notices on Acas or the Acas Arbitration Section

172 Any notice or other document required or authorised to be given or served on Acas or the Acas Arbitration Section for the purposes of the arbitral proceedings shall be sent by pre-paid post to the following address:

Acas Arbitration Section
Acas Head Office
Brandon House
180 Borough High Street
London
SE1 1LW

(a) 1996 c23.
Sections 80(1), (2), (4), (5), (6) and (7) of the Arbitration Act 1996 provide as follows:
   (1) References in this Part to an application, appeal or other step in relation to legal proceedings being taken 'upon notice' to the other parties to the arbitral proceedings, or to the tribunal, are to such notice of the originating process as is required by rules of court and do not impose any separate requirement.
   (2) Rules of court shall be made –
      (a) requiring such notice to be given as indicated by any provision of this Part, and
      (b) as to the manner, form and content of any such notice.
      ...
   (4) References in this Part to making an application or appeal to the court within a specified period are to the issue within that period of the appropriate originating process in accordance with rules of court.
   (5) Where any provision of this Part requires an application or appeal to be made to the court within a specified time, the rules of court relating to the reckoning of periods, the extending or abridging of periods, and the consequences of not taking a step within the period prescribed by the rules, apply in relation to that requirement.
   (6) Provision may be made by rules of court amending the provisions of this Part –
      (a) with respect to the time within which any application or appeal to the court must be made,
      (b) so as to keep any provision made by this Part in relation to arbitral proceedings in step with the corresponding provision of rules of court applying in relation to proceedings in the court, or
      (c) so as to keep any provision made by this Part in relation to legal proceedings in step with the corresponding provision of rules of court applying generally in relation to proceedings in the court
   (7) Nothing in this section affects the generality of the power to make rules of court.

or transmitted by facsimile, addressed to the Acas Arbitration Section, at the number stipulated in the Acas Guide to the Scheme,

or by electronic mail, at the address stipulated in the Acas Guide to the Scheme.

173 Paragraph 172 (above) does not apply to the service of documents on the Acas Arbitration Section for the purposes of legal proceedings.

Service of documents or notices on any other person or entity (other than Acas or the Acas Arbitration Section)

174 Any notice or other document required or authorised to be given or served on any person or entity (other than Acas or the Acas Arbitration Section) for the purposes of the arbitral proceedings may be served by any effective means.

175 If such a notice or other document is addressed, pre-paid and delivered by post:

i   to the addressee's last known principal residence or, if he or she is or has been carrying on a trade, profession or business, his or her last known principal business address, or

ii where the address is a body corporate, to the body's registered or principal office, it shall be treated as effectively served.

176 Paragraphs 174 and 175 (above) do not apply to the service of documents for the purposes of legal proceedings, for which provision is made by rules of court.

Powers of court in relation to service of documents

177 *(1) Section 77 of the Arbitration Act 1996[(a)] shall apply to arbitrations conducted in accordance with the Scheme, subject to the following modifications:*

(2) In subsection (1) omit 'in the manner agreed by the parties, or in accordance with provisions of section 76 having effect in default of agreement,'.

(3) In subsection (2) for 'Unless otherwise agreed by the parties, the court' substitute 'The High Court or Central London County Court'.

(4) In subsection (3) for 'Any party to the arbitration agreement may apply' substitute 'Acas or any party to the arbitration agreement may apply'.

(a) 1996 c23.

Section 77 of the Arbitration Act 1996 provides as follows:

(1) This section applies where service of a document on a person in the manner agreed by the parties, or in accordance with provisions of section 76 having effect in default of agreement, is not reasonably practicable.

(2) Unless otherwise agreed by the parties, the court may make such order as it thinks fit –

(a) for service in such manner as the court may direct, or

(b) dispensing with service of the document.

(3) Any party to the arbitration agreement may apply for an order, but only after exhausting any available arbitral process for resolving the matter.

(4) The leave of the court is required for any appeal from a decision of the court under this section.

Reckoning periods of time

178 (1) Sections 78(2), (3), (4) and (5) of the Arbitration Act 1996[a] shall apply to arbitrations conducted in accordance with the Scheme, subject to the following modification:

(2) In subsection (2) –

(a) omit 'If or to the extent that there is no such agreement,';

(b) after 'periods of time' insert 'provided for in any provision of this Part'.

XXVIII TERRITORIAL OPERATION OF THE SCHEME

179 The Scheme applies to disputes involving an Employer who resides or carries on business in England and Wales.

(a) 1996 c23.

Sections 78(2), (3), (4) and (5) of the Arbitration Act 1996 provide as follows:

(2) If or to the extent there is no such agreement, periods of time shall be reckoned in accordance with the following provisions.

(3) Where the act is required to be done within a specified period after or from a specified date, the period begins immediately after that date.

(4) Where the act is required to be done a specified number of clear days after a specified date, at least that number of days must intervene between the day on which the act is done and that date.

(5) Where the period is a period of seven days or less which would include a Saturday, Sunday or a public holiday in the place where anything which has to be done within the period falls to be done, that day shall be excluded.

In relation to England and Wales or Northern Ireland, a 'public holiday' means Christmas Day, Good Friday or a day which under the Banking and Financial Dealings Act 1971 is a bank holiday.

APPENDIX A
WAIVER OF RIGHTS

The Acas Arbitration Scheme ('the Scheme') is entirely voluntary. In agreeing to refer a dispute to arbitration under the Scheme, both parties agree to waive rights that they would otherwise have if, for example, they had referred their dispute to the employment tribunal. This follows from the informal nature of the Scheme, which is designed to be a confidential, relatively fast, cost-efficient and non-legalistic process.

As required by section VI of the Scheme, as a confirmation of the parties' agreement to waive their rights, this form must be completed by each party and submitted to Acas together with the agreement to arbitration.

A detailed description of the informal nature of arbitration under the Scheme, and the important differences between this and the employment tribunal, is contained in the Acas Guide to the Scheme ('the Acas Guide'), which should be read by each party before completing this form.

The Scheme is not intended for disputes involving complex legal issues, or questions of EC law. Parties to such disputes are strongly advised to consider applying to the employment tribunal, or settling their dispute by other means.

This form does not list all the differences between the Scheme and the employment tribunal, or all of the features of the Scheme to which each party agrees in referring their dispute to arbitration.

I, ..., the **Applicant/Respondent/Respondent's duly authorised**

representative [delete as appropriate] **confirm my agreement to each of the following points:**

1	Unlike proceedings in the employment tribunal, all proceedings under the Scheme, including all hearings, are conducted in private. There are no public hearings, and the final award will be confidential.
2	All arbitrators under the Scheme are appointed by Acas from the Acas Arbitration Panel (which is a panel of impartial, mainly non-lawyer, arbitrators appointed by Acas on fixed, but renewable, terms). The appointment process and the Acas Arbitration Panel is described in the Scheme and the Acas Guide. Neither party will have any choice of arbitrator.
3	Proceedings under the Scheme are conducted differently from the employment tribunal. In particular: -- arbitrators will conduct proceedings in an informal manner in all cases; -- the attendance of witnesses and the production of documents cannot be compelled (although failure to co-operate may be taken into account by the arbitrator); -- there will be no oaths or affirmations, and no cross-examination of witnesses by parties or their representatives; -- the arbitrator will take the initiative in asking questions and ascertaining the facts (with the aim of ensuring that all relevant issues are considered), as well as hearing each side's arguments; -- the arbitrator's decision will only contain the main considerations that have led to the result; it will not contain full or detailed reasons; -- the arbitrator has no power to order interim relief.
4	Once parties have agreed to refer their dispute to arbitration in accordance with the Scheme, the parties cannot then return to the employment tribunal.
5	In deciding whether or not the dismissal was fair or unfair, the arbitrator shall have regard to general principles of fairness and good conduct in employment relations (including, for example, principles referred to in any relevant Acas *Disciplinary and Grievance Procedures* Code of Practice or *Discipline at Work* Handbook). Unlike the employment tribunal, the arbitrator will not apply strict legal tests or rules (for example court decisions or legislation), with certain limited exceptions set out in the Scheme (see for example paragraph 12). Similarly, in cases that do not involve EC law, the arbitrator will calculate compensation or award any other remedy in accordance with the terms of the Scheme, instead of applying strict legal tests or rules.

6	Unlike the employment tribunal, there is no right of appeal from awards of arbitrators under the Scheme (except for a limited right to appeal questions of EC law and, aside from procedural matters set out in the Scheme, questions concerning the Human Rights Act 1998).
7	Unlike the employment tribunal, in agreeing to arbitration under the Scheme, parties agree that there is no jurisdictional argument, ie no reason why the claim cannot be heard and determined by the arbitrator. In particular, the arbitrator will assume that a dismissal has taken place, and will only consider whether or not this was unfair. This is explained further in the Scheme and in the Acas Guide.

SIGNED: ....

DATED: ....

IN THE PRESENCE OF

Signature: ....

Full Name: ....

Position: ....

Address: ....

....

APPENDIX 3

ARBITRATION ACT 1996 (OF ENGLAND)
CHAPTER 23 (17 JUNE 1996)

[PREAMBLE]

An Act to restate and improve the law relating to arbitration pursuant to an arbitration agreement; to make other provision relating to arbitration and arbitration awards; and for connected purposes.

Be it enacted by the Queen's most Excellent Majesty, by and with the advice and consent of the Lords Spiritual and Temporal, and Commons, in this present Parliament assembled, and by the authority of the same, as follows:

PART 1 – ARBITRATION PURSUANT TO AN ARBITRATION AGREEMENT

Introductory

Section 1 – General principles

The provisions of this Part are founded on the following principles, and shall be construed accordingly –

(a) the object of arbitration is to obtain the fair resolution of disputes by an impartial tribunal without unnecessary delay or expense;

(b) the parties should be free to agree how their disputes are resolved, subject only to such safeguards as are necessary in the public interest;

(c) in matters governed by this Part the court should not intervene except as provided by this Part.

Section 2 – Scope of application of provisions

(1) The provisions of this Part apply where the seat of the arbitration is in England and Wales or Northern Ireland.

(2) The following sections apply even if the seat of the arbitration is outside England and Wales or Northern Ireland or no seat has been designated or determined –

    (a) sections 9 to 11 (stay of legal proceedings, etc), and

    (b) section 66 (enforcement of arbitral awards).

(3) The powers conferred by the following sections apply even if the seat of the arbitration is outside England and Wales or Northern Ireland or no seat has been designated or determined –

    (a) section 43 (securing the attendance of witnesses), and

    (b) section 44 (court powers exercisable in support of arbitral proceedings); but the court may refuse to exercise any such power if, in the opinion of the court, the fact that the seat of the arbitration is outside England and Wales or Northern Ireland, or that when designated or determined the seat is likely to be outside England and Wales or Northern Ireland, makes it inappropriate to do so.

(4) The court may exercise a power conferred by any provision of this Part 20 not mentioned in subsection (2) or (3) for the purpose of supporting the arbitral process where –

(a) no seat of the arbitration has been designated or determined, and

(b) by reason of a connection with England and Wales or Northern Ireland the court is satisfied that it is appropriate to do so.

(5) Section 7 (separability of arbitration agreement) and section 8 (death of a party) apply where the law applicable to the arbitration agreement is the law of England and Wales or Northern Ireland even if the seat of the arbitration is outside England and Wales or Northern Ireland or has not been designated or determined.

Section 3 – The seat of the arbitration

In this Part 'the seat of the arbitration' means the juridical seat of the arbitration designated –

(a) by the parties to the arbitration agreement, or

(b) by any arbitral or other institution or person vested by the parties with powers in that regard, or

(c) by the arbitral tribunal if so authorised by the parties, or determined, in the absence of any such designation, having regard to the parties' agreement and all the relevant circumstances.

Section 4 – Mandatory and non-mandatory provisions

(1) The mandatory provisions of this Part are listed in Schedule 1 and have effect notwithstanding any agreement to the contrary.

(2) The other provisions of this Part (the 'non-mandatory provisions') allow the parties to make their own arrangements by agreement but provide rules which apply in the absence of such agreement.

(3) The parties may make such arrangements by agreeing to the application of institutional rules or providing any other means by which a matter may be decided.

(4) It is immaterial whether or not the law applicable to the parties' agreement is the law of England and Wales or, as the case may be, Northern Ireland.

(5) The choice of a law other than the law of England and Wales or Northern Ireland as the applicable law in respect of a matter provided for by a non-mandatory provision of this Part is equivalent to an agreement making provision about that matter. For this purpose an applicable law determined in accordance with the parties' agreement, or which is objectively determined in the absence of any express or implied choice, shall be treated as chosen by the parties.

Section 5 – Agreements to be in writing

(1) The provisions of this Part apply only where the arbitration agreement is in writing, and any other agreement between the parties as to any matter is effective for the purposes of this Part only if in writing. The expressions 'agreement', 'agree' and 'agreed' shall be construed accordingly.

(2) There is an agreement in writing –

(a) if the agreement is made in writing (whether or not it is signed by the parties),

(b) if the agreement is made by exchange of communications in writing, or

(c) if the agreement is evidenced in writing.

(3) Where parties agree otherwise than in writing by reference to terms which are in writing, they make an agreement in writing.

(4) An agreement is evidenced in writing if an agreement made otherwise than in writing is recorded by one of the parties, or by a third party, with the authority of the parties to the agreement.

(5) An exchange of written submissions in arbitral or legal proceedings in which the existence of an agreement otherwise than in writing is alleged by one party against another party and not denied by the other party in his response constitutes as between those parties an agreement in writing to the effect alleged.

(6) References in this Part to anything being written or in writing include its being recorded by any means.

Definition of arbitration agreement

Section 6 – The arbitration agreement

(1) In this Part an 'arbitration agreement' means an agreement to submit to arbitration present or future disputes (whether they are contractual or not).

(2) The reference in an agreement to a written form of arbitration clause or to a document containing an arbitration clause constitutes an arbitration agreement if the reference is such as to make that clause part of the agreement.

Section 7 – Separability of arbitration agreement

Unless otherwise agreed by the parties, an arbitration agreement which forms or was intended to form part of another agreement (whether or not in writing) shall not be regarded as invalid, non-existent or ineffective because that other agreement is invalid, or did not come into existence or has become ineffective, and it shall for that purpose be treated as a distinct agreement.

Section 8 – Whether agreement discharged by death of a party

(1) Unless otherwise agreed by the parties, an arbitration agreement is not discharged by the death of a party and may be enforced by or against the personal representatives of that party.

(2) Subsection (1) does not affect the operation of any enactment or rule of law by virtue of which a substantive right or obligation is extinguished by death.

Stay of legal proceedings

Section 9 – Stay of legal proceedings

(1) A party to an arbitration agreement against whom legal proceedings are brought (whether by way of claim or counterclaim) in respect of a matter which under the agreement is to be referred to arbitration may (upon notice to the other parties to the proceedings) apply to

the court in which the proceedings have been brought to stay the proceedings so far as they concern that matter.

(2) An application may be made notwithstanding that the matter is to be referred to arbitration only after the exhaustion of other dispute resolution procedures.

(3) An application may not be made by a person before taking the appropriate procedural step (if any) to acknowledge the legal proceedings against him or after he has taken any step in those proceedings to answer the substantive claim.

(4) On an application under this section the court shall grant a stay unless satisfied that the arbitration agreement is null and void, inoperative, or incapable of being performed.

(5) If the court refuses to stay the legal proceedings, any provision that an award is a condition precedent to the bringing of legal proceedings in respect of any matter is of no effect in relation to those proceedings.

Section 10 – Reference of interpleader issue to arbitration

(1) Where in legal proceedings relief by way of interpleader is granted and any issue between the claimants is one in respect of which there is an arbitration agreement between them, the court granting the relief shall direct that the issue be determined in accordance with the agreement unless the circumstances are such that proceedings brought by a claimant in respect of the matter would not be stayed.

(2) Where subsection (1) applies but the court does not direct that the issue be determined in accordance with the arbitration agreement, any provision that an award is a condition precedent to the bringing of legal proceedings in respect of any matter shall not affect the determination of that issue by the court.

Section 11 – Retention of security where Admiralty proceedings stayed

(1) Where Admiralty proceedings are stayed on the ground that the dispute in question should be submitted to arbitration, the court granting the stay may, if in those proceedings property has been arrested or bail or other security has been given to prevent or obtain release from arrest –

(a) order that the property arrested be retained as security for the satisfaction of any award given in the arbitration in respect of that dispute, or

(b) order that the stay of those proceedings be conditional on the provision of equivalent security for the satisfaction of any such award.

(2) Subject to any provision made by rules of court and to any necessary modifications, the same law and practice shall apply in relation to property retained in pursuance of an order as would apply if it were held for the purposes of proceedings in the court making the order.

Commencement of arbitral proceedings

Section 12 – Power of court to extend time for beginning arbitral proceedings, etc

(1) Where an arbitration agreement to refer future disputes to arbitration provides that a claim shall be barred, or the claimant's right extinguished, unless the claimant takes within a time fixed by the agreement some step

(a) to begin arbitral proceedings, or

(b) to begin other dispute resolution procedures which must be exhausted before arbitral proceedings can be begun, the court may by order extend the time for taking that step.

(2) Any party to the arbitration agreement may apply for such an order (upon notice to the other parties), but only after a claim has arisen and after exhausting any available arbitral process for obtaining an extension of time.

(3) The court shall make an order only if satisfied –

(a) that the circumstances are such as were outside the reasonable contemplation of the parties when they agreed the provision in question, and that it would be just to extend the time, or

(b) that the conduct of one party makes it unjust to hold the other party to the strict terms of the provision in question.

(4) The court may extend the time for such period and on such terms as it thinks fit, and may do so whether or not the time previously fixed (by agreement or by a previous order) has expired.

(5) An order under this section does not affect the operation of the Limitation Acts (see section 13).

(6) The leave of the court is required for any appeal from a decision of the court under this section.

Section 13 – Application of Limitation Acts

(1) The Limitation Acts apply to arbitral proceedings as they apply to legal proceedings.

(2) The court may order that in computing the time prescribed by the Limitation Acts for the commencement of proceedings (including arbitral proceedings) in respect of a dispute which was the subject matter –

(a) of an award which the court orders to be set aside or declares to be of no effect, or

(b) of the affected part of an award which the court orders to be set aside in part, or declares to be in part of no effect, the period between the commencement of the arbitration and the date of the order referred to in paragraph (a) or (b) shall be excluded.

(3) In determining for the purposes of the Limitation Acts when a cause of action accrued, any provision that an award is a condition precedent to the bringing of legal proceedings in respect of a matter to which an arbitration agreement applies shall be disregarded.

(4) In this Part 'the Limitation Acts' means –

(a) in England and Wales, the Limitation Act 1980, the Foreign Limitation Periods Act 1984 and any other enactment (whenever passed) relating to the limitation of actions;

(b) in Northern Ireland, the Limitation (Northern Ireland) Order 1989, the Foreign Limitation Periods (Northern Ireland) Order 1985 and any other enactment (whenever passed) relating to the limitation of actions.

1980 c58 93

1984 c16 94

SI 1989/1339 (NI 11) 95

SI 1985/754 (NI 5) 96

Section 14 – Commencement of arbitral proceedings

(1) The parties are free to agree when arbitral proceedings are to be regarded as commenced for the purposes of this Part and for the purposes of the Limitation Acts.

(2) If there is no such agreement the following provisions apply.

(3) Where the arbitrator is named or designated in the arbitration agreement, arbitral proceedings are commenced in respect of a matter when one party serves on the other party or parties a notice in writing requiring him or them to submit that matter to the person so named or designated.

(4) Where the arbitrator or arbitrators are to be appointed by the parties, arbitral proceedings are commenced in respect of a matter when one party serves on the other party or parties notice in writing requiring him or them to appoint an arbitrator or to agree to the appointment of an arbitrator in respect of that matter.

(5) Where the arbitrator or arbitrators are to be appointed by a person other than a party to the proceedings, arbitral proceedings are commenced in respect of a matter when one party gives notice in writing to that person requesting him to make the appointment in respect of that matter.

The arbitral tribunal

Section 15 – The arbitral tribunal

(1) The parties are free to agree on the number of arbitrators to form the tribunal and whether there is to be a chairman or umpire.

(2) Unless otherwise agreed by the parties, an agreement that the number of arbitrators shall be two or any other even number shall be understood as requiring the appointment of an additional arbitrator as chairman of the tribunal.

(3) If there is no agreement as to the number of arbitrators, the tribunal shall consist of a sole arbitrator.

Section 16 – Procedure for appointment of arbitrators

(1) The parties are free to agree on the procedure for appointing the arbitrator or arbitrators, including the procedure for appointing any chairman or umpire.

(2) If or to the extent that there is no such agreement, the following provisions apply.

(3) If the tribunal is to consist of a sole arbitrator, the parties shall jointly appoint the arbitrator not later than 28 days after service of a request in writing by either party to do so.

(4) If the tribunal is to consist of two arbitrators, each party shall appoint one arbitrator not later than 14 days after service of a request in writing by either party to do so.

(5) If the tribunal is to consist of three arbitrators –

    (a) each party shall appoint one arbitrator not later than 14 days after service of a request in writing by either party to do so, and

    (b) the two so appointed shall forthwith appoint a third arbitrator as the chairman of the tribunal.

(6) If the tribunal is to consist of two arbitrators and an umpire –

  (a) each party shall appoint one arbitrator not later than 14 days after service of a request in writing by either party to do so, and

  (b) the two so appointed may appoint an umpire at any time after they themselves are appointed and shall do so before any substantive hearing or forthwith if they cannot agree on a matter relating to the arbitration.

(7) In any other case (in particular, if there are more than two parties) section 18 applies as in the case of a failure of the agreed appointment procedure.

Section 17 – Power in case of default to appoint sole arbitrator

(1) Unless the parties otherwise agree, where each of two parties to an arbitration agreement is to appoint an arbitrator and one party ('the party in default') refuses to do so, or fails to do so within the time specified, the other party, having duly appointed his arbitrator, may give notice in writing to the party in default that he proposes to appoint his arbitrator to act as sole arbitrator.

(2) If the party in default does not within seven clear days of that notice being given –

  (a) make the required appointment, and

  (b) notify the other party that he has done so, the other party may appoint his arbitrator as sole arbitrator whose award shall be binding on both parties as if he had been so appointed by agreement.

(3) Where a sole arbitrator has been appointed under subsection (2), the party in default may (upon notice to the appointing party) apply to the court which may set aside the appointment.

(4) The leave of the court is required for any appeal from a decision of the court under this section.

Section 18 – Failure of appointment procedure

(1) The parties are free to agree what is to happen in the event of a failure of the procedure for the appointment of the arbitral tribunal. There is no failure if an appointment is duly made under section 17 (power in case of default to appoint sole arbitrator), unless that appointment is set aside.

(2) If or to the extent that there is no such agreement any party to the arbitration agreement may (upon notice to the other parties) apply to the court to exercise its powers under this section.

(3) Those powers are –

  (a) to give directions as to the making of any necessary appointments;

  (b) to direct that the tribunal shall be constituted by such appointments (or any one or more of them) as have been made;

  (c) to revoke any appointments already made;

  (d) to make any necessary appointments itself.

(4) An appointment made by the court under this section has effect as if made with the agreement of the parties.

(5) The leave of the court is required for any appeal from a decision of the court under this section.

Section 19 – Court to have regard to agreed qualifications

In deciding whether to exercise, and in considering how to exercise, any of its powers under section 16 (procedure for appointment of arbitrators) or section 18 (failure of appointment procedure), the court shall have due regard to any agreement of the parties as to the qualifications required of the arbitrators.

Section 20 – Chairman

(1) Where the parties have agreed that there is to be a chairman, they are free to agree what the functions of the chairman are to be in relation to the making of decisions, orders and awards.

(2) If or to the extent that there is no such agreement, the following provisions apply.

(3) Decisions, orders and awards shall be made by all or a majority of the arbitrators (including the chairman).

(4) The view of the chairman shall prevail in relation to a decision, order or award in respect of which there is neither unanimity nor a majority under subsection (3).

Section 21 – Umpire

(1) Where the parties have agreed that there is to be an umpire, they are free to agree what the functions of the umpire are to be, and in particular –

  (a) whether he is to attend the proceedings, and

  (b) when he is to replace the other arbitrators as the tribunal with power to make decisions, orders and awards.

(2) If or to the extent that there is no such agreement, the following provisions apply.

(3) The umpire shall attend the proceedings and be supplied with the same documents and other materials as are supplied to the other arbitrators.

(4) Decisions, orders and awards shall be made by the other arbitrators unless and until they cannot agree on a matter relating to the arbitration. In that event they shall forthwith give notice in writing to the parties and the umpire, whereupon the umpire shall replace them as the tribunal with power to make decisions, orders and awards as if he were sole arbitrator.

(5) If the arbitrators cannot agree but fail to give notice of that fact, or if any of them fails to join in the giving of notice, any party to the arbitral proceedings may (upon notice to the other parties and to the tribunal) apply to the court which may order that the umpire shall replace the other arbitrators as the tribunal with power to make decisions, orders and awards as if he were sole arbitrator.

(6) The leave of the court is required for any appeal from a decision of the court under this section.

Section 22 – Decision-making where no chairman or umpire

(1) Where the parties agree that there shall be two or more arbitrators with no chairman or umpire, the parties are free to agree how the tribunal is to make decisions, orders and awards.

(2) If there is no such agreement, decisions, orders and awards shall be made by all or a majority of the arbitrators.

Section 23 – Revocation of arbitrator's authority

(1) The parties are free to agree in what circumstances the authority of an arbitrator may be revoked.

(2) If or to the extent that there is no such agreement the following provisions apply.

(3) The authority of an arbitrator may not be revoked except –

    (a) by the parties acting jointly, or

    (b) by an arbitral or other institution or person vested by the parties with powers in that regard.

(4) Revocation of the authority of an arbitrator by the parties acting jointly must be agreed in writing unless the parties also agree (whether or not in writing) to terminate the arbitration agreement.

(5) Nothing in this section affects the power of the court –

    (a) to revoke an appointment under section 18 (powers exercisable in case of failure of appointment procedure), or

    (b) to remove an arbitrator on the grounds specified in section 24.

Section 24 – Power of court to remove arbitrator

(1) A party to arbitral proceedings may (upon notice to the other parties, to the arbitrator concerned and to any other arbitrator) apply to the court to remove an arbitrator on any of the following grounds –

    (a) that circumstances exist that give rise to justifiable doubts as to his impartiality;

    (b) that he does not possess the qualifications required by the arbitration agreement;

    (c) that he is physically or mentally incapable of conducting the proceedings or there are justifiable doubts as to his capacity to do so;

    (d) that he has refused or failed –

        (i) properly to conduct the proceedings, or

        (ii) to use all reasonable despatch in conducting the proceedings or making an award, and that substantial injustice has been or will be caused to the applicant.

(2) If there is an arbitral or other institution or person vested by the parties with power to remove an arbitrator, the court shall not exercise its power of removal unless satisfied that the applicant has first exhausted any available recourse to that institution or person.

(3) The arbitral tribunal may continue the arbitral proceedings and make an award while an application to the court under this section is pending.

(4) Where the court removes an arbitrator, it may make such order as it thinks fit with respect to his entitlement (if any) to fees or expenses, or the repayment of any fees or expenses already paid.

(5) The arbitrator concerned is entitled to appear and be heard by the court before it makes any order under this section.

(6) The leave of the court is required for any appeal from a decision of the court under this section.

Section 25 – Resignation of arbitrator

(1) The parties are free to agree with an arbitrator as to the consequences of his resignation as regards –

(a) his entitlement (if any) to fees or expenses, and

(b) any liability thereby incurred by him.

(2) If or to the extent that there is no such agreement the following provisions apply.

(3) An arbitrator who resigns his appointment may (upon notice to the parties) apply to the court –

(a) to grant him relief from any liability thereby incurred by him, and

(b) to make such order as it thinks fit with respect to his entitlement (if any) to fees or expenses or the repayment of any fees or expenses already paid.

(4) If the court is satisfied that in all the circumstances it was reasonable for the arbitrator to resign, it may grant such relief as is mentioned in subsection (3)(a) on such terms as it thinks fit.

(5) The leave of the court is required for any appeal from a decision of the court under this section.

Section 26 – Death of arbitrator or person appointing him

(1) The authority of an arbitrator is personal and ceases on his death.

(2) Unless otherwise agreed by the parties, the death of the person by whom an arbitrator was appointed does not revoke the arbitrator's authority.

Section 27 – Filling of vacancy, etc

(1) Where an arbitrator ceases to hold office, the parties are free to agree –

(a) whether and if so how the vacancy is to be filled,

(b) whether and if so to what extent the previous proceedings should stand, and

(c) what effect (if any) his ceasing to hold office has on any appointment made by him (alone or jointly).

(2) If or to the extent that there is no such agreement, the following provisions apply.

(3) The provisions of sections 16 (procedure for appointment of arbitrators) and 18 (failure of appointment procedure) apply in relation to the filling of the vacancy as in relation to an original appointment.

(4) The tribunal (when reconstituted) shall determine whether and if so to what extent the previous proceedings should stand. This does not affect any right of a party to challenge those proceedings on any ground which had arisen before the arbitrator ceased to hold office.

(5) His ceasing to hold office does not affect any appointment by him (alone or jointly) of another arbitrator, in particular any appointment of a chairman or umpire.

Section 28 – Joint and several liability of parties to arbitrators for fees and expenses

(1) The parties are jointly and severally liable to pay to the arbitrators such reasonable fees and expenses (if any) as are appropriate in the circumstances.

(2) Any party may apply to the court (upon notice to the other parties and to the arbitrators) which may order that the amount of the arbitrators' fees and expenses shall be considered and adjusted by such means and upon such terms as it may direct.

(3) If the application is made after any amount has been paid to the arbitrators by way of fees or expenses, the court may order the repayment of such amount (if any) as is shown to be excessive, but shall not do so unless it is shown that it is reasonable in the circumstances to order repayment.

(4) The above provisions have effect subject to any order of the court under section 24(4) or 25(3)(b) (order as to entitlement to fees or expenses in case of removal or resignation of arbitrator).

(5) Nothing in this section affects any liability of a party to any other party to pay all or any of the costs of the arbitration (see sections 59 to 65) or any contractual right of an arbitrator to payment of his fees and expenses.

(6) In this section references to arbitrators include an arbitrator who has ceased to act and an umpire who has not replaced the other arbitrators.

Section 29 – Immunity of arbitrator

(1) An arbitrator is not liable for anything done or omitted in the discharge or purported discharge of his functions as arbitrator unless the act or omission is shown to have been in bad faith.

(2) Subsection (1) applies to an employee or agent of an arbitrator as it applies to the arbitrator himself.

(3) This section does not affect any liability incurred by an arbitrator by reason of his resigning (but see section 25).

Jurisdiction of the arbitral tribunal

Section 30 – Competence of tribunal to rule on its own jurisdiction

(1) Unless otherwise agreed by the parties, the arbitral tribunal may rule on its own substantive jurisdiction, that is, as to –

(a) whether there is a valid arbitration agreement,

(b) whether the tribunal is properly constituted, and

(c) what matters have been submitted to arbitration in accordance with the arbitration agreement.

(2) Any such ruling may be challenged by any available arbitral process of appeal or review or in accordance with the provisions of this Part.

Section 31 – Objection to substantive jurisdiction of tribunal

(1) An objection that the arbitral tribunal lacks substantive jurisdiction at the outset of the proceedings must be raised by a party not later than the time he takes the first step in the proceedings to contest the merits of any matter in relation to which he challenges the tribunal's jurisdiction. A party is not precluded from raising such an objection by the fact that he has appointed or participated in the appointment of an arbitrator.

(2) Any objection during the course of the arbitral proceedings that the arbitral tribunal is exceeding its substantive jurisdiction must be made as soon as possible after the matter alleged to be beyond its jurisdiction is raised.

(3) The arbitral tribunal may admit an objection later than the time specified in subsection (1) or (2) if it considers the delay justified.

(4) Where an objection is duly taken to the tribunal's substantive jurisdiction and the tribunal has power to rule on its own jurisdiction, it may –

(a) rule on the matter in an award as to jurisdiction, or

(b) deal with the objection in its award on the merits. If the parties agree which of these courses the tribunal should take, the tribunal shall proceed accordingly.

(5) The tribunal may in any case, and shall if the parties so agree, stay proceedings whilst an application is made to the court under section 32 (determination of preliminary point of jurisdiction).

Section 32 – Determination of preliminary point of jurisdiction

(1) The court may, on the application of a party to arbitral proceedings (upon notice to the other parties), determine any question as to the substantive jurisdiction of the tribunal. A party may lose the right to object (see section 73).

(2) An application under this section shall not be considered unless –

(a) it is made with the agreement in writing of all the other parties to the proceedings, or

(b) it is made with the permission of the tribunal and the court is satisfied

(i) that the determination of the question is likely to produce substantial savings in costs,

(ii) that the application was made without delay, and

(iii) that there is good reason why the matter should be decided by the court.

(3) An application under this section, unless made with the agreement of all the other parties to the proceedings, shall state the grounds on which it is said that the matter should be decided by the court.

(4) Unless otherwise agreed by the parties, the arbitral tribunal may continue the arbitral proceedings and make an award while an application to the court under this section is pending.

(5) Unless the court gives leave, no appeal lies from a decision of the court whether the conditions specified in subsection (2) are met.

(6) The decision of the court on the question of jurisdiction shall be treated as a judgment of

the court for the purposes of an appeal. But no appeal lies without the leave of the court which shall not be given unless the court considers that the question involves a point of law which is one of general importance or is one which for some other special reason should be considered by the Court of Appeal.

The arbitral proceedings

Section 33 – General duty of the tribunal

(1) The tribunal shall –

    (a) act fairly and impartially as between the parties, giving each party a reasonable opportunity of putting his case and dealing with that of his opponent, and

    (b) adopt procedures suitable to the circumstances of the particular case, avoiding unnecessary delay or expense, so as to provide a fair means for the resolution of the matters falling to be determined.

(2) The tribunal shall comply with that general duty in conducting the arbitral proceedings, in its decisions on matters of procedure and evidence and in the exercise of all other powers conferred on it.

Section 34 – Procedural and evidential matters

(1) It shall be for the tribunal to decide all procedural and evidential matters, subject to the right of the parties to agree any matter.

(2) Procedural and evidential matters include –

    (a) when and where any part of the proceedings is to be held;

    (b) the language or languages to be used in the proceedings and whether translations of any relevant documents are to be supplied;

    (c) whether any and if so what form of written statements of claim and defence are to be used, when these should be supplied and the extent to which such statements can be later amended;

    (d) whether any and if so which documents or classes of documents should be disclosed between and produced by the parties and at what stage;

    (e) whether any and if so what questions should be put to and answered by the respective parties and when and in what form this should be done;

    (f) whether to apply strict rules of evidence (or any other rules) as to the admissibility, relevance or weight of any material (oral, written or other) sought to be tendered on any matters of fact or opinion, and the time, manner and form in which such material should be exchanged and presented;

    (g) whether and to what extent the tribunal should itself take the initiative in ascertaining the facts and the law;

    (h) whether and to what extent there should be oral or written evidence or submissions.

(3) The tribunal may fix the time within which any directions given by it are to be complied with, and may if it thinks fit extend the time so fixed (whether or not it has expired).

Section 35 – Consolidation of proceedings and concurrent hearings

(1) The parties are free to agree –

    (a) that the arbitral proceedings shall be consolidated with other arbitral proceedings, or

    (b) that concurrent hearings shall be held, on such terms as may be agreed.

(2) Unless the parties agree to confer such power on the tribunal, the tribunal has no power to order consolidation of proceedings or concurrent hearings.

Section 36 – Legal or other representation

Unless otherwise agreed by the parties, a party to arbitral proceedings may be represented in the proceedings by a lawyer or other person chosen by him.

Section 37 – Power to appoint experts, legal advisers or assessors

(1) Unless otherwise agreed by the parties –

    (a) the tribunal may –

        (i) appoint experts or legal advisers to report to it and the parties, or

        (ii) appoint assessors to assist it on technical matters, and may allow any such expert, legal adviser or assessor to attend the proceedings; and

    (b) the parties shall be given a reasonable opportunity to comment on any information, opinion or advice offered by any such person.

(2) The fees and expenses of an expert, legal adviser or assessor appointed by the tribunal for which the arbitrators are liable are expenses of the arbitrators for the purposes of this Part.

Section 38 – General powers exercisable by the tribunal

(1) The parties are free to agree on the powers exercisable by the arbitral tribunal for the purposes of and in relation to the proceedings.

(2) Unless otherwise agreed by the parties the tribunal has the following powers.

(3) The tribunal may order a claimant to provide security for the costs of the arbitration. This power shall not be exercised on the ground that the claimant is –

    (a) an individual ordinarily resident outside the United Kingdom, or

    (b) a corporation or association incorporated or formed under the law of a country outside the United Kingdom, or whose central management and control is exercised outside the United Kingdom.

(4) The tribunal may give directions in relation to any property which is the subject of the proceedings or as to which any question arises in the proceedings, and which is owned by or is in the possession of a party to the proceedings –

    (a) for the inspection, photographing, preservation, custody or detention of the property by the tribunal, an expert or a party, or

    (b) ordering that samples be taken from, or any observation be made of or experiment conducted upon, the property.

(5) The tribunal may direct that a party or witness shall be examined on oath or affirmation, and may for that purpose administer any necessary oath or take any necessary affirmation.

(6) The tribunal may give directions to a party for the preservation for the purposes of the proceedings of any evidence in his custody or control.

Section 39 – Power to make provisional awards

(1) The parties are free to agree that the tribunal shall have power to order on a provisional basis any relief which it would have power to grant in a final award.

(2) This includes, for instance, making –

(a) a provisional order for the payment of money or the disposition of property as between the parties, or

(b) an order to make an interim payment on account of the costs of the arbitration.

(3) Any such order shall be subject to the tribunal's final adjudication; and the tribunal's final award, on the merits or as to costs, shall take account of any such order.

(4) Unless the parties agree to confer such power on the tribunal, the tribunal has no such power. This does not affect its powers under section 47 (awards on different issues, etc).

Section 40 – General duty of parties

(1) The parties shall do all things necessary for the proper and expeditious conduct of the arbitral proceedings.

(2) This includes –

(a) complying without delay with any determination of the tribunal as to procedural or evidential matters, or with any order or directions of the tribunal, and

(b) where appropriate, taking without delay any necessary steps to obtain a decision of the court on a preliminary question of jurisdiction or law (see sections 32 and 45).

Section 41 – Powers of tribunal in case of party's default

(1) The parties are free to agree on the powers of the tribunal in case of a party's failure to do something necessary for the proper and expeditious conduct of the arbitration.

(2) Unless otherwise agreed by the parties, the following provisions apply.

(3) If the tribunal is satisfied that there has been inordinate and inexcusable delay on the part of the claimant in pursuing his claim and that the delay –

(a) gives rise, or is likely to give rise, to a substantial risk that it is not possible to have a fair resolution of the issues in that claim, or

(b) has caused, or is likely to cause, serious prejudice to the respondent, the tribunal may make an award dismissing the claim.

(4) If without showing sufficient cause a party –

(a) fails to attend or be represented at an oral hearing of which due notice was given, or

(b) where matters are to be dealt with in writing, fails after due notice to submit written evidence or make written submissions, the tribunal may continue the proceedings in the absence of that party or, as the case may be, without any written evidence or submissions on his behalf, and may make an award on the basis of the evidence before it.

(5) If without showing sufficient cause a party fails to comply with any order or directions of the tribunal, the tribunal may make a peremptory order to the same effect, prescribing such time for compliance with it as the tribunal considers appropriate.

(6) If a claimant fails to comply with a peremptory order of the tribunal to provide security for costs, the tribunal may make an award dismissing his claim.

(7) If a party fails to comply with any other kind of peremptory order, then, without prejudice to section 42 (enforcement by court of tribunal's peremptory orders), the tribunal may do any of the following –

   (a) direct that the party in default shall not be entitled to rely upon any allegation or material which was the subject matter of the order;

   (b) draw such adverse inferences from the act of non-compliance as the circumstances justify;

   (c) proceed to an award on the basis of such materials as have been properly provided to it;

   (d) make such order as it thinks fit as to the payment of costs of the arbitration incurred in consequence of the non-compliance.

Powers of court in relation to arbitral proceedings

Section 42 – Enforcement of peremptory orders of tribunal

(1) Unless otherwise agreed by the parties, the court may make an order requiring a party to comply with a peremptory order made by the tribunal.

(2) An application for an order under this section may be made –

   (a) by the tribunal (upon notice to the parties),

   (b) by a party to the arbitral proceedings with the permission of the tribunal (and upon notice to the other parties), or

   (c) where the parties have agreed that the powers of the court under this section shall be available.

(3) The court shall not act unless it is satisfied that the applicant has exhausted any available arbitral process in respect of failure to comply with the tribunal's order.

(4) No order shall be made under this section unless the court is satisfied that the person to whom the tribunal's order was directed has failed to comply with it within the time prescribed in the order or, if no time was prescribed, within a reasonable time.

(5) The leave of the court is required for any appeal from a decision of the court under this section.

Section 43 – Securing the attendance of witnesses

(1) A party to arbitral proceedings may use the same court procedures as are available in relation to legal proceedings to secure the attendance before the tribunal of a witness in order to give oral testimony or to produce documents or other material evidence.

(2) This may only be done with the permission of the tribunal or the agreement of the other parties.

(3) The court procedures may only be used if –

(a) the witness is in the United Kingdom, and

(b) the arbitral proceedings are being conducted in England and Wales or, as the case may be, Northern Ireland.

(4) A person shall not be compelled by virtue of this section to produce any document or other material evidence which he could not be compelled to produce in legal proceedings.

Section 44 – Court powers exercisable in support of arbitral proceedings

(1) Unless otherwise agreed by the parties, the court has for the purposes of and in relation to arbitral proceedings the same power of making orders about the matters listed below as it has for the purposes of and in relation to legal proceedings.

(2) Those matters are –

(a) the taking of the evidence of witnesses;

(b) the preservation of evidence;

(c) making orders relating to property which is the subject of the proceedings or as to which any question arises in the proceedings –

(i) for the inspection, photographing, preservation, custody or detention of the property, or

(ii) ordering that samples be taken from, or any observation be made of or experiment conducted upon, the property;

and for that purpose authorising any person to enter any premises in the possession or control of a party to the arbitration;

(d) the sale of any goods the subject of the proceedings;

(e) the granting of an interim injunction or the appointment of a receiver.

(3) If the case is one of urgency, the court may, on the application of a party or proposed party to the arbitral proceedings, make such orders as it thinks necessary for the purpose of preserving evidence or assets.

(4) If the case is not one of urgency, the court shall act only on the application of a party to the arbitral proceedings (upon notice to the other parties and to the tribunal) made with the permission of the tribunal or the agreement in writing of the other parties.

(5) In any case the court shall act only if or to the extent that the arbitral tribunal, and any arbitral or other institution or person vested by the parties with power in that regard, has no power or is unable for the time being to act effectively.

(6) If the court so orders, an order made by it under this section shall cease to have effect in whole or in part on the order of the tribunal or of any such arbitral or other institution or person having power to act in relation to the subject matter of the order.

(7) The leave of the court is required for any appeal from a decision of the court under this section.

Section 45 – Determination of preliminary point of law

(1) Unless otherwise agreed by the parties, the court may on the application of a party to arbitral proceedings (upon notice to the other parties) determine any question of law arising in the course of the proceedings which the court is satisfied substantially affects

the rights of one or more of the parties. An agreement to dispense with reasons for the tribunal's award shall be considered an agreement to exclude the court's jurisdiction under this section.

(2) An application under this section shall not be considered unless –

    (a) it is made with the agreement of all the other parties to the proceedings, or

    (b) it is made with the permission of the tribunal and the court is satisfied –

        (i) that the determination of the question is likely to produce substantial savings in costs, and

        (ii) that the application was made without delay.

(3) The application shall identify the question of law to be determined and, unless made with the agreement of all the other parties to the proceedings, shall state the grounds on which it is said that the question should be decided by the court.

(4) Unless otherwise agreed by the parties, the arbitral tribunal may continue the arbitral proceedings and make an award while an application to the court under this section is pending.

(5) Unless the court gives leave, no appeal lies from a decision of the court whether the conditions specified in subsection (2) are met.

(6) The decision of the court on the question of law shall be treated as a judgment of the court for the purposes of an appeal. But no appeal lies without the leave of the court which shall not be given unless the court considers that the question is one of general importance, or is one which for some other special reason should be considered by the Court of Appeal.

The award

Section 46 – Rules applicable to substance of dispute

(1) The arbitral tribunal shall decide the dispute –

    (a) in accordance with the law chosen by the parties as applicable to the substance of the dispute, or

    (b) if the parties so agree, in accordance with such other considerations as are agreed by them or determined by the tribunal.

(2) For this purpose the choice of the laws of a country shall be understood to refer to the substantive laws of that country and not its conflict of laws rules.

(3) If or to the extent that there is no such choice or agreement, the tribunal shall apply the law determined by the conflict of laws rules which it considers applicable.

Section 47 – Awards on different issues, etc

(1) Unless otherwise agreed by the parties, the tribunal may make more than one award at different times on different aspects of the matters to be determined.

(2) The tribunal may, in particular, make an award relating –

    (a) to an issue affecting the whole claim, or

    (b) to a part only of the claims or cross-claims submitted to it for decision.

(3) If the tribunal does so, it shall specify in its award the issue, or the claim or part of a claim, which is the subject matter of the award.

Section 48 – Remedies

(1) The parties are free to agree on the powers exercisable by the arbitral tribunal as regards remedies.

(2) Unless otherwise agreed by the parties, the tribunal has the following powers.

(3) The tribunal may make a declaration as to any matter to be determined in the proceedings.

(4) The tribunal may order the payment of a sum of money, in any currency.

(5) The tribunal has the same powers as the court –

    (a) to order a party to do or refrain from doing anything;

    (b) to order specific performance of a contract (other than a contract relating to land);

    (c) to order the rectification, setting aside or cancellation of a deed or other document.

Section 49 – Interest

(1) The parties are free to agree on the powers of the tribunal as regards the award of interest.

(2) Unless otherwise agreed by the parties the following provisions apply.

(3) The tribunal may award simple or compound interest from such dates, at such rates and with such rests as it considers meets the justice of the case –

    (a) on the whole or part of any amount awarded by the tribunal, in respect of any period up to the date of the award;

    (b) on the whole or part of any amount claimed in the arbitration and outstanding at the commencement of the arbitral proceedings but paid before the award was made, in respect of any period up to the date of payment.

(4) The tribunal may award simple or compound interest from the date of the award (or any later date) until payment, at such rates and with such rests as it considers meets the justice of the case, on the outstanding amount of any award (including any award of interest under subsection (3) and any award as to costs).

(5) References in this section to an amount awarded by the tribunal include an amount payable in consequence of a declaratory award by the tribunal.

(6) The above provisions do not affect any other power of the tribunal to award interest.

Section 50 – Extension of time for making award

(1) Where the time for making an award is limited by or in pursuance of the arbitration agreement, then, unless otherwise agreed by the parties, the court may in accordance with the following provisions by order extend that time.

(2) An application for an order under this section may be made –

    (a) by the tribunal (upon notice to the parties), or

    (b) by any party to the proceedings (upon notice to the tribunal and the other parties), but only after exhausting any available arbitral process for obtaining an extension of time.

(3) The court shall only make an order if satisfied that a substantial injustice would otherwise be done.

(4) The court may extend the time for such period and on such terms as it thinks fit, and may do so whether or not the time previously fixed (by or under the agreement or by a previous order) has expired.

(5) The leave of the court is required for any appeal from a decision of the court under this section.

Section 51 – Settlement

(1) If during arbitral proceedings the parties settle the dispute, the following provisions apply unless otherwise agreed by the parties.

(2) The tribunal shall terminate the substantive proceedings and, if so requested by the parties and not objected to by the tribunal, shall record the settlement in the form of an agreed award.

(3) An agreed award shall state that it is an award of the tribunal and shall have the same status and effect as any other award on the merits of the case.

(4) The following provisions of this Part relating to awards (sections 52 to 58) apply to an agreed award.

(5) Unless the parties have also settled the matter of the payment of the costs of the arbitration, the provisions of this Part relating to costs (sections 59 to 65) continue to apply.

Section 52 – Form of award

(1) The parties are free to agree on the form of an award.

(2) If or to the extent that there is no such agreement, the following provisions apply.

(3) The award shall be in writing signed by all the arbitrators or all those assenting to the award.

(4) The award shall contain the reasons for the award unless it is an agreed award or the parties have agreed to dispense with reasons.

(5) The award shall state the seat of the arbitration and the date when the award is made.

Section 53 – Place where award treated as made

Unless otherwise agreed by the parties, where the seat of the arbitration is in England and Wales or Northern Ireland, any award in the proceedings shall be treated as made there, regardless of where it was signed, despatched or delivered to any of the parties.

Section 54 – Date of award

(1) Unless otherwise agreed by the parties, the tribunal may decide what is to be taken to be the date on which the award was made.

(2) In the absence of any such decision, the date of the award shall be taken to be the date on which it is signed by the arbitrator or, where more than one arbitrator signs the award, by the last of them.

Section 55 – Notification of award

(1) The parties are free to agree on the requirements as to notification of the award to the parties.

(2) If there is no such agreement, the award shall be notified to the parties by service on them of copies of the award, which shall be done without delay after the award is made.

(3) Nothing in this section affects section 56 (power to withhold award in case of non-payment).

Section 56 – Power to withhold award in case of non-payment

(1) The tribunal may refuse to deliver an award to the parties except upon full payment of the fees and expenses of the arbitrators.

(2) If the tribunal refuses on that ground to deliver an award, a party to the arbitral proceedings may (upon notice to the other parties and the tribunal) apply to the court, which may order that –

    (a) the tribunal shall deliver the award on the payment into court by the applicant of the fees and expenses demanded, or such lesser amount as the court may specify,

    (b) the amount of the fees and expenses properly payable shall be determined by such means and upon such terms as the court may direct, and

    (c) out of the money paid into court there shall be paid out such fees and expenses as may be found to be properly payable and the balance of the money (if any) shall be paid out to the applicant.

(3) For this purpose the amount of fees and expenses properly payable is the amount the applicant is liable to pay under section 28 or any agreement relating to the payment of the arbitrators.

(4) No application to the court may be made where there is any available arbitral process for appeal or review of the amount of the fees or expenses demanded.

(5) References in this section to arbitrators include an arbitrator who has ceased to act and an umpire who has not replaced the other arbitrators.

(6) The above provisions of this section also apply in relation to any arbitral or other institution or person vested by the parties with powers in relation to the delivery of the tribunal's award. As they so apply, the references to the fees and expenses of the arbitrators shall be construed as including the fees and expenses of that institution or person.

(7) The leave of the court is required for any appeal from a decision of the court under this section.

(8) Nothing in this section shall be construed as excluding an application under section 28 where payment has been made to the arbitrators in order to obtain the award.

Section 57 – Correction of award or additional award

(1) The parties are free to agree on the powers of the tribunal to correct an award or make an additional award.

(2) If or to the extent there is no such agreement, the following provisions apply.

(3) The tribunal may on its own initiative or on the application of a party –

   (a) correct an award so as to remove any clerical mistake or error arising from an accidental slip or omission or clarify or remove any ambiguity in the award, or

   (b) make an additional award in respect of any claim (including a claim for interest or costs) which was presented to the tribunal but was not dealt with in the award. These powers shall not be exercised without first affording the other parties a reasonable opportunity to make representations to the tribunal.

(4) Any application for the exercise of those powers must be made within 28 days of the date of the award or such longer period as the parties may agree.

(5) Any correction of an award shall be made within 28 days of the date the application was received by the tribunal or, where the correction is made by the tribunal on its own initiative, within 28 days of the date of the award or, in either case, such longer period as the parties may agree.

(6) Any additional award shall be made within 56 days of the date of the original award or such longer period as the parties may agree.

(7) Any correction of an award shall form part of the award.

Section 58 – Effect of award

(1) Unless otherwise agreed by the parties, an award made by the tribunal pursuant to an arbitration agreement is final and binding both on the parties and on any persons claiming through or under them.

(2) This does not affect the right of a person to challenge the award by any available arbitral process of appeal or review or in accordance with the provisions of this Part.

Costs of the arbitration

Section 59 – Costs of the arbitration

(1) References in this Part to the costs of the arbitration are to –

   (a) the arbitrators' fees and expenses,

   (b) the fees and expenses of any arbitral institution concerned, and

   (c) the legal or other costs of the parties.

(2) Any such reference includes the costs of or incidental to any proceedings to determine the amount of the recoverable costs of the arbitration (see section 63).

Section 60 – Agreement to pay costs in any event

An agreement which has the effect that a party is to pay the whole or part of the costs of the arbitration in any event is only valid if made after the dispute in question has arisen.

Section 61 – Award of costs

(1) The tribunal may make an award allocating the costs of the arbitration as between the parties, subject to any agreement of the parties.

(2) Unless the parties otherwise agree, the tribunal shall award costs on the general principle that costs should follow the event except where it appears to the tribunal that in the circumstances this is not appropriate in relation to the whole or part of the costs.

Section 62 – Effect of agreement or award about costs

Unless the parties otherwise agree, any obligation under an agreement between them as to how the costs of the arbitration are to be borne, or under an award allocating the costs of the arbitration, extends only to such costs as are recoverable.

Section 63 – The recoverable costs of the arbitration

(1) The parties are free to agree what costs of the arbitration are recoverable.

(2) If or to the extent there is no such agreement, the following provisions apply.

(3) The tribunal may determine by award the recoverable costs of the arbitration on such basis as it thinks fit. If it does so, it shall specify –

(a) the basis on which it has acted, and

(b) the items of recoverable costs and the amount referable to each.

(4) If the tribunal does not determine the recoverable costs of the arbitration, any party to the arbitral proceedings may apply to the court (upon notice to the other parties) which may –

(a) determine the recoverable costs of the arbitration on such basis as it thinks fit, or

(b) order that they shall be determined by such means and upon such terms as it may specify.

(5) Unless the tribunal or the court determines otherwise –

(a) the recoverable costs of the arbitration shall be determined on the basis that there shall be allowed a reasonable amount in respect of all costs reasonably incurred, and

(b) any doubt as to whether costs were reasonably incurred or were reasonable in amount shall be resolved in favour of the paying party.

(6) The above provisions have effect subject to section 64 (recoverable fees and expenses of arbitrators).

(7) Nothing in this section affects any right of the arbitrators, any expert, legal adviser or assessor appointed by the tribunal, or any arbitral institution, to payment of their fees and expenses.

Section 64 – Recoverable fees and expenses of arbitrators

(1) Unless otherwise agreed by the parties, the recoverable costs of the arbitration shall include in respect of the fees and expenses of the arbitrators only such reasonable fees and expenses as are appropriate in the circumstances.

(2) If there is any question as to what reasonable fees and expenses are appropriate in the circumstances, and the matter is not already before the court on an application under section 63(4), the court may on the application of any party (upon notice to the other parties) –

    (a) determine the matter, or

    (b) order that it be determined by such means and upon such terms as the court may specify.

(3) Subsection (1) has effect subject to any order of the court under section 24(4) or 25(3)(b) (order as to entitlement to fees or expenses in case of removal or resignation of arbitrator).

(4) Nothing in this section affects any right of the arbitrator to payment of his fees and expenses.

Section 65 – Power to limit recoverable costs

(1) Unless otherwise agreed by the parties, the tribunal may direct that the recoverable costs of the arbitration, or of any part of the arbitral proceedings, shall be limited to a specified amount.

(2) Any direction may be made or varied at any stage, but this must be done sufficiently in advance of the incurring of costs to which it relates, or the taking of any steps in the proceedings which may be affected by it, for the limit to be taken into account.

Powers of the court in relation to award

Section 66 – Enforcement of the award

(1) An award made by the tribunal pursuant to an arbitration agreement may, by leave of the court, be enforced in the same manner as a judgment or order of the court to the same effect.

(2) Where leave is so given, judgment may be entered in terms of the award.

(3) Leave to enforce an award shall not be given where, or to the extent that, the person against whom it is sought to be enforced shows that the tribunal lacked substantive jurisdiction to make the award. The right to raise such an objection may have been lost (see section 73).

    1950 c27 489

(4) Nothing in this section affects the recognition or enforcement of an award under any other enactment or rule of law, in particular under Part II of the Arbitration Act 1950 (enforcement of awards under Geneva Convention) or the provisions of Part III of this Act relating to the recognition and enforcement of awards under the New York Convention or by an action on the award.

Section 67 – Challenging the award: substantive jurisdiction

(1) A party to arbitral proceedings may (upon notice to the other parties and to the tribunal) apply to the court –

    (a) challenging any award of the arbitral tribunal as to its substantive jurisdiction; or

    (b) for an order declaring an award made by the tribunal on the merits to be of no effect, in whole or in part, because the tribunal did not have substantive jurisdiction. A party may lose the right to object (see section 73) and the right to apply is subject to the restrictions in section 70(2) and (3).

(2) The arbitral tribunal may continue the arbitral proceedings and make a further award while an application to the court under this section is pending in relation to an award as to jurisdiction.

(3) On an application under this section challenging an award of the arbitral tribunal as to its substantive jurisdiction, the court may by order –

(a) confirm the award,

(b) vary the award, or

(c) set aside the award in whole or in part.

(4) The leave of the court is required for any appeal from a decision of the court under this section.

Section 68 – Challenging the award: serious irregularity

(1) A party to arbitral proceedings may (upon notice to the other parties and to the tribunal) apply to the court challenging an award in the proceedings on the ground of serious irregularity affecting the tribunal, the proceedings or the award. A party may lose the right to object (see section 73) and the right to apply is subject to the restrictions in section 70(2) and (3).

(2) Serious irregularity means an irregularity of one or more of the following kinds which the court considers has caused or will cause substantial injustice to the applicant –

(a) failure by the tribunal to comply with section 33 (general duty of tribunal);

(b) the tribunal exceeding its powers (otherwise than by exceeding its substantive jurisdiction: see section 67);

(c) failure by the tribunal to conduct the proceedings in accordance with the procedure agreed by the parties;

(d) failure by the tribunal to deal with all the issues that were put to it;

(e) any arbitral or other institution or person vested by the parties with powers in relation to the proceedings or the award exceeding its powers;

(f) uncertainty or ambiguity as to the effect of the award;

(g) the award being obtained by fraud or the award or the way in which it was procured being contrary to public policy;

(h) failure to comply with the requirements as to the form of the award; or

(i) any irregularity in the conduct of the proceedings or in the award which is admitted by the tribunal or by any arbitral or other institution or person vested by the parties with powers in relation to the proceedings or the award.

(3) If there is shown to be serious irregularity affecting the tribunal, the proceedings or the award, the court may –

(a) remit the award to the tribunal, in whole or in part, for reconsideration,

(b) set the award aside in whole or in part, or

(c) declare the award to be of no effect, in whole or in part. The court shall not exercise its power to set aside or to declare an award to be of no effect, in whole or in part, unless it is satisfied that it would be inappropriate to remit the matters in question to the tribunal for reconsideration.

(4) The leave of the court is required for any appeal from a decision of the court under this section.

Section 69 – Appeal on point of law

(1) Unless otherwise agreed by the parties, a party to arbitral proceedings may (upon notice to the other parties and to the tribunal) appeal to the court on a question of law arising out of an award made in the proceedings. An agreement to dispense with reasons for the tribunal's award shall be considered an agreement to exclude the court's jurisdiction under this section.

(2) An appeal shall not be brought under this section except –

   (a) with the agreement of all the other parties to the proceedings, or

   (b) with the leave of the court. The right to appeal is also subject to the restrictions in section 70(2) and (3).

(3) Leave to appeal shall be given only if the court is satisfied –

   (a) that the determination of the question will substantially affect the rights of one or more of the parties,

   (b) that the question is one which the tribunal was asked to determine,

   (c) that, on the basis of the findings of fact in the award –

      (i) the decision of the tribunal on the question is obviously wrong, or

      (ii) the question is one of general public importance and the decision of the tribunal is at least open to serious doubt, and

   (d) that, despite the agreement of the parties to resolve the matter by arbitration, it is just and proper in all the circumstances for the court to determine the question.

(4) An application for leave to appeal under this section shall identify the question of law to be determined and state the grounds on which it is alleged that leave to appeal should be granted.

(5) The court shall determine an application for leave to appeal under this section without a hearing unless it appears to the court that a hearing is required.

(6) The leave of the court is required for any appeal from a decision of the court under this section to grant or refuse leave to appeal.

(7) On an appeal under this section the court may by order –

   (a) confirm the award,

   (b) vary the award,

   (c) remit the award to the tribunal, in whole or in part, for reconsideration in the light of the court's determination, or

   (d) set aside the award in whole or in part. The court shall not exercise its power to set aside an award, in whole or in part, unless it is satisfied that it would be inappropriate to remit the matters in question to the tribunal for reconsideration.

(8) The decision of the court on an appeal under this section shall be treated as a judgment of the court for the purposes of a further appeal. But no such appeal lies without the leave of the court which shall not be given unless the court considers that the question is one of general importance or is one which for some other special reason should be considered by the Court of Appeal.

Section 70 – Challenge or appeal: supplementary provisions

(1) The following provisions apply to an application or appeal under section 67, 68 or 69.

(2) An application or appeal may not be brought if the applicant or appellant has not first exhausted –

   (a) any available arbitral process of appeal or review, and

   (b) any available recourse under section 57 (correction of award or additional award).

(3) Any application or appeal must be brought within 28 days of the date of the award or, if there has been any arbitral process of appeal or review, of the date when the applicant or appellant was notified of the result of that process.

(4) If on an application or appeal it appears to the court that the award –

   (a) does not contain the tribunal's reasons, or

   (b) does not set out the tribunal's reasons in sufficient detail to enable the court properly to consider the application or appeal, the court may order the tribunal to state the reasons for its award in sufficient detail for that purpose.

(5) Where the court makes an order under subsection (4), it may make such further order as it thinks fit with respect to any additional costs of the arbitration resulting from its order.

(6) The court may order the applicant or appellant to provide security for the costs of the application or appeal, and may direct that the application or appeal be dismissed if the order is not complied with. The power to order security for costs shall not be exercised on the ground that the applicant or appellant is –

   (a) an individual ordinarily resident outside the United Kingdom, or

   (b) a corporation or association incorporated or formed under the law of a country outside the United Kingdom, or whose central management and control is exercised outside the United Kingdom.

(7) The court may order that any money payable under the award shall be brought into court or otherwise secured pending the determination of the application or appeal, and may direct that the application or appeal be dismissed if the order is not complied with.

(8) The court may grant leave to appeal subject to conditions to the same or similar effect as an order under subsection (6) or (7). This does not affect the general discretion of the court to grant leave subject to conditions.

Section 71 – Challenge or appeal: effect of order of court

(1) The following provisions have effect where the court makes an order under section 67, 68 or 69 with respect to an award.

(2) Where the award is varied, the variation has effect as part of the tribunal's award.

(3) Where the award is remitted to the tribunal, in whole or in part, for reconsideration, the tribunal shall make a fresh award in respect of the matters remitted within three months of the date of the order for remission or such longer or shorter period as the court may direct.

(4) Where the award is set aside or declared to be of no effect, in whole or in part, the court may also order that any provision that an award is a condition precedent to the bringing of legal proceedings in respect of a matter to which the arbitration agreement applies, is of no effect as regards the subject matter of the award or, as the case may be, the relevant part of the award.

Miscellaneous

Section 72 – Saving for rights of person who takes no part in proceedings

(1) A person alleged to be a party to arbitral proceedings but who takes no part in the proceedings may question –

   (a) whether there is a valid arbitration agreement,

   (b) whether the tribunal is properly constituted, or

   (c) what matters have been submitted to arbitration in accordance with the arbitration agreement, by proceedings in the court for a declaration or injunction or other appropriate relief.

(2) He also has the same right as a party to the arbitral proceedings to challenge an award –

   (a) by an application under section 67 on the ground of lack of substantive jurisdiction in relation to him, or

   (b) by an application under section 68 on the ground of serious irregularity (within the meaning of that section) affecting him; and section 70(2) (duty to exhaust arbitral procedures) does not apply in his case.

Section 73 – Loss of right to object

(1) If a party to arbitral proceedings takes part, or continues to take part, in the proceedings without making, either forthwith or within such time as is allowed by the arbitration agreement or the tribunal or by any provision of this Part, any objection –

   (a) that the tribunal lacks substantive jurisdiction,

   (b) that the proceedings have been improperly conducted,

   (c) that there has been a failure to comply with the arbitration agreement or with any provision of this Part, or

   (d) that there has been any other irregularity affecting the tribunal or the proceedings, he may not raise that objection later, before the tribunal or the court, unless he shows that, at the time he took part or continued to take part in the proceedings, he did not know and could not with reasonable diligence have discovered the grounds for the objection.

(2) Where the arbitral tribunal rules that it has substantive jurisdiction and a party to arbitral proceedings who could have questioned that ruling –

   (a) by any available arbitral process of appeal or review, or

   (b) by challenging the award, does not do so, or does not do so within the time allowed by the arbitration agreement or any provision of this Part, he may not object later to the tribunal's substantive jurisdiction on any ground which was the subject of that ruling.

Section 74 – Immunity of arbitral institutions, etc

(1) An arbitral or other institution or person designated or requested by the parties to appoint or nominate an arbitrator is not liable for anything done or omitted in the discharge or purported discharge of that function unless the act or omission is shown to have been in bad faith.

(2) An arbitral or other institution or person by whom an arbitrator is appointed or nominated is not liable, by reason of having appointed or nominated him, for anything done or omitted by the arbitrator (or his employees or agents) in the discharge or purported discharge of his functions as arbitrator.

(3) The above provisions apply to an employee or agent of an arbitral or other institution or person as they apply to the institution or person himself.

Section 75 – Charge to secure payment of solicitors' costs

The powers of the court to make declarations and orders under section 73 of the Solicitors Act 1974 or Article 71H of the Solicitors (Northern Ireland) Order 1976 (power to charge property recovered in the proceedings with the payment of solicitors' costs) may be exercised in relation to arbitral proceedings as if those proceedings were proceedings in the court.

1974 c47 588

SI 1976/582 (NI 12) 589

Supplementary

Section 76 – Service of notices, etc

(1) The parties are free to agree on the manner of service of any notice or other document required or authorised to be given or served in pursuance of the arbitration agreement or for the purposes of the arbitral proceedings.

(2) If or to the extent that there is no such agreement the following provisions apply.

(3) A notice or other document may be served on a person by any effective means.

(4) If a notice or other document is addressed, pre-paid and delivered by post –

(a) to the addressee's last known principal residence or, if he is or has been carrying on a trade, profession or business, his last known principal business address, or

(b) where the addressee is a body corporate, to the body's registered or principal office, it shall be treated as effectively served.

(5) This section does not apply to the service of documents for the purposes of legal proceedings, for which provision is made by rules of court.

(6) References in this Part to a notice or other document include any form of communication in writing and references to giving or serving a notice or other document shall be construed accordingly.

Section 77 – Powers of court in relation to service of documents.

(1) This section applies where service of a document on a person in the manner agreed by the parties, or in accordance with provisions of section 76 having effect in default of agreement, is not reasonably practicable.

(2) Unless otherwise agreed by the parties, the court may make such order as it thinks fit –

(a) for service in such manner as the court may direct, or

(b) dispensing with service of the document.

(3) Any party to the arbitration agreement may apply for an order, but only after exhausting any available arbitral process for resolving the matter.

(4) The leave of the court is required for any appeal from a decision of the court under this section.

Section 78 – Reckoning periods of time

(1) The parties are free to agree on the method of reckoning periods of time for the purposes of any provision agreed by them or any provision of this Part having effect in default of such agreement.

(2) If or to the extent there is no such agreement, periods of time shall be reckoned in accordance with the following provisions.

(3) Where the act is required to be done within a specified period after or from a specified date, the period begins immediately after that date.

(4) Where the act is required to be done a specified number of clear days after a specified date, at least that number of days must intervene between the day on which the act is done and that date.

1971 c80 613

(5) Where the period is a period of seven days or less which would include a Saturday, Sunday or a public holiday in the place where anything which has to be done within the period falls to be done, that day shall be excluded. In relation to England and Wales or Northern Ireland, a 'public holiday' means Christmas Day, Good Friday or a day which under the Banking and Financial Dealings Act 1971 is a bank holiday.

Section 79 – Power of court to extend time limits relating to arbitral proceedings

(1) Unless the parties otherwise agree, the court may by order extend any time limit agreed by them in relation to any matter relating to the arbitral proceedings or specified in any provision of this Part having effect in default of such agreement. This section does not apply to a time limit to which section 12 applies (power of court to extend time for beginning arbitral proceedings, etc).

(2) An application for an order may be made –

   (a) by any party to the arbitral proceedings (upon notice to the other parties and to the tribunal), or

   (b) by the arbitral tribunal (upon notice to the parties).

(3) The court shall not exercise its power to extend a time limit unless it is satisfied –

   (a) that any available recourse to the tribunal, or to any arbitral or other institution or person vested by the parties with power in that regard, has first been exhausted, and

   (b) that a substantial injustice would otherwise be done.

(4) The court's power under this section may be exercised whether or not the time has already expired.

(5) An order under this section may be made on such terms as the court thinks fit.

(6) The leave of the court is required for any appeal from a decision of the court under this section.

Section 80 – Notice and other requirements in connection with legal proceedings

(1) References in this Part to an application, appeal or other step in relation to legal proceedings being taken 'upon notice' to the other parties to the arbitral proceedings, or to the tribunal, are to such notice of the originating process as is required by rules of court and do not impose any separate requirement.

(2) Rules of court shall be made –

(a) requiring such notice to be given as indicated by any provision of this Part, and

(b) as to the manner, form and content of any such notice.

(3) Subject to any provision made by rules of court, a requirement to give notice to the tribunal of legal proceedings shall be construed –

(a) if there is more than one arbitrator, as a requirement to give notice to each of them; and

(b) if the tribunal is not fully constituted, as a requirement to give notice to any arbitrator who has been appointed.

(4) References in this Part to making an application or appeal to the court within a specified period are to the issue within that period of the appropriate originating process in accordance with rules of court.

(5) Where any provision of this Part requires an application or appeal to be made to the court within a specified time, the rules of court relating to the reckoning of periods, the extending or abridging of periods, and the consequences of not taking a step within the period prescribed by the rules, apply in relation to that requirement.

(6) Provision may be made by rules of court amending the provisions of this Part –

(a) with respect to the time within which any application or appeal to the court must be made,

(b) so as to keep any provision made by this Part in relation to arbitral proceedings in step with the corresponding provision of rules of court applying in relation to proceedings in the court, or

(c) so as to keep any provision made by this Part in relation to legal proceedings in step with the corresponding provision of rules of court applying generally in relation to proceedings in the court.

(7) Nothing in this section affects the generality of the power to make rules of court.

Section 81 – Saving for certain matters governed by common law

(1) Nothing in this Part shall be construed as excluding the operation of any rule of law consistent with the provisions of this Part, in particular, any rule of law as to –

(a) matters which are not capable of settlement by arbitration;

(b) the effect of an oral arbitration agreement; or

(c) the refusal of recognition or enforcement of an arbitral award on grounds of public policy.

(2) Nothing in this Act shall be construed as reviving any jurisdiction of the court to set aside or remit an award on the ground of errors of fact or law on the face of the award.

Section 82 – Minor definitions

(1) In this Part –

'arbitrator', unless the context otherwise requires, includes an umpire;

'available arbitral process', in relation to any matter, includes any process of appeal to or review by an arbitral or other institution or person vested by the parties with powers in relation to that matter;

'claimant', unless the context otherwise requires, includes a counter-claimant, and related expressions shall be construed accordingly;

'dispute' includes any difference;

'enactment' includes an enactment contained in Northern Ireland legislation;

'legal proceedings' means civil proceedings in the High Court or a county court;

'peremptory order' means an order made under section 41(5) or made in exercise of any corresponding power conferred by the parties;

'premises' includes land, buildings, moveable structures, vehicles, vessels, aircraft and hovercraft;

'question of law' means –

(a) for a court in England and Wales, a question of the law of England and Wales, and

(b) for a court in Northern Ireland, a question of the law of Northern Ireland;

'substantive jurisdiction', in relation to an arbitral tribunal, refers to the matters specified in section 30(1)(a) to (c), and references to the tribunal exceeding its substantive jurisdiction shall be construed accordingly.

(2) References in this Part to a party to an arbitration agreement include any person claiming under or through a party to the agreement.

Section 83 – Index of defined expressions: Part I

In this Part the expressions listed below are defined or otherwise explained by the provisions indicated –

agreement, agree and agreed	section 5(1)
agreement in writing	section 5(2) to (5)
arbitration agreement	sections 6 and 5(1)
arbitrator	section 82(1)
available arbitral process	section 82(1)
claimant	section 82(1)
commencement (in relation to arbitral proceedings)	section 14
costs of the arbitration	section 59
the court	section 105
dispute	section 82(1)
enactment	section 82(1)
legal proceedings	section 82(1)
Limitation Acts	section 13(4)
notice (or other document)	section 76(6)
party –	
– in relation to an arbitration agreement	section 82(2)

– where section 106(2) or (3) applies	section 106(4)
peremptory order	section 82(1) (and see section 41(5))
premises	section 82(1)
question of law	section 82(1)
recoverable costs	sections 63 and 64
seat of the arbitration	section 3
serve and service (of notice or other document)	section 76(6)
substantive jurisdiction	
(in relation to an arbitral tribunal)	section 82(1) (and see section 30(1)(a) to (c))
upon notice (to the parties or the tribunal)	section 80
written and in writing	section 5(6)

Section 84 – Transitional provisions

(1) The provisions of this Part do not apply to arbitral proceedings commenced before the date on which this Part comes into force.

(2) They apply to arbitral proceedings commenced on or after that date under an arbitration agreement whenever made.

(3) The above provisions have effect subject to any transitional provision made by an order under section 109(2) (power to include transitional provisions in commencement order).

PART II – OTHER PROVISIONS RELATING TO ARBITRATION

Domestic arbitration agreements

Section 85 – Modification of Part I in relation to domestic arbitration agreement

(1) In the case of a domestic arbitration agreement the provisions of Part I are modified in accordance with the following sections.

(2) For this purpose a 'domestic arbitration agreement' means an arbitration agreement to which none of the parties is –

(a) an individual who is a national of, or habitually resident in, a state other than the United Kingdom, or

(b) a body corporate which is incorporated in, or whose central control and management is exercised in, a state other than the United Kingdom, and under which the seat of the arbitration (if the seat has been designated or determined) is in the United Kingdom.

(3) In subsection (2) 'arbitration agreement' and 'seat of the arbitration' have the same meaning as in Part I (see sections 3, 5(1) and 6).

Section 86 – Staying of legal proceedings

(1) In section 9 (stay of legal proceedings), subsection (4) (stay unless the arbitration agreement is null and void, inoperative, or incapable of being performed) does not apply to a domestic arbitration agreement.

(2) On an application under that section in relation to a domestic arbitration agreement the court shall grant a stay unless satisfied –

(a) that the arbitration agreement is null and void, inoperative, or incapable of being performed, or

(b) that there are other sufficient grounds for not requiring the parties to abide by the arbitration agreement.

(3) The court may treat as a sufficient ground under subsection (2)(b) the fact that the applicant is or was at any material time not ready and willing to do all things necessary for the proper conduct of the arbitration or of any other dispute resolution procedures required to be exhausted before resorting to arbitration.

(4) For the purposes of this section the question whether an arbitration agreement is a domestic arbitration agreement shall be determined by reference to the facts at the time the legal proceedings are commenced.

Section 87 – Effectiveness of agreement to exclude court's jurisdiction

(1) In the case of a domestic arbitration agreement any agreement to exclude the jurisdiction of the court under –

(a) section 45 (determination of preliminary point of law), or

(b) section 69 (challenging the award: appeal on point of law), is not effective unless entered into after the commencement of the arbitral proceedings in which the question arises or the award is made.

(2) For this purpose the commencement of the arbitral proceedings has the same meaning as in Part I (see section 14).

(3) For the purposes of this section the question whether an arbitration agreement is a domestic arbitration agreement shall be determined by reference to the facts at the time the agreement is entered into.

Section 88 – Power to repeal or amend sections 85 to 87

(1) The Secretary of State may by order repeal or amend the provisions of sections 85 to 87.

(2) An order under this section may contain such supplementary, incidental and transitional provisions as appear to the Secretary of State to be appropriate.

(3) An order under this section shall be made by statutory instrument and no such order shall be made unless a draft of it has been laid before and approved by a resolution of each House of Parliament.

Consumer arbitration agreements

Section 89 – Application of unfair terms regulations to consumer arbitration agreements

(1) The following sections extend the application of the Unfair Terms in Consumer Contracts Regulations 1994 in relation to a term which constitutes an arbitration agreement. For this purpose 'arbitration agreement' means an agreement to submit to arbitration present or future disputes or differences (whether or not contractual).

SI 1994/3159 698

(2) In those sections 'the Regulations' means those regulations and includes any regulations amending or replacing those regulations.

(3) Those sections apply whatever the law applicable to the arbitration agreement.

Section 90 – Regulations apply where consumer is a legal person

The Regulations apply where the consumer is a legal person as they apply where the consumer is a natural person.

Section 91 – Arbitration agreement unfair where modest amount sought

(1) A term which constitutes an arbitration agreement is unfair for the purposes of the Regulations so far as it relates to a claim for a pecuniary remedy which does not exceed the amount specified by order for the purposes of this section.

(2) Orders under this section may make different provision for different cases and for different purposes.

(3) The power to make orders under this section is exercisable –

(a) for England and Wales, by the Secretary of State with the concurrence of the Lord Chancellor,

(b) for Scotland, by the Secretary of State with the concurrence of the Lord Advocate, and

(c) for Northern Ireland, by the Department of Economic Development for Northern Ireland with the concurrence of the Lord Chancellor.

(4) Any such order for England and Wales or Scotland shall be made by statutory instrument which shall be subject to annulment in pursuance of a resolution of either House of Parliament.

SI 1979/1573 (NI 12) 711

1954 c33 (NI) 712

(5) Any such order for Northern Ireland shall be a statutory rule for the purposes of the Statutory Rules (Northern Ireland) Order 1979 and shall be subject to negative resolution, within the meaning of section 41(6) of the Interpretation Act (Northern Ireland) 1954.

Small claims arbitration in the county court

Section 92 – Exclusion of Part I in relation to small claims arbitration in the county court

Nothing in Part I of this Act applies to arbitration under section 64 of the County Courts Act 1984.

1984 c28 717

Section 93 – Appointment of judges as arbitrators

(1) A judge of the Commercial Court or an official referee may, if in all the circumstances he thinks fit, accept appointment as a sole arbitrator or as umpire by or by virtue of an arbitration agreement.

(2) A judge of the Commercial Court shall not do so unless the Lord Chief Justice has informed him that, having regard to the state of business in the High Court and the Crown Court, he can be made available.

(3) An official referee shall not do so unless the Lord Chief Justice has informed him that, having regard to the state of official referees' business, he can be made available.

(4) The fees payable for the services of a judge of the Commercial Court or official referee as arbitrator or umpire shall be taken in the High Court.

(5) In this section –

'arbitration agreement' has the same meaning as in Part I; and

1981 c54

'official referee' means a person nominated under section 68(1)(a) of the Supreme Court Act 1981 to deal with official referees' business.

(6) The provisions of Part I of this Act apply to arbitration before a person appointed under this section with the modifications specified in Schedule 2.

Statutory arbitrations

Section 94 – Application of Part I to statutory arbitrations

(1) The provisions of Part I apply to every arbitration under an enactment (a 'statutory arbitration'), whether the enactment was passed or made before or after the commencement of this Act, subject to the adaptations and exclusions specified in sections 95 to 98.

(2) The provisions of Part I do not apply to a statutory arbitration if or to the extent that their application –

   (a) is inconsistent with the provisions of the enactment concerned, with any rules or procedure authorised or recognised by it, or

   (b) is excluded by any other enactment.

(3) In this section and the following provisions of this Part 'enactment' – 1978 c30 735

   (a) in England and Wales, includes an enactment contained in subordinate legislation within the meaning of the Interpretation Act 1978; 1954 c33 (NI) 737

   (b) in Northern Ireland, means a statutory provision within the meaning of section 1(f) of the Interpretation Act (Northern Ireland) 1954.

Section 95 – General adaptation of provisions in relation to statutory arbitrations

(1) The provisions of Part I apply to a statutory arbitration –

   (a) as if the arbitration were pursuant to an arbitration agreement and as if the enactment were that agreement, and

   (b) as if the persons by and against whom a claim subject to arbitration in pursuance of the enactment may be or has been made were parties to that agreement.

(2) Every statutory arbitration shall be taken to have its seat in England and Wales or, as the case may be, in Northern Ireland.

Section 96 – Specific adaptations of provisions in relation to statutory arbitrations

(1) The following provisions of Part I apply to a statutory arbitration with the following adaptations.

(2) In section 30(1) (competence of tribunal to rule on its own jurisdiction), the reference in paragraph (a) to whether there is a valid arbitration agreement shall be construed as a reference to whether the enactment applies to the dispute or difference in question.

(3) Section 35 (consolidation of proceedings and concurrent hearings) applies only so as to authorise the consolidation of proceedings, or concurrent hearings in proceedings, under the same enactment.

(4) Section 46 (rules applicable to substance of dispute) applies with the omission of subsection (1)(b) (determination in accordance with considerations agreed by parties).

Section 97 – Provisions excluded from applying to statutory arbitrations

The following provisions of Part I do not apply in relation to a statutory arbitration –

(a) section 8 (whether agreement discharged by death of a party);

(b) section 12 (power of court to extend agreed time limits);

(c) sections 9(5), 10(2) and 71(4) (restrictions on effect of provision that award condition precedent to right to bring legal proceedings).

Section 98 – Power to make further provision by regulations

(1) The Secretary of State may make provision by regulations for adapting or excluding any provision of Part I in relation to statutory arbitrations in general or statutory arbitrations of any particular description.

(2) The power is exercisable whether the enactment concerned is passed or made before or after the commencement of this Act.

(3) Regulations under this section shall be made by statutory instrument which shall be subject to annulment in pursuance of a resolution of either House of Parliament.

PART III – RECOGNITION AND ENFORCEMENT OF CERTAIN FOREIGN AWARDS

Enforcement of Geneva Convention awards

Section 99 – Continuation of Part II of the Arbitration Act 1950

Part II of the Arbitration Act 1950 (enforcement of certain foreign awards) continues to apply in relation to foreign awards within the meaning of that Part which are not also New York Convention awards.

1950 c27 762

Recognition and enforcement of New York Convention awards

Section 100 – New York Convention awards

(1) In this Part a 'New York Convention award' means an award made, in pursuance of an arbitration agreement, in the territory of a state (other than the United Kingdom) which is a party to the New York Convention.

(2) For the purposes of subsection (1) and of the provisions of this Part relating to such awards –

(a) 'arbitration agreement' means an arbitration agreement in writing, and

(b) an award shall be treated as made at the seat of the arbitration, regardless of where it was signed, despatched or delivered to any of the parties.

In this subsection 'agreement in writing' and 'seat of the arbitration' have the same meaning as in Part I.

(3) If Her Majesty by Order in Council declares that a state specified in the Order is a party to the New York Convention, or is a party in respect of any territory so specified, the Order shall, while in force, be conclusive evidence of that fact.

(4) In this section 'the New York Convention' means the Convention on the Recognition and Enforcement of Foreign Arbitral Awards adopted by the United Nations Conference on International Commercial Arbitration on 10th June 1958.

Section 101 – Recognition and enforcement of awards

(1) A New York Convention award shall be recognised as binding on the persons as between whom it was made, and may accordingly be relied on by those persons by way of defence, set-off or otherwise in any legal proceedings in England and Wales or Northern Ireland.

(2) A New York Convention award may, by leave of the court, be enforced in the same manner as a judgment or order of the court to the same effect. As to the meaning of 'the court' see section 105.

(3) Where leave is so given, judgment may be entered in terms of the award.

Section 102 – Evidence to be produced by party seeking recognition or enforcement

(1) A party seeking the recognition or enforcement of a New York Convention award must produce –

(a) the duly authenticated original award or a duly certified copy of it, and

(b) the original arbitration agreement or a duly certified copy of it.

(2) If the award or agreement is in a foreign language, the party must also produce a translation of it certified by an official or sworn translator or by a diplomatic or consular agent.

Section 103 – Refusal of recognition or enforcement

(1) Recognition or enforcement of a New York Convention award shall not be refused except in the following cases.

(2) Recognition or enforcement of the award may be refused if the person against whom it is invoked proves –

(a) that a party to the arbitration agreement was (under the law applicable to him) under some incapacity;

(b) that the arbitration agreement was not valid under the law to which the parties subjected it or, failing any indication thereon, under the law of the country where the award was made;

(c) that he was not given proper notice of the appointment of the arbitrator or of the arbitration proceedings or was otherwise unable to present his case;

(d) that the award deals with a difference not contemplated by or not falling within the terms of the submission to arbitration or contains decisions on matters beyond the scope of the submission to arbitration (but see subsection (4));

(e) that the composition of the arbitral tribunal or the arbitral procedure was not in accordance with the agreement of the parties or, failing such agreement, with the law of the country in which the arbitration took place;

(f) that the award has not yet become binding on the parties, or has been set aside or suspended by a competent authority of the country in which, or under the law of which, it was made.

(3) Recognition or enforcement of the award may also be refused if the award is in respect of a matter which is not capable of settlement by arbitration, or if it would be contrary to public policy to recognise or enforce the award.

(4) An award which contains decisions on matters not submitted to arbitration may be recognised or enforced to the extent that it contains decisions on matters submitted to arbitration which can be separated from those on matters not so submitted.

(5) Where an application for the setting aside or suspension of the award has been made to such a competent authority as is mentioned in subsection (2)(f), the court before which the award is sought to be relied upon may, if it considers it proper, adjourn the decision on the recognition or enforcement of the award. It may also on the application of the party claiming recognition or enforcement of the award order the other party to give suitable security.

Section 104 – Saving for other bases of recognition or enforcement

Nothing in the preceding provisions of this Part affects any right to rely upon or enforce a New York Convention award at common law or under section 66.

PART IV - GENERAL PROVISIONS

Section 105 – Meaning of 'the court': jurisdiction of High Court and county court

(1) In this Act 'the court' means the High Court or a county court, subject to the following provisions.

(2) The Lord Chancellor may by order make provision –

(a) allocating proceedings under this Act to the High Court or to county courts; or

(b) specifying proceedings under this Act which may be commenced or taken only in the High Court or in a county court.

(3) The Lord Chancellor may by order make provision requiring proceedings of any specified description under this Act in relation to which a county court has jurisdiction to be commenced or taken in one or more specified county courts. Any jurisdiction so exercisable by a specified county court is exercisable throughout England and Wales or, as the case may be, Northern Ireland.

(4) An order under this section –

   (a) may differentiate between categories of proceedings by reference to such criteria as the Lord Chancellor sees fit to specify, and

   (b) may make such incidental or transitional provision as the Lord Chancellor considers necessary or expedient.

(5) An order under this section for England and Wales shall be made by statutory instrument which shall be subject to annulment in pursuance of a resolution of either House of Parliament.

   SI 1979/1573 (NI 12) 805

   1946 c36 806

(6) An order under this section for Northern Ireland shall be a statutory rule for the purposes of the Statutory Rules (Northern Ireland) Order 1979 which shall be subject to annulment in pursuance of a resolution of either House of Parliament in like manner as a statutory instrument and section 5 of the Statutory Instruments Act 1946 shall apply accordingly.

Section 106 – Crown application

(1) Part I of this Act applies to any arbitration agreement to which Her Majesty, either in right of the Crown or of the Duchy of Lancaster or otherwise, or the Duke of Cornwall, is a party.

(2) Where Her Majesty is party to an arbitration agreement otherwise than in right of the Crown, Her Majesty shall be represented for the purposes of any arbitral proceedings –

   (a) where the agreement was entered into by Her Majesty in right of the Duchy of Lancaster, by the Chancellor of the Duchy or such person as he may appoint, and

   (b) in any other case, by such person as Her Majesty may appoint in writing under the Royal Sign Manual.

(3) Where the Duke of Cornwall is party to an arbitration agreement, he shall be represented for the purposes of any arbitral proceedings by such person as he may appoint.

(4) References in Part I to a party or the parties to the arbitration agreement or to arbitral proceedings shall be construed, where subsection (2) or (3) applies, as references to the person representing Her Majesty or the Duke of Cornwall.

Section 107 – Consequential amendments and repeals

(1) The enactments specified in Schedule 3 are amended in accordance with that Schedule, the amendments being consequential on the provisions of this Act.

(2) The enactments specified in Schedule 4 are repealed to the extent specified.

Section 108 – Extent

(1) The provisions of this Act extend to England and Wales and, except as mentioned below, to Northern Ireland.

(2) The following provisions of Part II do not extend to Northern Ireland – section 92 (exclusion of Part I in relation to small claims arbitration in the county court), and section 93 and Schedule 2 (appointment of judges as arbitrators).

(3) Sections 89, 90 and 91 (consumer arbitration agreements) extend to Scotland and the provisions of Schedules 3 and 4 (consequential amendments and repeals) extend to Scotland so far as they relate to enactments which so extend, subject as follows.

   1975 c3 824

(4) The repeal of the Arbitration Act 1975 extends only to England and Wales and Northern Ireland.

Section 109 – Commencement

(1) The provisions of this Act come into force on such day as the Secretary of State may appoint by order made by statutory instrument, and different days may be appointed for different purposes.

(2) An order under subsection (1) may contain such transitional provisions as appear to the Secretary of State to be appropriate.

Section 110 – Short title

This Act may be cited as the Arbitration Act 1996.

SCHEDULES

SCHEDULE 1
MANDATORY PROVISIONS OF PART I

sections 9 to 11 (stay of legal proceedings);

section 12 (power of court to extend agreed time limits);

section 13 (application of Limitation Acts);

section 24 (power of court to remove arbitrator);

section 26(1) (effect of death of arbitrator);

section 28 (liability of parties for fees and expenses of arbitrators);

section 29 (immunity of arbitrator);

section 31 (objection to substantive jurisdiction of tribunal);

section 32 (determination of preliminary point of jurisdiction);

section 33 (general duty of tribunal);

section 37(2) (items to be treated as expenses of arbitrators);

section 40 (general duty of parties);

section 43 (securing the attendance of witnesses);

section 56 (power to withhold award in case of non-payment);

section 60 (effectiveness of agreement for payment of costs in any event);

section 66 (enforcement of award);

sections 67 and 68 (challenging the award: substantive jurisdiction and serious irregularity), and sections 70 and 71 (supplementary provisions; effect of order of court) so far as relating to those sections;

section 72 (saving for rights of person who takes no part in proceedings);

section 73 (loss of right to object);

section 74 (immunity of arbitral institutions, etc);

section 75 (charge to secure payment of solicitors' costs).

SCHEDULE 2
MODIFICATIONS OF PART I IN RELATION TO JUDGE-ARBITRATORS

Introductory

1   In this Schedule 'judge-arbitrator' means a judge of the Commercial Court or official referee appointed as arbitrator or umpire under section 93.

General

2 (1) Subject to the following provisions of this Schedule, references in Part I to the court shall be construed in relation to a judge-arbitrator, or in relation to the appointment of a judge-arbitrator, as references to the Court of Appeal.

(2) The references in sections 32(6), 45(6) and 69(8) to the Court of Appeal shall in such a case be construed as references to the House of Lords.

Arbitrator's fees

3 (1) The power of the court in section 28(2) to order consideration and adjustment of the liability of a party for the fees of an arbitrator may be exercised by a judge-arbitrator.

(2) Any such exercise of the power is subject to the powers of the Court of Appeal under sections 24(4) and 25(3)(b) (directions as to entitlement to fees or expenses in case of removal or resignation).

Exercise of court powers in support of arbitration

4 (1) Where the arbitral tribunal consists of or includes a judge-arbitrator the powers of the court under sections 42 to 44 (enforcement of peremptory orders, summoning witnesses, and other court powers) are exercisable by the High Court and also by the judge-arbitrator himself.

(2) Anything done by a judge-arbitrator in the exercise of those powers shall be regarded as done by him in his capacity as judge of the High Court and have effect as if done by that court.

Nothing in this sub-paragraph prejudices any power vested in him as arbitrator or umpire.

Extension of time for making award

5 (1) The power conferred by section 50 (extension of time for making award) is exercisable by the judge-arbitrator himself.

(2) Any appeal from a decision of a judge-arbitrator under that section lies to the Court of Appeal with the leave of that court.

Withholding award in case of non-payment

6 (1) The provisions of paragraph 7 apply in place of the provisions of section 56 (power to withhold award in the case of non-payment) in relation to the withholding of an award for non-payment of the fees and expenses of a judge-arbitrator.

(2) This does not affect the application of section 56 in relation to the delivery of such an award by an arbitral or other institution or person vested by the parties with powers in relation to the delivery of the award.

7 (1) A judge-arbitrator may refuse to deliver an award except upon payment of the fees and expenses mentioned in section 56(1).

(2) The judge-arbitrator may, on an application by a party to the arbitral proceedings, order that if he pays into the High Court the fees and expenses demanded, or such lesser amount as the judge-arbitrator may specify –

(a) the award shall be delivered,

(b) the amount of the fees and expenses properly payable shall be determined by such means and upon such terms as he may direct, and

(c) out of the money paid into court there shall be paid out such fees and expenses as may be found to be properly payable and the balance of the money (if any) shall be paid out to the applicant.

(3) For this purpose the amount of fees and expenses properly payable is the amount the applicant is liable to pay under section 28 or any agreement relating to the payment of the arbitrator.

(4) No application to the judge-arbitrator under this paragraph may be made where there is any available arbitral process for appeal or review of the amount of the fees or expenses demanded.

(5) Any appeal from a decision of a judge-arbitrator under this paragraph lies to the Court of Appeal with the leave of that court.

(6) Where a party to arbitral proceedings appeals under sub-paragraph (5), an arbitrator is entitled to appear and be heard.

Correction of award or additional award

8   Subsections (4) to (6) of section 57 (correction of award or additional award: time limit for application or exercise of power) do not apply to a judge-arbitrator.

Costs

9   Where the arbitral tribunal consists of or includes a judge-arbitrator the powers of the court under section 63(4) (determination of recoverable costs) shall be exercised by the High Court.

10 (1) The power of the court under section 64 to determine an arbitrator's reasonable fees and expenses may be exercised by a judge-arbitrator.

(2) Any such exercise of the power is subject to the powers of the Court of Appeal under sections 24(4) and 25(3)(b) (directions as to entitlement to fees or expenses in case of removal or resignation).

Enforcement of award

11   The leave of the court required by section 66 (enforcement of award) may in the case of an award of a judge-arbitrator be given by the judge-arbitrator himself.

Solicitors' costs

12   The powers of the court to make declarations and orders under the provisions applied by section 75 (power to charge property recovered in arbitral proceedings with the payment of solicitors' costs) may be exercised by the judge-arbitrator.

Powers of court in relation to service of documents

13 (1) The power of the court under section 77(2) (powers of court in relation to service of documents) is exercisable by the judge-arbitrator.

(2) Any appeal from a decision of a judge-arbitrator under that section lies to the Court of Appeal with the leave of that court.

Powers of court to extend time limits relating to arbitral proceedings

14 (1) The power conferred by section 79 (power of court to extend time limits relating to arbitral proceedings) is exercisable by the judge-arbitrator himself.

(2) Any appeal from a decision of a judge-arbitrator under that section lies to the Court of Appeal with the leave of that court.

SCHEDULE 3
CONSEQUENTIAL AMENDMENTS

Merchant Shipping Act 1894 (c60)

1   In section 496 of the Merchant Shipping Act 1894 (provisions as to deposits by owners of goods), after subsection (4) insert –

'(5) In subsection (3) the expression "legal proceedings" includes arbitral proceedings and as respects England and Wales and Northern Ireland the provisions of section 14 of the Arbitration Act 1996 apply to determine when such proceedings are commenced.'

Stannaries Court (Abolition) Act 1896 (c45)

2   In section 4(1) of the Stannaries Court (Abolition) Act 1896 (references of certain disputes to arbitration), for the words from 'tried before' to 'any such reference' substitute 'referred to arbitration before himself or before an arbitrator agreed on by the parties or an officer of the court'.

Tithe Act 1936 (c43)

3   In section 39(1) of the Tithe Act 1936 (proceedings of Tithe Redemption Commission) –

(a)   for 'the Arbitration Acts 1889 to 1934' substitute 'Part I of the Arbitration Act 1996';

(b)   for paragraph (e) substitute –

'(e) the making of an application to the court to determine a preliminary point of law and the bringing of an appeal to the court on a point of law';

(c)   for 'the said Acts' substitute 'Part I of the Arbitration Act 1996'.

Education Act 1944 (c31)

4   In section 75(2) of the Education Act 1944 (proceedings of Independent School Tribunals) for 'the Arbitration Acts 1889 to 1934' substitute 'Part I of the Arbitration Act 1996'.

Commonwealth Telegraphs Act 1949 (c39)

5   In section 8(2) of the Commonwealth Telegraphs Act 1949 (proceedings of referees under the Act) for 'the Arbitration Acts 1889 to 1934, or the Arbitration Act (Northern Ireland) 1937,' substitute 'Part I of the Arbitration Act 1996'.

Lands Tribunal Act 1949 (c42)

6   In section 3 of the Lands Tribunal Act 1949 (proceedings before the Lands Tribunal) –

(a) in subsection (6)(c) (procedural rules: power to apply Arbitration Acts), and

(b) in subsection (8) (exclusion of Arbitration Acts except as applied by rules),

for 'the Arbitration Acts 1889 to 1934' substitute 'Part I of the Arbitration Act 1996'.

Wireless Telegraphy Act 1949 (c54)

7   In the Wireless Telegraphy Act 1949, Schedule 2 (procedure of appeals tribunal), in paragraph 3(1) –

(a) for the words 'the Arbitration Acts 1889 to 1934' substitute 'Part I of the Arbitration Act 1996';

(b) after the word 'Wales' insert 'or Northern Ireland'; and

(c) for 'the said Acts' substitute 'Part I of that Act'.

Patents Act 1949 (c87)

8   In section 67 of the Patents Act 1949 (proceedings as to infringement of pre-1978 patents referred to comptroller), for 'The Arbitration Acts 1889 to 1934' substitute 'Part I of the Arbitration Act 1996'.

National Health Service (Amendment) Act 1949 (c93)

9   In section 7(8) of the National Health Service (Amendment) Act 1949 (arbitration in relation to hardship arising from the National Health Service Act 1946 or the Act), for 'the Arbitration Acts 1889 to 1934' substitute 'Part I of the Arbitration Act 1996' and for 'the said Acts' substitute 'Part I of that Act'.

Arbitration Act 1950 (c27)

10   In section 36(1) of the Arbitration Act 1950 (effect of foreign awards enforceable under Part II of that Act) for 'section 26 of this Act' substitute 'section 66 of the Arbitration Act 1996'.

Interpretation Act (Northern Ireland) 1954 (c33 (NI))

11   In section 46(2) of the Interpretation Act (Northern Ireland) 1954 (miscellaneous definitions), for the definition of 'arbitrator' substitute –

'"arbitrator" has the same meaning as in Part I of the Arbitration Act 1996'.

Agricultural Marketing Act 1958 (c47)

12 In section 12(1) of the Agricultural Marketing Act 1958 (application of provisions of Arbitration Act 1950) –

(a) for the words from the beginning to 'shall apply' substitute 'Sections 45 and 69 of the Arbitration Act 1996 (which relate to the determination by the court of questions of law) and section 66 of that Act (enforcement of awards) apply'; and

(b) for 'an arbitration' substitute 'arbitral proceedings'.

Carriage by Air Act 1961 (c27)

13 (1) The Carriage by Air Act 1961 is amended as follows.

(2) In section 5(3) (time for bringing proceedings) –

(a) for 'an arbitration' in the first place where it occurs substitute 'arbitral proceedings'; and

(b) for the words from 'and subsections (3) and (4)' to the end substitute 'and the provisions of section 14 of the Arbitration Act 1996 apply to determine when such proceedings are commenced'.

(3) In section 11(c) (application of section 5 to Scotland) –

(a) for 'subsections (3) and (4)' substitute 'the provisions of section 14 of the Arbitration Act 1996'; and

(b) for 'an arbitration' substitute 'arbitral proceedings'.

Factories Act 1961 (c34)

14 In the Factories Act 1961, for section 171 (application of Arbitration Act 1950), substitute –

'Application of the Arbitration Act 1996.

171 Part I of the Arbitration Act 1996 does not apply to proceedings under this Act except in so far as it may be applied by regulations made under this Act.'

Clergy Pensions Measure 1961 (No 3)

15 In the Clergy Pensions Measure 1961, section 38(4) (determination of questions), for the words 'The Arbitration Act 1950' substitute 'Part I of the Arbitration Act 1996'.

Transport Act 1962 (c46)

16 (1) The Transport Act 1962 is amended as follows.

(2) In section 74(6)(f) (proceedings before referees in pension disputes), for the words 'the Arbitration Act 1950' substitute 'Part I of the Arbitration Act 1996'.

(3) In section 81(7) (proceedings before referees in compensation disputes), for the words 'the Arbitration Act 1950' substitute 'Part I of the Arbitration Act 1996'.

(4) In Schedule 7, Part IV (pensions), in paragraph 17(5) for the words 'the Arbitration Act 1950' substitute 'Part I of the Arbitration Act 1996'.

Corn Rents Act 1963 (c14)

17 In the Corn Rents Act 1963, section 1(5) (schemes for apportioning corn rents, etc), for the words 'the Arbitration Act 1950' substitute 'Part I of the Arbitration Act 1996'.

Plant Varieties and Seeds Act 1964 (c14)

18 In section 10(6) of the Plant Varieties and Seeds Act 1964 (meaning of 'arbitration agreement'), for 'the meaning given by section 32 of the Arbitration Act 1950' substitute 'the same meaning as in Part I of the Arbitration Act 1996'.

Lands Tribunal and Compensation Act (Northern Ireland) 1964 (c29 (NI))

19 In section 9 of the Lands Tribunal and Compensation Act (Northern Ireland) 1964 (proceedings of Lands Tribunal), in subsection (3) (where Tribunal acts as arbitrator) for 'the Arbitration Act (Northern Ireland) 1937' substitute 'Part I of the Arbitration Act 1996'.

Industrial and Provident Societies Act 1965 (c12)

20 (1) Section 60 of the Industrial and Provident Societies Act 1965 is amended as follows.

(2) In subsection (8) (procedure for hearing disputes between society and member, etc) –

(a) in paragraph (a) for 'the Arbitration Act 1950' substitute 'Part I of the Arbitration Act 1996'; and

(b) in paragraph (b) omit 'by virtue of section 12 of the said Act of 1950'.

(3) For subsection (9) substitute –

'(9) The court or registrar to whom any dispute is referred under subsections (2) to (7) may at the request of either party state a case on any question of law arising in the dispute for the opinion of the High Court or, as the case may be, the Court of Session.'

Carriage of Goods by Road Act 1965 (c37)

21 In section 7(2) of the Carriage of Goods by Road Act 1965 (arbitrations: time at which deemed to commence), for paragraphs (a) and (b) substitute –

'(a) as respects England and Wales and Northern Ireland, the provisions of section 14(3) to (5) of the Arbitration Act 1996 (which determine the time at which an arbitration is commenced) apply'.

Factories Act (Northern Ireland) 1965 (c20 (NI))

22 In section 171 of the Factories Act (Northern Ireland) 1965 (application of Arbitration Act), for 'The Arbitration Act (Northern Ireland) 1937' substitute 'Part I of the Arbitration Act 1996'.

Commonwealth Secretariat Act 1966 (c10)

23 In section 1(3) of the Commonwealth Secretariat Act 1966 (contracts with Commonwealth Secretariat to be deemed to contain provision for arbitration), for 'the Arbitration Act 1950 and the Arbitration Act (Northern Ireland) 1937' substitute 'Part I of the Arbitration Act 1996'.

Arbitration (International Investment Disputes) Act 1966 (c41)

24 In the Arbitration (International Investment Disputes) Act 1966, for section 3 (application of Arbitration Act 1950 and other enactments) substitute –

'Application of provisions of Arbitration Act 1996.

3   (1) The Lord Chancellor may by order direct that any of the provisions contained in sections 36 and 38 to 44 of the Arbitration Act 1996 (provisions concerning the conduct of arbitral proceedings, etc) shall apply to such proceedings pursuant to the Convention as are specified in the order with or without any modifications or exceptions specified in the order.

(2) Subject to subsection (1), the Arbitration Act 1996 shall not apply to proceedings pursuant to the Convention, but this subsection shall not be taken as affecting section 9 of that Act (stay of legal proceedings in respect of matter subject to arbitration).

(3) An order made under this section –

(a) may be varied or revoked by a subsequent order so made, and

(b) shall be contained in a statutory instrument.'

Poultry Improvement Act (Northern Ireland) 1968 (c12 (NI))

25 In paragraph 10(4) of the Schedule to the Poultry Improvement Act (Northern Ireland) 1968 (reference of disputes), for 'The Arbitration Act (Northern Ireland) 1937' substitute 'Part I of the Arbitration Act 1996'.

Industrial and Provident Societies Act (Northern Ireland) 1969 (c24 (NI))

26 (1) Section 69 of the Industrial and Provident Societies Act (Northern Ireland) 1969 (decision of disputes) is amended as follows.

(2) In subsection (7) (decision of disputes) –

(a) in the opening words, omit the words from 'and without prejudice' to '1937';

(b) at the beginning of paragraph (a) insert 'without prejudice to any powers exercisable by virtue of Part I of the Arbitration Act 1996'; and

(c) in paragraph (b) omit 'the registrar or' and 'registrar or' and for the words from 'as might have been granted by the High Court' to the end substitute 'as might be granted by the registrar'.

(3) For subsection (8) substitute –

'(8) The court or registrar to whom any dispute is referred under subsections (2) to (6) may at the request of either party state a case on any question of law arising in the dispute for the opinion of the High Court.'

Health and Personal Social Services (Northern Ireland) Order 1972 (NI 14)

27 In Article 105(6) of the Health and Personal Social Services (Northern Ireland) Order 1972 (arbitrations under the Order), for 'the Arbitration Act (Northern Ireland) 1937' substitute 'Part I of the Arbitration Act 1996'.

Consumer Credit Act 1974 (c39)

28 (1) Section 146 of the Consumer Credit Act 1974 is amended as follows.

(2) In subsection (2) (solicitor engaged in contentious business), for 'section 86(1) of the Solicitors Act 1957' substitute 'section 87(1) of the Solicitors Act 1974'.

(3) In subsection (4) (solicitor in Northern Ireland engaged in contentious business), for the words from 'business done' to 'Administration of Estates (Northern Ireland) Order 1979' substitute 'contentious business (as defined in Article 3(2) of the Solicitors (Northern Ireland) Order 1976'.

Friendly Societies Act 1974 (c46)

29 (1) The Friendly Societies Act 1974 is amended as follows.

(2) For section 78(1) (statement of case) substitute –

'(1) Any arbitrator, arbiter or umpire to whom a dispute falling within section 76 above is referred under the rules of a registered society or branch may at the request of either party state a case on any question of law arising in the dispute for the opinion of the High Court or, as the case may be, the Court of Session.'

(3) In section 83(3) (procedure on objections to amalgamations etc of friendly societies), for 'the Arbitration Act 1950 or, in Northern Ireland, the Arbitration Act (Northern Ireland) 1937' substitute 'Part I of the Arbitration Act 1996'.

Industry Act 1975 (c68)

30 In Schedule 3 to the Industry Act (arbitration of disputes relating to vesting and compensation orders), in paragraph 14 (application of certain provisions of Arbitration Acts) –

(a) for 'the Arbitration Act 1950 or, in Northern Ireland, the Arbitration Act (Northern Ireland) 1937' substitute 'Part I of the Arbitration Act 1996', and

(b) for 'that Act' substitute 'that Part'.

Industrial Relations (Northern Ireland) Order 1976 (NI 16)

31 In Article 59(9) of the Industrial Relations (Northern Ireland) Order 1976 (proceedings of industrial tribunal), for 'The Arbitration Act (Northern Ireland) 1937' substitute 'Part I of the Arbitration Act 1996'.

Aircraft and Shipbuilding Industries Act 1977 (c3)

32 In Schedule 7 to the Aircraft and Shipbuilding Industries Act 1977 (procedure of Arbitration Tribunal), in paragraph 2 –

(a) for 'the Arbitration Act 1950 or, in Northern Ireland, the Arbitration Act (Northern Ireland) 1937' substitute 'Part I of the Arbitration Act 1996', and

(b) for 'that Act' substitute 'that Part'.

Patents Act 1977 (c37)

33 In section 130 of the Patents Act 1977 (interpretation), in subsection (8) (exclusion of Arbitration Act) for 'The Arbitration Act 1950' substitute 'Part I of the Arbitration Act 1996'.

Judicature (Northern Ireland) Act 1978 (c23)

34 (1) The Judicature (Northern Ireland) Act 1978 is amended as follows.

(2) In section 35(2) (restrictions on appeals to the Court of Appeal), after paragraph (f) insert –

'(fa) except as provided by Part I of the Arbitration Act 1996, from any decision of the High Court under that Part'.

(3) In section 55(2) (rules of court) after paragraph (c) insert –

'(cc) providing for any prescribed part of the jurisdiction of the High Court in relation to the trial of any action involving matters of account to be exercised in the prescribed manner by a person agreed by the parties and for the remuneration of any such person'.

Health and Safety at Work (Northern Ireland) Order 1978 (NI 9)

35 In Schedule 4 to the Health and Safety at Work (Northern Ireland) Order 1978 (licensing provisions), in paragraph 3, for 'The Arbitration Act (Northern Ireland) 1937' substitute 'Part I of the Arbitration Act 1996'.

County Courts (Northern Ireland) Order 1980 (NI 3)

36 (1) The County Courts (Northern Ireland) Order 1980 is amended as follows.

(2) In Article 30 (civil jurisdiction exercisable by district judge) –

(a) for paragraph (2) substitute –

'(2) Any order, decision or determination made by a district judge under this Article (other than one made in dealing with a claim by way of arbitration under paragraph (3)) shall be embodied in a decree which for all purposes (including the right of appeal under Part VI) shall have the like effect as a decree pronounced by a county court judge';

(b) for paragraphs (4) and (5) substitute –

'(4) Where in any action to which paragraph (1) applies the claim is dealt with by way of arbitration under paragraph (3) –

(a) any award made by the district judge in dealing with the claim shall be embodied in a decree which for all purposes (except the right of appeal under Part VI) shall have the like effect as a decree pronounced by a county court judge;

(b) the district judge may, and shall if so required by the High Court, state for the determination of the High Court any question of law arising out of an award so made;

(c) except as provided by sub-paragraph (b), any award so made shall be final; and

(d) except as otherwise provided by county court rules, no costs shall be awarded in connection with the action.

(5) Subject to paragraph (4), county court rules may –

(a) apply any of the provisions of Part I of the Arbitration Act 1996 to arbitrations under paragraph (3) with such modifications as may be prescribed;

(b) prescribe the rules of evidence to be followed on any arbitration under paragraph (3) and, in particular, make provision with respect to the manner of taking and questioning evidence.

(5A)Except as provided by virtue of paragraph (5)(a), Part I of the Arbitration Act 1996 shall not apply to an arbitration under paragraph (3).'

(3) After Article 61 insert –

'Appeals from decisions under Part I of Arbitration Act 1996

61A (1) Article 61 does not apply to a decision of a county court judge made in the exercise of the jurisdiction conferred by Part I of the Arbitration Act 1996.

(2) Any party dissatisfied with a decision of the county court made in the exercise of the jurisdiction conferred by any of the following provisions of Part I of the Arbitration Act 1996, namely –

(a) section 32 (question as to substantive jurisdiction of arbitral tribunal);

(b) section 45 (question of law arising in course of arbitral proceedings);

(c) section 67 (challenging award of arbitral tribunal: substantive jurisdiction);

(d) section 68 (challenging award of arbitral tribunal: serious irregularity);

(e) section 69 (appeal on point of law),

may, subject to the provisions of that Part, appeal from that decision to the Court of Appeal.

(3) Any party dissatisfied with any decision of a county court made in the exercise of the jurisdiction conferred by any other provision of Part I of the Arbitration Act 1996 may, subject to the provisions of that Part, appeal from that decision to the High Court.

(4) The decision of the Court of Appeal on an appeal under paragraph (2) shall be final.'

Supreme Court Act 1981 (c54)

37 (1) The Supreme Court Act 1981 is amended as follows.

(2) In section 18(1) (restrictions on appeals to the Court of Appeal), for paragraph (g) substitute –

'(g) except as provided by Part I of the Arbitration Act 1996, from any decision of the High Court under that Part'.

(3) In section 151 (interpretation, etc), in the definition of 'arbitration agreement', for 'the Arbitration Act 1950 by virtue of section 32 of that Act'; substitute 'Part I of the Arbitration Act 1996'.

Merchant Shipping (Liner Conferences) Act 1982 (c37)

38   In section 7(5) of the Merchant Shipping (Liner Conferences) Act 1982 (stay of legal proceedings), for the words from 'section 4(1)' to the end substitute 'section 9 of the Arbitration Act 1996 (which also provides for the staying of legal proceedings)'.

Agricultural Marketing (Northern Ireland) Order 1982 (NI 12)

39   In Article 14 of the Agricultural Marketing (Northern Ireland) Order 1982 (application of provisions of Arbitration Act (Northern Ireland) 1937) –

(a)   for the words from the beginning to 'shall apply' substitute 'Sections 45 and 69 of the Arbitration Act 1996 (which relate to the determination by the court of questions of law) and section 66 of that Act (enforcement of awards)' apply; and

(b)   for 'an arbitration' substitute 'arbitral proceedings'.

Mental Health Act 1983 (c20)

40   In section 78 of the Mental Health Act 1983 (procedure of Mental Health Review Tribunals), in subsection (9) for 'The Arbitration Act 1950' substitute 'Part I of the Arbitration Act 1996'.

Registered Homes Act 1984 (c23)

41   In section 43 of the Registered Homes Act 1984 (procedure of Registered Homes Tribunals), in subsection (3) for 'The Arbitration Act 1950' substitute 'Part I of the Arbitration Act 1996'.

Housing Act 1985 (c68)

42   In section 47(3) of the Housing Act 1985 (agreement as to determination of matters relating to service charges) for 'section 32 of the Arbitration Act 1950' substitute 'Part I of the Arbitration Act 1996'.

Landlord and Tenant Act 1985 (c70)

43   In section 19(3) of the Landlord and Tenant Act 1985 (agreement as to determination of matters relating to service charges), for 'section 32 of the Arbitration Act 1950' substitute 'Part I of the Arbitration Act 1996'.

Credit Unions (Northern Ireland) Order 1985 (NI 12)

44 (1) Article 72 of the Credit Unions (Northern Ireland) Order 1985 (decision of disputes) is amended as follows.

(2)   In paragraph (7) –

(a)   in the opening words, omit the words from 'and without prejudice' to '1937';

(b)   at the beginning of sub-paragraph (a) insert 'without prejudice to any powers exercisable by virtue of Part I of the Arbitration Act 1996'; and

(c) in sub-paragraph (b) omit 'the registrar or' and 'registrar or' and for the words from 'as might have been granted by the High Court' to the end substitute 'as might be granted by the registrar'.

(3) For paragraph (8) substitute –

'(8) The court or registrar to whom any dispute is referred under paragraphs (2) to (6) may at the request of either party state a case on any question of law arising in the dispute for the opinion of the High Court.'

Agricultural Holdings Act 1986 (c5)

45   In section 84(1) of the Agricultural Holdings Act 1986 (provisions relating to arbitration), for 'the Arbitration Act 1950' substitute 'Part I of the Arbitration Act 1996'.

Insolvency Act 1986 (c45)

46   In the Insolvency Act 1986, after section 349 insert –

'Arbitration agreements to which bankrupt is party.

349A (1) This section applies where a bankrupt had become party to a contract containing an arbitration agreement before the commencement of his bankruptcy.

(2) If the trustee in bankruptcy adopts the contract, the arbitration agreement is enforceable by or against the trustee in relation to matters arising from or connected with the contract.

(3) If the trustee in bankruptcy does not adopt the contract and a matter to which the arbitration agreement applies requires to be determined in connection with or for the purposes of the bankruptcy proceedings –

(a) the trustee with the consent of the creditors' committee, or

(b) any other party to the agreement,

may apply to the court which may, if it thinks fit in all the circumstances of the case, order that the matter be referred to arbitration in accordance with the arbitration agreement.

(4) In this section –

"arbitration agreement" has the same meaning as in Part I of the Arbitration Act 1996; and

"the court" means the court which has jurisdiction in the bankruptcy proceedings.'

Building Societies Act 1986 (c53)

47   In Part II of Schedule 14 to the Building Societies Act 1986 (settlement of disputes: arbitration), in paragraph 5(6) for 'the Arbitration Act 1950 and the Arbitration Act 1979 or, in Northern Ireland, the Arbitration Act (Northern Ireland) 1937' substitute 'Part I of the Arbitration Act 1996'.

Mental Health (Northern Ireland) Order 1986 (NI 4)

48   In Article 83 of the Mental Health (Northern Ireland) Order 1986 (procedure of Mental Health Review Tribunal), in paragraph (8) for 'The Arbitration Act (Northern Ireland) 1937' substitute 'Part I of the Arbitration Act 1996'.

Multilateral Investment Guarantee Agency Act 1988 (c8)

49   For section 6 of the Multilateral Investment Guarantee Agency Act 1988 (application of Arbitration Act) substitute –

'Application of Arbitration Act.

6 (1) The Lord Chancellor may by order made by statutory instrument direct that any of the provisions of sections 36 and 38 to 44 of the Arbitration Act 1996 (provisions in relation to the conduct of the arbitral proceedings, etc) apply, with such modifications or exceptions as are specified in the order, to such arbitration proceedings pursuant to Annex II to the Convention as are specified in the order.

(2)   Except as provided by an order under subsection (1) above, no provision of Part I of the Arbitration Act 1996 other than section 9 (stay of legal proceedings) applies to any such proceedings.'

Copyright, Designs and Patents Act 1988 (c48)

50   In section 150 of the Copyright, Designs and Patents Act 1988 (Lord Chancellor's power to make rules for Copyright Tribunal), for subsection (2) substitute –

'(2) The rules may apply in relation to the Tribunal, as respects proceedings in England and Wales or Northern Ireland, any of the provisions of Part I of the Arbitration Act 1996.'

Fair Employment (Northern Ireland) Act 1989 (c32)

51   In the Fair Employment (Northern Ireland) Act 1989, section 5(7) (procedure of Fair Employment Tribunal), for 'The Arbitration Act (Northern Ireland) 1937' substitute 'Part I of the Arbitration Act 1996'.

Limitation (Northern Ireland) Order 1989 (NI 11)

52   In Article 2(2) of the Limitation (Northern Ireland) Order 1989 (interpretation), in the definition of 'arbitration agreement', for 'the Arbitration Act (Northern Ireland) 1937' substitute 'Part I of the Arbitration Act 1996'.

Insolvency (Northern Ireland) Order 1989 (NI 19)

53   In the Insolvency (Northern Ireland) Order 1989, after Article 320 insert –

'Arbitration agreements to which bankrupt is party

320A (1) This Article applies where a bankrupt had become party to a contract containing an arbitration agreement before the commencement of his bankruptcy.

(2)   If the trustee in bankruptcy adopts the contract, the arbitration agreement is enforceable by or against the trustee in relation to matters arising from or connected with the contract.

(3)   If the trustee in bankruptcy does not adopt the contract and a matter to which the arbitration agreement applies requires to be determined in connection with or for the purposes of the bankruptcy proceedings –

(a)   the trustee with the consent of the creditors' committee, or

(b)   any other party to the agreement,

may apply to the court which may, if it thinks fit in all the circumstances of the case, order that the matter be referred to arbitration in accordance with the arbitration agreement.

(4) In this Article –

"arbitration agreement" has the same meaning as in Part I of the Arbitration Act 1996; and

"the court" means the court which has jurisdiction in the bankruptcy proceedings.'

Social Security Administration Act 1992 (c5)

54 In section 59 of the Social Security Administration Act 1992 (procedure for inquiries, etc), in subsection (7), for 'The Arbitration Act 1950' substitute 'Part I of the Arbitration Act 1996'.

Social Security Administration (Northern Ireland) Act 1992 (c8)

55 In section 57 of the Social Security Administration (Northern Ireland) Act 1992 (procedure for inquiries, etc), in subsection (6) for 'the Arbitration Act (Northern Ireland) 1937' substitute 'Part I of the Arbitration Act 1996'.

Trade Union and Labour Relations (Consolidation) Act 1992 (c52)

56 In sections 212(5) and 263(6) of the Trade Union and Labour Relations (Consolidation) Act 1992 (application of Arbitration Act) for 'the Arbitration Act 1950' substitute 'Part I of the Arbitration Act 1996'.

Industrial Relations (Northern Ireland) Order 1992 (NI 5)

57 In Articles 84(9) and 92(5) of the Industrial Relations (Northern Ireland) Order 1992 (application of Arbitration Act) for 'The Arbitration Act (Northern Ireland) 1937' substitute 'Part I of the Arbitration Act 1996'.

Registered Homes (Northern Ireland) Order 1992 (NI 20)

58 In Article 33(3) of the Registered Homes (Northern Ireland) Order 1992 (procedure of Registered Homes Tribunal) for 'The Arbitration Act (Northern Ireland) 1937' substitute 'Part I of the Arbitration Act 1996'.

Education Act 1993 (c35)

59 In section 180(4) of the Education Act 1993 (procedure of Special Educational Needs Tribunal), for 'The Arbitration Act 1950' substitute 'Part I of the Arbitration Act 1996'.

Roads (Northern Ireland) Order 1993 (NI 15)

60 (1) The Roads (Northern Ireland) Order 1993 is amended as follows.

(2) In Article 131 (application of Arbitration Act) for 'the Arbitration Act (Northern Ireland) 1937' substitute 'Part I of the Arbitration Act 1996'.

(3) In Schedule 4 (disputes), in paragraph 3(2) for 'the Arbitration Act (Northern Ireland) 1937' substitute 'Part I of the Arbitration Act 1996'.

Merchant Shipping Act 1995 (c21)

61 In Part II of Schedule 6 to the Merchant Shipping Act 1995 (provisions having effect in connection with the Convention Relating to the Carriage of Passengers and Their Luggage by Sea), for paragraph 7 substitute –

'7 Article 16 shall apply to arbitral proceedings as it applies to an action; and, as respects England and Wales and Northern Ireland, the provisions of section 14 of the Arbitration Act 1996 apply to determine for the purposes of that Article when an arbitration is commenced.'

Industrial Tribunals Act 1996 (c17)

62 In section 6(2) of the Industrial Tribunals Act 1996 (procedure of industrial tribunals), for 'The Arbitration Act 1950' substitute 'Part I of the Arbitration Act 1996'.

SCHEDULE 4
REPEALS

Chapter	Short title	Extent of repeal
1892 c43	Military Lands Act 1892	In section 21(b), the words 'under the Arbitration Act 1889'
1922 c51	Allotments Act 1922	In section 21(3), the words 'under the Arbitration Act 1889'
1937 c8 (NI)	Arbitration Act (Northern Ireland) 1937	The whole Act
1949 c54	Wireless Telegraphy Act 1949	In Schedule 2, paragraph 3(3)
1949 c97	National Parks and Access to the Countryside Act 1949	In section 18(4), the words from 'Without prejudice' to 'England or Wales'
1950 c27	Arbitration Act 1950	Part I section 42(3)
1958 c47	Agricultural Marketing Act 1958	Section 53(8)
1962 c46	Transport Act 1962	In Schedule 11, Part II, paragraph 7
1964 c14	Plant Varieties and Seeds Act 1964	In section 10(4) the words from 'or in section 9' to 'three arbitrators'
		Section 39(3)(b)(i)
1964 c29 (NI)	Lands Tribunal and Compensation Act (Northern Ireland) 1964	In section 9(3) the words from 'so, however, that' to the end
1965 c12	Industrial and Provident Societies Act 1965	In section 60(8)(b), the words 'by virtue of section 12 of the said Act of 1950'
1965 c37	Carriage of Goods by Road Act 1965	Section 7(2)(b)

Chapter	Short title	Extent of repeal
1965 c13 (NI)	New Towns Act (Northern Ireland) 1965	In section 27(2), the words from 'under and in accordance with' to the end
1969 c24 (NI)	Industrial and Provident Societies Act (Northern Ireland) 1969	In section 69(7) – (a) in the opening words, the words from 'and without prejudice' to '1937'; (b) in paragraph (b), the words 'the registrar or' and 'registrar or'
1970 c31	Administration of Justice Act 1970	Section 4 Schedule 3
1973 c41	Fair Trading Act 1973	Section 33(2)(d)
1973 NI 1	Drainage (Northern Ireland) Order 1973	In Article 15(4), the words from 'under and in accordance' to the end Article 40(4) In Schedule 7, in paragraph 9(2), the words from 'under and in accordance' to the end
1974 c47	Solicitors Act 1974	In section 87(1), in the definition of 'contentious business', the words 'appointed under the Arbitration Act 1950'
1975 c3	Arbitration Act 1975	The whole Act
1975 c74	Petroleum and Submarine Pipe-Lines Act 1975	In Part II of Schedule 2 – (a) in model clause 40(2), the words 'in accordance with the Arbitration Act 1950'; (b) in model clause 40(2B), the words 'in accordance with the Arbitration Act (Northern Ireland) 1937' In Part II of Schedule 3, in model clause 38(2), the words 'in accordance with the Arbitration Act 1950'
1976 NI 12	Solicitors (Northern Ireland) Order 1976	In Article 3(2), in the entry 'contentious business', the words 'appointed under the Arbitration Act (Northern Ireland) 1937' Article 71H(3)

Chapter	Short title	Extent of repeal
1977 c37	Patents Act 1977	In section 52(4) the words 'section 21 of the Arbitration Act 1950 or, as the case may be, section 22 of the Arbitration Act (Northern Ireland) 1937 (statement of cases by arbitrators); but' Section 131(e)
1977 c38	Administration of Justice Act 1977	Section 17(2)
1978 c23	Judicature (Northern Ireland) Act 1978	In section 35(2), paragraph (g)(v) In Schedule 5, the amendment to the Arbitration Act 1950
1979 c42	Arbitration Act 1979	The whole Act
1980 c58	Limitation Act 1980	Section 34
1980 NI 3	County Courts (Northern Ireland) Order 1980	Article 31(3)
1981 c54	Supreme Court Act 1981	Section 148
1982 c27	Civil Jurisdiction and Judgments Act 1982	Section 25(3)(c) and (5) In section 26 – (a) in subsection (1), the words 'to arbitration or'; (b) in subsection (1)(a)(i), the words 'arbitration or'; (c) in subsection (2), the words 'arbitration or'
1982 c53	Administration of Justice Act 1982	Section 15(6) In Schedule 1, Part IV
1984 c5	Merchant Shipping Act 1984	Section 4(8)
1984 c12	Telecommunications Act 1984	Schedule 2, paragraph 13(8)
1984 c16	Foreign Limitation Periods Act 1984	Section 5
1984 c28	County Courts Act 1984	In Schedule 2, paragraph 70
1985 c61	Administration of Justice Act 1985	Section 58 In Schedule 9, paragraph 15
1985 c68	Housing Act 1985	In Schedule 18, in paragraph 6(2) the words from 'and the Arbitration Act 1950' to the end

Chapter	Short title	Extent of repeal
1985 NI 12	Credit Unions (Northern Ireland) Order 1985	In Article 72(7)(a) in the opening words, the words from 'and without prejudice' to '1937'; (b) in sub-paragraph (b), the words 'the registrar or' and 'registrar or'
1986 c45	Insolvency Act 1986	In Schedule 14, the entry relating to the Arbitration Act 1950
1988 c8	Multilateral Investment Guarantee Agency Act 1988	Section 8(3)
1988 c21	Consumer Arbitration Agreements Act 1988	The whole Act
1989 NI 11	Limitation (Northern Ireland) Order 1989	Article 72 In Schedule 3, paragraph 1
1989 NI 19	Insolvency (Northern Ireland) Order 1989	In Part II of Schedule 9, paragraph 66
1990 c41	Courts and Legal Services Act 1990	Sections 99 and 101 to 103
1991 NI 7	Food Safety (Northern Ireland) Order 1991	In Articles 8(8) and 11(10), the words from 'and the provisions' to the end
1992 c40	Friendly Societies Act 1992	In Schedule 16, paragraph 30(1)
1995 c8	Agricultural Tenancies Act 1995	Section 28(4)
1995 c21	Merchant Shipping Act 1995	Section 96(10) Section 264(9)
1995 c42	Private International Law (Miscellaneous Provisions) Act 1995	Section 3

APPENDIX 4

EMPLOYMENT ACT 2002

PART 3 OF THE EMPLOYMENT ACT 2002

Statutory procedures

29 Statutory dispute resolution procedures

(1) Schedule 2 (which sets out the statutory dispute resolution procedures) shall have effect.

(2) The Secretary of State may by order –

    (a) amend Schedule 2;

    (b) make provision for the Schedule to apply, with or without modifications, as if –

        (i) any individual of a description specified in the order who would not otherwise be an employee for the purposes of the Schedule were an employee for those purposes; and

        (ii) a person of a description specified in the order were, in the case of any such individual, the individual's employer for those purposes.

(3) Before making an order under this section, the Secretary of State must consult the Advisory, Conciliation and Arbitration Service.

30 Contracts of employment

(1) Every contract of employment shall have effect to require the employer and employee to comply, in relation to any matter to which a statutory procedure applies, with the requirements of the procedure.

(2) Subsection (1) shall have effect notwithstanding any agreement to the contrary, but does not affect so much of an agreement to follow a particular procedure as requires the employer or employee to comply with a requirement which is additional to, and not inconsistent with, the requirements of the statutory procedure.

(3) The Secretary of State may for the purpose of this section by regulations make provision about the application of the statutory procedures.

(4) In this section, 'contract of employment' has the same meaning as in the Employment Rights Act 1996 (c18).

31 Non-completion of statutory procedure: adjustment of awards

(1) This section applies to proceedings before an employment tribunal relating to a claim under any of the jurisdictions listed in Schedule 3 by an employee.

(2) If, in the case of proceedings to which this section applies, it appears to the employment tribunal that –

    (a) the claim to which the proceedings relate concerns a matter to which one of the statutory procedures applies,

    (b) the statutory procedure was not completed before the proceedings were begun, and

(c) the non-completion of the statutory procedure was wholly or mainly attributable to failure by the employee –

(i) to comply with a requirement of the procedure, or

(ii) to exercise a right of appeal under it,

it must, subject to subsection (4), reduce any award which it makes to the employee by 10 per cent, and may, if it considers it just and equitable in all the circumstances to do so, reduce it by a further amount, but not so as to make a total reduction of more than 50 per cent.

(3) If, in the case of proceedings to which this section applies, it appears to the employment tribunal that –

(a) the claim to which the proceedings relate concerns a matter to which one of the statutory procedures applies,

(b) the statutory procedure was not completed before the proceedings were begun, and

(c) the non-completion of the statutory procedure was wholly or mainly attributable to failure by the employer to comply with a requirement of the procedure,

it must, subject to subsection (4), increase any award which it makes to the employee by 10 per cent and may, if it considers it just and equitable in all the circumstances to do so, increase it by a further amount, but not so as to make a total increase of more than 50 per cent.

(4) The duty under subsection (2) or (3) to make a reduction or increase of 10 per cent does not apply if there are exceptional circumstances which would make a reduction or increase of that percentage unjust or inequitable, in which case the tribunal may make no reduction or increase or a reduction or increase of such lesser percentage as it considers just and equitable in all the circumstances.

(5) Where an award falls to be adjusted under this section and under section 38, the adjustment under this section shall be made before the adjustment under that section.

(6) The Secretary of State may for the purposes of this section by regulations –

(a) make provision about the application of the statutory procedures;

(b) make provision about when a statutory procedure is to be taken to be completed;

(c) make provision about what constitutes compliance with a requirement of a statutory procedure;

(d) make provision about circumstances in which a person is to be treated as not subject to, or as having complied with, such a requirement;

(e) make provision for a statutory procedure to have effect in such circumstances as may be specified by the regulations with such modifications as may be so specified;

(f) make provision about when an employee is required to exercise a right of appeal under a statutory procedure.

(7) The Secretary of State may by order –

(a) amend Schedule 3 for the purpose of –

(i) adding a jurisdiction to the list in that Schedule, or

(ii) removing a jurisdiction from that list;

(b) make provision, in relation to a jurisdiction listed in Schedule 3, for this section not to apply to proceedings relating to claims of a description specified in the order;

(c) make provision for this section to apply, with or without modifications, as if –

    (i) any individual of a description specified in the order who would not otherwise be an employee for the purposes of this section were an employee for those purposes, and

    (ii) a person of a description specified in the order were, in the case of any such individual, the individual's employer for those purposes.

32 *Complaints about grievances*

(1) This section applies to the jurisdictions listed in Schedule 4.

(2) An employee shall not present a complaint to an employment tribunal under a jurisdiction to which this section applies if –

    (a) it concerns a matter in relation to which the requirement in paragraph 6 or 9 of Schedule 2 applies, and

    (b) the requirement has not been complied with.

(3) An employee shall not present a complaint to an employment tribunal under a jurisdiction to which this section applies if –

    (a) it concerns a matter in relation to which the requirement in paragraph 6 or 9 of Schedule 2 has been complied with, and

    (b) less than 28 days have passed since the day on which the requirement was complied with.

(4) An employee shall not present a complaint to an employment tribunal under a jurisdiction to which this section applies if –

    (a) it concerns a matter in relation to which the requirement in paragraph 6 or 9 of Schedule 2 has been complied with, and

    (b) the day on which the requirement was complied with was more than one month after the end of the original time limit for making the complaint.

(5) In such circumstances as the Secretary of State may specify by regulations, an employment tribunal may direct that subsection (4) shall not apply in relation to a particular matter.

(6) An employment tribunal shall be prevented from considering a complaint presented in breach of subsections (2) to (4), but only if –

    (a) the breach is apparent to the tribunal from the information supplied to it by the employee in connection with the bringing of the proceedings, or

    (b) the tribunal is satisfied of the breach as a result of his employer raising the issue of compliance with those provisions in accordance with regulations under section 7 of the Employment Tribunals Act 1996 (c17) (employment tribunal procedure regulations).

(7) The Secretary of State may for the purposes of this section by regulations –

    (a) make provision about the application of the procedures set out in Part 2 of Schedule 2;

    (b) make provision about what constitutes compliance with paragraph 6 or 9 of that Schedule;

    (c) make provision about circumstances in which a person is to be treated as having complied with paragraph 6 or 9 of that Schedule;

(d) make provision for paragraph 6 or 9 of that Schedule to have effect in such circumstances as may be specified by the regulations with such modifications as may be so specified.

(8) The Secretary of State may by order –

(a) amend, repeal or replace any of subsections (2) to (4);

(b) amend Schedule 4;

(c) make provision for this section to apply, with or without modifications, as if –

(i) any individual of a description specified in the order who would not otherwise be an employee for the purposes of this section were an employee for those purposes, and

(ii) a person of a description specified in the order were, in the case of any such individual, the individual's employer for those purposes.

(9) Before making an order under subsection (8)(a), the Secretary of State must consult the Advisory, Conciliation and Arbitration Service.

(10) In its application to orders under subsection (8)(a), section 51(1)(b) includes power to amend this section.

33 Consequential adjustment of time limits

(1) The Secretary of State may, in relation to a jurisdiction listed in Schedule 3 or 4, by regulations make provision about the time limit for beginning proceedings in respect of a claim concerning a matter to which a statutory procedure applies.

(2) Regulations under this section may, in particular –

(a) make provision extending, or authorising the extension of, the time for beginning proceedings,

(b) make provision about the exercise of a discretion to extend the time for beginning proceedings, or

(c) make provision treating proceedings begun out of time as begun within time.

34 Procedural fairness in unfair dismissal

(1) Part 10 of the Employment Rights Act 1996 (c18) (unfair dismissal) is amended as follows.

(2) After section 98 there is inserted –

'98A Procedural fairness

(1) An employee who is dismissed shall be regarded for the purposes of this Part as unfairly dismissed if –

(a) one of the procedures set out in Part 1 of Schedule 2 to the Employment Act 2002 (dismissal and disciplinary procedures) applies in relation to the dismissal,

(b) the procedure has not been completed, and

(c) the non-completion of the procedure is wholly or mainly attributable to failure by the employer to comply with its requirements.

(2) Subject to subsection (1), failure by an employer to follow a procedure in relation to the dismissal of an employee shall not be regarded for the purposes of section 98(4)(a) as by itself making the employer's action unreasonable if he shows that he would

have decided to dismiss the employee if he had followed the procedure.

(3) For the purposes of this section, any question as to the application of a procedure set out in Part 1 of Schedule 2 to the Employment Act 2002, completion of such a procedure or failure to comply with the requirements of such a procedure shall be determined by reference to regulations under section 31 of that Act.'

(3) In section 112 (the remedies: orders and compensation), at the end there is inserted –

'(5) Where –

(a) an employee is regarded as unfairly dismissed by virtue of section 98A(1) (whether or not his dismissal is unfair or regarded as unfair for any other reason), and

(b) an order is made in respect of the employee under section 113,

the employment tribunal shall, subject to subsection (6), also make an award of four weeks' pay to be paid by the employer to the employee.

(6) An employment tribunal shall not be required to make an award under subsection (5) if it considers that such an award would result in injustice to the employer.'

(4) In section 117 (under which an award of compensation falls to be made if an employee is reinstated or re-engaged in pursuance of an order under section 113, but the terms of the order are not fully complied with), after subsection (2) there is inserted –

'(2A) There shall be deducted from any award under subsection (1) the amount of any award made under section 112(5) at the time of the order under section 113.'

(5) In section 123 (compensatory award) at the end there is inserted –

'(8) Where the amount of the compensatory award falls to be calculated for the purposes of an award under section 117(3)(a), there shall be deducted from the compensatory award any award made under section 112(5) at the time of the order under section 113.'

(6) In section 120 (basic award: minimum in certain cases) after subsection (1) there is inserted –

'(1A) Where –

(a) an employee is regarded as unfairly dismissed by virtue of section 98A(1) (whether or not his dismissal is unfair or regarded as unfair for any other reason),

(b) an award of compensation falls to be made under section 112(4), and

(c) the amount of the award under section 118(1)(a), before any reduction under section 122(3A) or (4), is less than the amount of four weeks' pay,

the employment tribunal shall, subject to subsection (1B), increase the award under section 118(1)(a) to the amount of four weeks' pay.

(1B) An employment tribunal shall not be required by subsection (1A) to increase the amount of an award if it considers that the increase would result in injustice to the employer.'

Employment particulars

35 *Particulars of procedures relating to discipline or dismissal*

(1) Section 3 of the Employment Rights Act 1996 (c18) (note about disciplinary rules and procedures) is amended as follows.

(2) In subsection (1) (which requires a statement under section 1 of that Act to include a note specifying the disciplinary rules and procedures applying to an employee), after paragraph (a) there is inserted –

'(aa) specifying any procedure applicable to the taking of disciplinary decisions relating to the employee, or to a decision to dismiss the employee, or referring the employee to the provisions of a document specifying such a procedure which is reasonably accessible to the employee'.

(3) In that subsection, in paragraph (b)(i) (which requires the note to specify a person for the employee to apply to if he is dissatisfied with a disciplinary decision) after 'him' there is inserted 'or any decision to dismiss him'.

(4) In subsection (2) (which provides that the note does not need to specify the rules and procedures relating to health and safety at work) after 'decisions,' there is inserted 'decisions to dismiss'.

36 Removal of exemption for small employers

In section 3 of the Employment Rights Act 1996 (c18) (note about disciplinary rules and procedures), subsections (3) and (4) (exemptions for undertakings with less than 20 employees) shall cease to have effect.

37 Use of alternative documents to give particulars

In Part 1 of the Employment Rights Act 1996 (employment particulars), after section 7 there is inserted –

'7A Use of alternative documents to give particulars

(1) Subsections (2) and (3) apply where –

(a) an employer gives an employee a document in writing in the form of a contract of employment or letter of engagement,

(b) the document contains information which, were the document in the form of a statement under section 1, would meet the employer's obligation under that section in relation to the matters mentioned in subsections (3) and (4)(a) to (c), (d)(i), (f) and (h) of that section, and

(c) the document is given after the beginning of the employment and before the end of the period for giving a statement under that section.

(2) The employer's duty under section 1 in relation to any matter shall be treated as met if the document given to the employee contains information which, were the document in the form of a statement under that section, would meet the employer's obligation under that section in relation to that matter.

(3) The employer's duty under section 3 shall be treated as met if the document given to the employee contains information which, were the document in the form of a statement under section 1 and the information included in the form of a note, would meet the employer's obligation under section 3.

(4) For the purposes of this section a document to which subsection (1)(a) applies shall be treated, in relation to information in respect of any of the matters mentioned in section 1(4), as specifying the date on which the document is given to the employee as the date as at which the information applies.

(5) Where subsection (2) applies in relation to any matter, the date on which the document by virtue of which that subsection applies is given to the employee shall be the material date in relation to that matter for the purposes of section 4(1).

(6) Where subsection (3) applies, the date on which the document by virtue of which that subsection applies is given to the employee shall be the material date for the purposes of section 4(1) in relation to the matters of which particulars are required to be given under section 3.

(7) The reference in section 4(6) to an employer having given a statement under section 1 shall be treated as including his having given a document by virtue of which his duty to give such a statement is treated as met.

7B Giving of alternative documents before start of employment

A document in the form of a contract of employment or letter of engagement given by an employer to an employee before the beginning of the employee's employment with the employer shall, when the employment begins, be treated for the purposes of section 7A as having been given at that time.'

38   Failure to give statement of employment particulars etc

(1) This section applies to proceedings before an employment tribunal relating to a claim by an employee under any of the jurisdictions listed in Schedule 5.

(2) If in the case of proceedings to which this section applies –

    (a) the employment tribunal finds in favour of the employee, but makes no award to him in respect of the claim to which the proceedings relate, and

    (b) when the proceedings were begun the employer was in breach of his duty to the employee under section 1(1) or 4(1) of the Employment Rights Act 1996 (c18) (duty to give a written statement of initial employment particulars or of particulars of change),

the tribunal must, subject to subsection (5), make an award of the minimum amount to be paid by the employer to the employee and may, if it considers it just and equitable in all the circumstances, award the higher amount instead.

(3) If in the case of proceedings to which this section applies –

    (a) the employment tribunal makes an award to the employee in respect of the claim to which the proceedings relate, and

    (b) when the proceedings were begun the employer was in breach of his duty to the employee under section 1(1) or 4(1) of the Employment Rights Act 1996,

the tribunal must, subject to subsection (5), increase the award by the minimum amount and may, if it considers it just and equitable in all the circumstances, increase the award by the higher amount instead.

(4) In subsections (2) and (3) –

    (a) references to the minimum amount are to an amount equal to two weeks' pay, and

    (b) references to the higher amount are to an amount equal to four weeks' pay.

(5) The duty under subsection (2) or (3) does not apply if there are exceptional circumstances which would make an award or increase under that subsection unjust or inequitable.

(6) The amount of a week's pay of an employee shall –

   (a) be calculated for the purposes of this section in accordance with Chapter 2 of Part 14 of the Employment Rights Act 1996 (c18), and

   (b) not exceed the amount for the time being specified in section 227 of that Act (maximum amount of a week's pay).

(7) For the purposes of Chapter 2 of Part 14 of the Employment Rights Act 1996 as applied by subsection (6), the calculation date shall be taken to be –

   (a) if the employee was employed by the employer on the date the proceedings were begun, that date, and

   (b) if he was not, the effective date of termination as defined by section 97 of that Act.

(8) The Secretary of State may by order –

   (a) amend Schedule 5 for the purpose of –

      (i) adding a jurisdiction to the list in that Schedule, or

      (ii) removing a jurisdiction from that list;

   (b) make provision, in relation to a jurisdiction listed in Schedule 5, for this section not to apply to proceedings relating to claims of a description specified in the order;

   (c) make provision for this section to apply, with or without modifications, as if –

      (i) any individual of a description specified in the order who would not otherwise be an employee for the purposes of this section were an employee for those purposes, and

      (ii) a person of a description specified in the order were, in the case of any such individual, the individual's employer for those purposes.

General

39 Unfair dismissal: adjustments under sections 31 and 38

In the Employment Rights Act 1996 (c18), after section 124 there is inserted –

'124A Adjustments under the Employment Act 2002

Where an award of compensation for unfair dismissal falls to be –

   (a) reduced or increased under section 31 of the Employment Act 2002 (non-completion of statutory procedures), or

   (b) increased under section 38 of that Act (failure to give statement of employment particulars),

the adjustment shall be in the amount awarded under section 118(1)(b) and shall be applied immediately before any reduction under section 123(6) or (7).'

40 Interpretation of Part 3

In this Part –

'employer' and 'employee' have the same meanings as in the Employment Rights Act 1996 (c18);

'statutory procedure' means a procedure set out in Schedule 2.

BIBLIOGRAPHY

Acas, *Acas Arbitration Scheme for the Resolution of Unfair Dismissal Disputes – A Consultation Document*, 1998, London: HMSO

Acas, Advisory Handbook, *Discipline and Grievances at Work*, 2001(a), London: HMSO

Acas, *The Acas Arbitration Scheme for the Resolution of Unfair Dismissal Disputes: A Guide to the Scheme*, 2001(b), London: HMSO

Acas, *Annual Report 2001–02*, 2002, London: HMSO

Baker, A, 'Access vs process in employment discrimination: why ADR suits the US but not the UK' [2002] 31(2) Ind LJ 113

Better Regulation Task Force, *Employment Regulation: Striking a Balance*, May 2001, London: HMSO

Brown, A, 'Acas arbitration: a case of consumer satisfaction?' (1992) 23 IRJ 224

Clark, J, 'Adversarial and investigative approaches to the arbitral resolution of dismissal disputes: a comparison of South Africa and the UK' [1999] 28(4) Ind LJ 319

Consumers' Association, *Alternatives to Court*, 2001 Community Legal Service Information Leaflet No 23

Corby, S, 'Resolving employment rights disputes through mediation: the New Zealand experience' (1999) Institute of Employment Rights

Doyle, M, *Advising on ADR: the Essential Guide to Appropriate Dispute Resolution*, 2000, London: Advice Services Alliance

Earnshaw, J, Goodman, J, Harrison, R and Marchington, M, 'Industrial tribunals, workplace disciplinary procedures and employment practices' (1998) DTI EMAR Series, No 2

Earnshaw, J and Hardy, S, 'Assessing an arbitral route for unfair dismissal' [2001] 30(3) Ind LJ 289

Employment Tribunal Task Force, *Moving Forward*, July 2002, London: HMSO

ETS (Employment Tribunals Service), *Annual Report 2001–02*, 2002, London: HMSO

Genn, H, 'Mediation in action: resolving court disputes without trial' (2002) LCD report

Hepple, B, *Report on the Reform of UK Industrial Tribunals*, 1987, London: JUSTICE

Hepple, B and Morris, G, 'The Employment Act 2002 and the crisis of individual employment rights' [2002] 31(3) Ind LJ 245

Lewis, R and Clark, J, 'Arbitration in dismissal disputes: the Acas scheme', Industrial Law Society Annual Conference, September 2000, unpublished (see www.industriallawsociety.org.uk/papers/lewisclark.htm)

Lewis, R and Clark, J, *Employment Rights, Industrial Tribunals and Arbitration; The Case for Alternative Dispute Resolution*, 1993, London: Institute of Employment Rights

Lewis, J and Legard, R, *Acas Individual Conciliation: a Qualitative Evaluation of the Service Provided in Industrial Tribunal Cases*, 1998, Acas, London: HMSO

MacMillan, J, 'Employment tribunals: philosophies and practicalities' [1999] 28(1) Ind LJ 33

Marshall, EA, *Gill on the Law of Arbitration*, 4th edn, 2001, London: Sweet & Maxwell

Merkin, R, *Guide to the 1996 Arbitration Act*, 1997, London: Butterworths

Merkin, R, *Arbitration Law*, 2000, London: Butterworths

Rees, W, Editorials (2000–02) Journal of ADR, Mediation and Negotiation

Rideout, R, 'Unfair dismissal: tribunal or arbitration?' [1986] 15(1) Ind LJ 84

St John Sutton, D, Kendall, J and Gill, J, *Russell on Arbitration*, 21st edn, 1997, London: Butterworths

Tweeddale, A and Tweeddale, K, *A Practical Approach to Arbitration Law*, 2001, London: Blackstone

Yorke, D, *Guide to Arbitration Law*, 2002, London: Sweet & Maxwell

INDEX